HARD WORK

Life in Low-Pay Britain

POLLY TOYNBEE

BLOOMSBURY

First published by Bloomsbury Publishing 2003

Copyright © by Polly Toynbee 2003

The moral right of the author has been asserted

Bloomsbury Publishing Plc, 38 Soho Square, London W1D 3HB

A CIP catalogue record for this book
is available from the British Library

ISBN 0 7475 6415 9

10 9 8 7 6 5 4 3 2

Typeset by Hewer Text Ltd, Edinburgh
Printed in Great Britain by Clays Ltd, St Ives Plc

ACKNOWLEDGEMENTS

Many thanks to all who helped in the writing of this book, especially: Andrew Dilnot, Carl Emmerson, Tom Clark, Mike Brewer of the Institute for Fiscal Studies; John Hills and Abigail McKnight of the LSE; Professor Mark Stewart, Warwick University; Sanjiv Sachdev, Kingston University; Alistair Hatchett of Income Data Services; Will Hutton and John Knell, The Work Foundation; John Wheatley, Social Policy Officer, Citizens Advice Bureau; Dr Richard Towers and Tim Bickerstaff, Low Pay Unit; Oliver Higgins, chair of Clapham Park Project board; Tom Bremner and Stuart Holton, Lambeth Housing Department; Faith Boardman, Chief Executive of Lambeth Council; PC Simon Cham, Community Officer, Clapham Park; Niall Cooper and Oliver Fernandes of Church Action on Poverty; Shan Rogbeer and Letticia Sabimana at the Shaftesbury Rescources Centre; Frances O'Grady, Head of Organisation at the TUC; Heather Wakefield, Maggie Jones and others at Unison; Jack Dromey at the Transport and General Workers' Union; TELCO, the East London Communities Organisation; Elaine Hazelhurst, Unilever; Sir Clive Thompson, Chief Executive, Rentokil-Initial; my editor at the Guardian, Alan Rusbridger, for giving me the time; Gordon Brown for his riposte to me that writers have as much duty as politicians to raise concern about poverty.

For my mother, my children and David.

CONTENTS

Chapter 1

Starting Out

When the letter arrived I thought briefly about it then dumped it in the cluttered tray of awkward ones where it lay unanswered on my desk for weeks. I would glance at it occasionally, then drop it back undecided. It was from Church Action on Poverty. As a patron of the National Secular Society and profoundly anti-religious, I should have had no problem in scribbling them a polite refusal.

But Church Action on Poverty has a strong claim on folk memory. In 1985 they inspired *Faith in the Cities*, a devastating report on what was happening to many ordinary people as unemployment soared in that calamitous decade. The gap between rich and poor yawned yet wider in the 1980s, when the market was the golden calf, greed was glorious and the Big Bang made heroes of City lads in Porsches. Private wealth and public squalor grew alongside each other but hardly a voice could make itself heard protesting about the rising poverty, so loud was the clatter of cash registers. The Labour party had silenced itself in a fit of its own madness, social research was about as influential as alchemy and the titanic struggle between Arthur Scargill and Mrs Thatcher was not about the meek of the earth. But suddenly up sprang the C of E, formerly known as the Conservative party at prayer, offering a moral critique that landed one of the few effective blows on the Conservative government. Only the bishops succeeded in poking Mrs Thatcher in the eye with their croziers for her social destructiveness. She ordered the troublesome clerics back into their pulpits to preach personal morality and render everything else unto Caesarena.

Now, in 2002, the church was taking on Labour, this time over

low pay. It was a well-chosen target. Yes, Labour had at last
introduced the minimum wage but the challenge Church Action
had set myself and others was this: try living on that £4.10 an hour
basic for Lent.

It was a brilliant idea. Work lies at the heart of Labour's approach.
Work was to be the salvation of the poor, their escape upwards:
everyone believes in its redemptive power. Workless households
have been the great social disaster of our time. Gordon Brown
promised full employment, believing work in itself would herald an
end to poverty: the economy boomed and a million more jobs were
created. But what if the pay offered is so low that however many
hours people work, no one can live on it? Live, not just get by and
have enough to eat, but pay the bills, feel secure, have a drink, afford
pleasures for the children, belong in the same consumer universe as
most other people. What if work, hard, demanding, important
work, does not liberate people from poverty at all? 'Work for those
who can, welfare for those who can't', 'A hand up, not a hand out',
'Work is the best welfare' – these were Labour's mantras and they
chimed with the spirit of the times. But what if they disguise the
awkward fact that work pays so little that those on the minimum
wage are still excluded, marginalised, locked out?

So I put the Church Action letter back in the tray. It would be
impossible. How could I possibly live on £4.10 an hour? That's
£164 a week, twice what two of us paid the other night for one
local restaurant meal in Clapham, nothing exceptional. Every time I
thought about my own gold-plated life as a journalist – the taxis, the
Guardian's car, my mobile phone, eating out, or the gifts for my
family and what's called 'discretionary spending' on pleasing non-
necessities – it seemed undoable. I had to carry out my ordinary
working life. How would I get from place to place in a hurry, to
press conferences, seminars or interviews, with just a bus pass? What
was it Mrs Thatcher said about only failures using buses?

I thought about my Victorian house bought decades ago and, like
most in London, now worth a fortune. I thought about how much
comes in each month, never needing to count the cost. It couldn't
be done. Or at least, nothing remotely resembling my life could be
lived on that sum.

But I was due a sabbatical from the *Guardian* which was to begin at the start of Lent. I picked up the book I wrote some thirty years ago when I was starting out in journalism, a personal exploration of a world of manual work I knew nothing about. In *A Working Life* I had travelled the country taking jobs as they came, describing the lives of people, many just getting by, with hardship lurking around the corner. I worked on the production line at Unilever's Port Sunlight soap factory, lodging in Lord Lever's model workers' village in Birkenhead. In Birmingham I assembled electrical car parts at Lucas's: there was one of the regular car industry strikes while I was there. In a Lyons factory I operated the cream spreader, watching the angel cakes fly past on the conveyor belt. I was a ward orderly in a West London hospital and I joined the WRAC, the women's royal army corps, to be bawled at and brutalised on the parade ground. For a while I lived in Rotherham, lodging with a steel-worker's family, visited a steel-works and the coalface down a coal mine. My book now seems redolent of another era, a time of strong trade unions and comforting but sometimes malign social solidarity. Pay rates were rising at a time of social progress and the chance of upward mobility for working-class children was in the air.

Then and now. There is no need for cloying nostalgia, but let's get it in perspective. The economic story of the last century was growth: national income multiplied by seven. After the last war the gap in income between rich and poor got steadily narrower: we have never been more equal than in the late 1970s. Wealth as well as income was shared more evenly: the richest were taxed progressively while more people started to acquire wealth by owning their own homes, building up pensions and savings. But that historic progress towards greater social justice stopped dead with Mrs Thatcher: instead the rich got richer and the poor were left behind, both in income and in wealth.[1]

Since I wrote *A Working Life* in 1970, national income (GDP) has doubled. As a nation we are now twice as well off.[2] How does that feel? Look around: cars, CDs, cornucopias of exotic food. But not for all, since the extra income has been so unevenly distributed. Imagine we are in a caravan, with the low-paid bringing up the rear. As the whole procession moved on into the 1980s, those at the back moved a little, too, but far slower than the sheikhs and their entourage at the front. The poorest fell ever further behind the rest, almost out of sight. When the front and the back are stretched so far apart, at what point can they no longer be said to be travelling together at all, breaking the community between them? If there is, in Margaret Thatcher's words, 'no such thing as society', why care? Because everyone needs a justification for the way we live. We can no longer muster anything that feels remotely credible as an excuse for paying so many people too little to live on for work that society depends on for its standard of living.

Something else happened in those years. It should have been as obvious as it was inevitable, yet until research was published recently, it was the wicked secret of the last twenty years. As the income gap between top and bottom widened, so social mobility up (and down) shuddered to a halt. It is as if the escalator has slowed, even jammed. The people at the bottom will never get any nearer the top.

The idea of meritocracy has sustained many generations of the privileged. Belief that the clever children of the poor could make their way in the world has exonerated inequality. So long as we could persuade ourselves that anyone could make it, the privileged could live comfortably with this moral justification for their way of life. That justification is dying. The ladders up into middle-class domains have been cut off. The middle classes have now secured everlasting wealth, status and success regardless of merit as never before. Their money and power guarantees class stability for their children more effectively than the Victorians or Edwardians could, with no fear of falling. The children of the low-paid workers in this book are much less likely to reach into better jobs than they were thirty years ago. A recent study comparing the fate of children born in 1958 with those born in 1970 found a sharp drop in social mobility between the two dates. The 1970 children are following more certainly in their fathers' footsteps, with less chance of movement either up or down the social or wages scale.[3]

To my generation this is hard to credit. It feels counter-intuitive; it runs against everything we have experienced in our own post-war lifetime. I went to the sixth form of one of London's first comprehensives at a time when opportunity was in the air. The new plate-glass universities opened their gleaming doors and comprehensive schools symbolised the ideal of upward mobility. All around us, as the children of blue-collar workers were moving upwards, a swathe of new middle-class jobs beckoned; a social earthquake was in progress that lifted a giant slice of my generation up far above their parents' income, education and expectations. That was what the sixties explosion was all about. That culture of progress seemed unstoppable, inevitable, the onward march of social history.

Every generation deludes itself that it is more classless than it is. Classlessness feels modern: the American anyone-can-make-it dream permeates all Western culture. Is the dream over? It can't be true, people exclaim: only consider how university places have multiplied. In the 1970s one in eight children took degrees; now it is one in three, and Tony Blair promises it will soon be 50 per cent. But it turns out that most extra university places are taken by the dimmer sons of the middle classes who would never have made it before. And, ironically, equality for women has meant less equality for others, as middle-class girls, previously denied higher education, have taken up many of the rest of the new places. What's more, the children of the well-off marry one another with even greater certainty than before. A new survey shows that marriage is now rarer between young middle- and working-class adults.[4]

In 1970, writing my first book, I was aware of living through a time when the number of blue-collar jobs was shrinking fast while the number of middle-class white-collar jobs was growing. Embourgeoisement was everywhere and a mass working class was dying out: it seemed as if this upward mobility could only accelerate. But it stopped.[5]

The end of the meritocratic idea changes everything. Many on the right and the market liberals always said: don't worry, it's quite fair if the poor are poor through lack of talent or ambition. No need to redistribute income when they could pull themselves up by the bootstraps if they would only work harder. Gross inequality is morally comfortable so long as there is a plausible story of the rise of the fittest. Low pay is also fair enough if these jobs can be labelled 'entry-level', just a first step on a ladder. But it is now clear that very

few of those in low-paid jobs can ever move far. Sometimes they
climb from the bottom tenth of earners into the next decile, but
often fall back down again. Few make it to the next step. They
inhabit a cycle of no-pay/low-pay job insecurity. This is indeed the
end of social progress.[6]

Post-Thatcher, fewer people seem to question why incomes are
distributed as they are. Conservative cultural domination of a
generation has atrophied natural sensitivity to the unfairness of
the accidents of birth or position. Thatcher's children were told the
iron laws of economics ordained their wealth: to question the
market was to risk the golden goose's demise. Some of her children,
grown queasy, voted Labour in 1997 but Tony Blair has been
anxious not to overtax their consciences. He did make that
remarkable pledge to abolish child poverty but, ever-ambivalent,
Labour were silent about it in the 2001 election, and certainly silent
about how it can ever be achieved without a far greater change in
relative rewards. So far money for the poor has been given
generously but only in quiet back-handers.

Opinions are formed in a small London village inhabited by
think-tankers and journalists, all of us living the same well-paid
affluent life, often forgetting just how exceptional our incomes are.
MPs earn more than 96 per cent of the population does, and many
of us earn yet more. It leads the media to foster a misleading, if not
downright dishonest, representation of a Britain where everyone
has lots of money. Turn on those television life-style shows about
interior decoration, holidays, cooking or gardening and they relay
images of living standards that reflect the programme-makers' own.
At least a third of viewers live no such lives, pressing their noses
against the panes of that society. How casually, with what insou-
ciance the magazine culture assumes that everyone in work these
days has a decent income and a home they own, everyone drinks in
expensive bars and eats out often, everyone goes on foreign holidays.

In the flourishing parts of London it is hard to believe that the
national median income is only £390 a week or £20,280 a year.
This is not to be confused with the average – a useless measure that
tots up all the incomes and divides them up as if we lived in an

egalitarian society. If, say, Bill Gates came to live here, the average measurement would make it look as if we had each of us suddenly got more in our pockets. The better measure is the median, which is the mid-point in the population where half the people earn less and half earn more. At just over £20,000 a year, that half-way mark is not high – after tax, national insurance, council tax, rent, gas, electricity and a tank full of petrol. But the media opinion-formers, who themselves earn so much more, develop a convenient social myopia, air-brushing out the low earners and most of those below the median. As for the obstinate one-third of the population for whom shopping is never a leisure activity but the opposite of retail therapy, they are dropped from the national portrait altogether for lack of advertising potential.

People do dress more alike these days, regardless of income. You can usually spot the very rich; you can sometimes spot the very poor. But clothes that look like everyone else's are cheap these days. Thanks to stores like Matalan, the low-paid rarely look different to the rest. People are upset by that small handful of street beggars sitting in their blankets under cash machines because they are all-too-visible and they ruffle the rhythm of life. But no one can see the invisible millions of hard-working poor people milling all around us. Social injustice is rarely thrust in our face on the bus or tube; it does not smell, it is well disguised. One in five of those people hurrying past in the street each morning is on the way to a job that will pay them less than £6 an hour, less than £240 a week. Just ponder what that does *not* buy – meals in restaurants that get written about, Manolo shoes or a haircut and highlights at Michaeljohn.

New Labour came to power with the work ethic as its core value. Its New Deal would get people back into work, ending the unemployment that fractured a generation. The quid pro quo was a minimum wage to ensure work offered at least a basic reward. This fulfilled a 100-year-old Labour objective. It did raise the wages of some 1.3 million people a little, but fewer than the government expected because it was set far too low. Introduced in April 1999 at an ultra-cautious £3.60 an hour, it has barely risen in relation to other wages since, now standing at £4.10 an hour.

Work, work, work is the message, but £4.10 does not free you from poverty.

Labour's 'Third Way' answer to this problem has been the Working Families' Tax Credit, designed to make sure work is always worth more than life on the dole, while at the same time not alarming business by forcing up the minimum wage to a genuine living wage. Those who work at these sub-survivable rates are now rewarded with extra benefits from the state. While it helps in the short term, in the long run it cannot bear the weight of compensating for huge income inequality.

First, as many as a third of families never claim it; some studies suggest more: all targeted benefits miss large numbers of would-be beneficiaries. Second, it goes only to families with children, though a lower rate will be brought in for some other low-paid people. Third, WFTC forbids more than one adult in the household from working, which forces wives to stay at home instead of developing their own careers. Fourth, if there is any intention of creating a serious increase in incomes at the bottom, to do this by increasing WFTC would make low-pay incomes surreally top-heavy – all top-up and no substance. It would grossly distort the market, encouraging employers to keep on paying well below the market rate, even where there was a shortage of workers, letting tax-payers pay out an ever heftier subsidy to low-paying employers.

But above all, it is a question of basic fairness. A wage should reflect the dignity and value of the work done. Low pay is low esteem. Ask top directors and they will admit that much of the pride they take in their huge salaries is in the way it looks as well as the way it feels in the pocket. That is just as true of people glumly surveying jobs at £4.10 an hour: it looks insultingly small. Studies show that those looking for work are more influenced by the headline rate than by complex calculations of how much they might win or lose in benefits when stepping from the dole into work. WFTC is fine as a stop-gap and it may always be needed for some situations and in some work sectors, but it cannot become the main motor driving for long-term fairer incomes.

So, what if work is not the great liberator? What if workers are treated so badly, paid so unfairly, that a job is not a route out of poverty? I wanted to go back again and look at the world of work as it is now. How much social progress has there been since 1970 in these jobs? After all, the greatest single group of poor people are already in work. 3.5 million poor people live in working households. There are more working poor than there are unemployed. There are more working poor than there are poor pensioners. As growing numbers of single mothers, people with disabilities and anyone else who possibly can is urged into work, it becomes ever clearer that most poor people are not the feckless/hopeless/helpless but people who work very hard for long hours and yet still fall below the official poverty line.

For them, working at these rates of pay, work is not the best welfare. Nor are they doing marginal, unimportant jobs but essential work without which things fall apart. They are the bedrock of the public services, the mainstay of the booming service economy, yet they are grossly under-rewarded. They are poor because the work they do is underpaid. Only consider the arbitrariness of current values. The lowest-paid occupations in 2002 were cleaners, caterers, carers, classroom assistants, launderers, dry-cleaners and check-out operators. The top-ten highest-paid occupations were: company financial managers, insurance brokers, solicitors, pilots, management consultants, data-processing managers, doctors, top-rank police officers and marketing and sales managers.[7]

Is that scale of rewards really down to market logic and market rationality or is it just prejudice, custom – and the domination of men? To clean the suit or scrub the steps of the management consultant, to care for his senile mother, to assist in the classroom of his daughter, these are called 'ancillary' to his mighty work, as if extraneous and not as necessary to the smooth running of society. Directly in cash or indirectly in taxes he is not paying a fair price to those upon whom he depends for everything. The word 'ancillary' comes from the Latin *ancilla*: a handmaid, work done by women slaves. Although this is now a service economy, service remains lowly, servile, womanly and worth less than traditional men's work. Note how there are no traditional men's jobs among the ten lowest-paid occupations, 80 per cent of which are occupied by women.

It is not revolutionary to suggest a fairer balancing of values and rewards. There is no need to reinvent socialism: there is a limit to what governments can and should do to intervene. Back in the days when government tried to set both prices and incomes centrally, I once had a conversation with the politician Tony Crosland – himself far from Old Labour – in which he advanced the serious policy proposal for a national tariff of merit and reward. It seemed improbable then, impossible now and is on no one's agenda. What has been done with great success by other countries is to bring incomes closer together without jeopardising prosperity for all, indeed with greater per capita wealth than Britain's. Steady social democratic gradualism has delivered more fairness in most other European countries, and considerably more in Norway, Finland and Sweden whose economies have outstripped ours partly because of the social cohesiveness they have fostered through fairer distribution of pay and status. At the very least, their social justice has done them no economic harm, in comparison with Britain.

So now seemed the right time to go back again and explore low-paid work. If I needed any further nudging in this direction, by chance I was asked to write the introduction to the British edition of Barbara Ehrenreich's excellent *Nickel and Dimed*.[8] Ehrenreich took minimum-wage jobs around the United States to see if she could survive on the pay. In her electifying exploration of American working destitution, she found it impossible to get by.

Reading her book with a British eye, I was struck most forcefully by how very much worse matters are in the US. The lack of social security forces everyone to work or die which, not surprisingly, creates high employment rates. But such forced labour also keeps wages pitifully low. America may be working, but the US has double Europe's poverty rate, a more important statistic than its employment rate. British politicians look across the Atlantic seeking the philosopher's stone, a gold-spinning alchemy that could combine US tax and pay rates with a European welfare and social justice ideal. But the only useful comparisons for the UK are within Europe, where there is a diversity of employment, welfare and poverty patterns. A graph plotting these shows that some countries can have high employment, high welfare and low poverty. What emerges is the extent to which countries have shaped their own social and economic destinies through the political choices they have made. The idea of some rigid economic determinism vanishes on close inspection. The only iron law appears to be a correlation between social spending as a percentage of GDP and poverty levels: Britain has the lowest social spending and the highest poverty; Sweden is the opposite way round, and France and Germany are half way between.[9]

By now coincidences were making this book seem unavoidable, and I decided to go with it. But how? For the last year I had been following the fortunes of a council estate near where I live. Clapham Park Estate had been picked as a New Deal for Communities project in Labour's flagship regeneration programme. As the biggest and worst estate in one of London's poorest boroughs, it had won a £56 million grant to see what the residents themselves could do with the money to breathe new life into a semi-derelict community. They had agreed to let me sit in on their meetings and get to know the local people who were trying to effect a miracle. I wanted to watch the scheme's progress at first hand, as a way of observing government targets close up, not just through reams of annual statistics. Now my connections on the estate gave me the chance to go and live there for a while, making my attempt at living on the minimum wage a little more realistic. At least it gave me an accounting base for estimating the true cost of living, since most people (the lucky ones) living on low pay are in social housing, either council- or housing-association-owned.

Oliver Higgins, estate resident and chair of the board, was enthusiastic about the idea. So was Lambeth council's Tom Bremner, manager of the estate's neighbourhood housing office which does all lettings and repairs. Without their approval I couldn't have done it. Yes, Tom said, as it happened he had one block on the estate that was about to be partially renovated. It had several empty flats that could not be let until the work was done so he could rent me one of those without depriving anyone on the housing waiting list. All I had to do was sign a contract, pay the rent and move in.

Living on the minimum wage would not be enough without working to earn it: work has its own costs. But getting jobs might be more difficult. I knew the general employment figures, but I had no idea how many jobs there were available within affordable reach of Clapham Park. Nor did I know whether I could get any jobs myself. Maybe at fifty-five I would be unemployable for anything except my own profession?

The more I thought about this project, the closer the time came, the more I was struck by the absurdity of it, too. Several times I almost abandoned the whole idea. It was play-acting, Marie Antoinette as a milk maid in the Petit Trianon. In all my life I have never experienced one moment's financial insecurity, nor even the remotest fear of it. I was born into rock-solid middle-class security reaching back as many generations as I know about on both sides of my family. Like most people who have had well-paid careers for many years, I find it hard to imagine falling far. To make that imaginative leap I have to devise some elaborate scenario that would deprive me of my ability to earn, losing my home, my pension, my savings, my family and friends. Middle-class destiny is safe as houses. We exist in our silos, they in theirs.

One reason to stay for a while in Clapham Park was to remind myself that most people who have to live in estates such as these are the working poor and they bear little resemblance to popular images of deprivation. Whenever the glare of cameras and headlines turns to poverty, it ignores the unpicturesque ordinary majority, preferring to ogle grossly dysfunctional families. How documentary-makers love the visual drama of neighbours from hell, demented drug addicts, tiny truants shoplifting in school hours, muggers, yobs and a whole Beggars' Opera of modern grotesques. Newspapers enjoy frightening their readers with tales of some twelve-year-old with a hair-raising criminal record, or of a family of six out-of-control children. All this is entertaining in a gruesome sort of way, a necessary fable to explore the social boundaries, but these images turn poverty into a social/psychological/criminological phenomenon. It makes the political personal. The better-off always relish the titillating sins of the underclasses as another way to justify their own lives.

To be sure, there are many people with serious problems, more since the social destruction of the 1980s. Low-paid workers who have to live among them suffer greatly from the resultant crime and vandalism, far more than the middle classes safely elsewhere. The government's own research shows that most crime is committed by a small number of bad boys and young men, maybe fifty in each area. But this book is not about the misfits and the outcasts, or at least not directly.

This book is about the millions of 'deserving' poor who live surrounded by the antisocial dangers to their children of the dysfunctional few. Working parents fear their children will fall down into the social abyss they see around them: that is often what keeps them working forty-eight or more hours a week, although they will never earn enough to escape these surroundings. They will never own their own homes, never save more than a pittance, never have pensions to make them independent in old age. Illness or accident will plunge them downwards, yet they work on until they die young. One small illumination: the life expectancy of the poor was brutally exposed when free TV licences were recently granted to the over-75s. On average, Class V low-paid male workers only live until seventy-one so they will never qualify. Men in the top social class live until over seventy-eight.

What is it to be poor now? Compared with 1970, people live better. Back then only 73 per cent had a fridge, but now it is 92 per cent. Only 37 per cent had central heating, now that, too, is 92 per cent. 42 per cent had telephones, now it is 98 per cent. Back then half of all households had access to a car, now it is 73 per cent, so while the poor now have central heating, most still lack cars. No, the poor do not live in Dickensian squalor and yes, they have a slightly higher standard of living. But remember the caravan with the low-paid bringing up the rear. Everyone has more – but the poor have less of it – less of what it takes to live the common life. There are now three times more children beneath the poverty line than in 1970. (The official poverty measure, then and now, is those living on less than 60 per cent of the national median income.) While the country grew twice as rich, they hardly gained. Excluded from the mainstream, these hard-working families cannot afford holidays, take train journeys, spend £35 on filling a tank with petrol, buy computers or join the great world of shopping for fun. Why are they still falling behind? Because the top tenth had a pay rise last year of 7.3 per cent while the bottom tenth only got 4.5 per cent – and it goes on happening year after year.

How will we justify the way we live now to future generations? Humans are born with an elemental sense of fairness and what we have now is not fair. The history of social progress, from factory acts and electoral reform to universal education and the welfare state, used to be a story of the onward march of social justice. But the clock seems to have stopped. Since Thatcher, Britain has skidded backwards and Labour has at best just about stopped the slide by doling out extra benefits. Does it matter so long as the poor don't starve? It does.

Chapter 2

A Home

Jenny from the housing office walked me over to my flat, swinging the keys in her hand as we picked our way across the estate between potholes and puddles. Yes, she said, there were plenty of empty flats in this block, unlettable in its present state. People who had waited years to reach the top of the council house list were given three choices, 'But no one would choose the White House. It's the hardest to let of them all.'

Its name was an irony not lost on its tenants. On the estate the White House was notorious for just about everything. Even among the grimmest blocks on the west side of Clapham Park, it was an eyesore. Its once-white façade was pockmarked all over with deep holes exposing concrete and metal wires, as if it had been bombarded in a long Balkan war, which was why the residents called it Little Kosovo. There was scaffolding around its first floor, holding up a green netting skirt into which had been flung rubbish from the windows above. There was an old iron, a chair, all kinds of trash which now hung there in permanent netted suspension, exhibited to the world like some Britart installation. On my first trip around the estate I had assumed the scaffolding was a sign that the block was in the process of much-needed repair, but an old man I met then laughed at the idea and said the netting had been there as long as anyone could remember, placed to catch falling chunks of concrete. A few years ago the other blocks down this end had been painted but the council ran out of funds before they reached the White House, leaving it looking yet worse by contrast. The old man told me he never let anyone know he lived there, he was too ashamed.

He always stood at the door of one of the better blocks and pretended to go inside when taking leave of anyone he knew.

Bad as the outside looked, it didn't prepare me for the inside. Jenny led the way into my staircase in the block. My nose told the rest of the story. The place stank and you could smell it before even stepping inside. The dustbins outside were overflowing, bags of rubbish lay stacked against them, and the front door with its shattered glass was hanging open at a disjointed angle like a broken limb, flapping to and fro in the wind. In the stairway there was a thick crusty aroma of decades of decaying detritus, only slightly masked by the heavier scent of urine. Jenny wrinkled her nose but said she'd smelled worse. There was a small lift just inside the passage with a battered graffiti-covered silver door. 'Sorry, but I never use the lifts in these places,' Jenny said. 'I was stuck in one once, never again.' So we walked up four floors past gaping broken windows on each stairway, past rubbish chutes clogged with filth. I noted the chutes were only big enough for a lightly filled plastic carrier bag, designed in an era before the days of heavy duty rubbish. Even an ordinary pedal bin bag would be enough to cause a blockage.

The stairway walls might once have been painted a pinkish beige but they had been overlaid with layer upon layer of brownish stuff scattered on the surface, something indescribable and horrible. The smell had seeped deep in and no one ever touched the walls as they walked past. The steps themselves were quite clean that morning: they were washed down every day by a cleaning contractor now more vigorously monitored under the New Deal regime. But while the whole block was open to any passer-by, day or night, there was nothing to stop these staircases being used as open public lavatories and rubbish tips.

My fourth-floor flat shared a dark cul-de-sac landing with two other closed front doors, but all was silent. Jenny could tell me nothing about my neighbours, though she did mention unspecified trouble on the ground floor that broke out from time to time. I questioned her nervously but she was vague, as if it might be breaking confidentiality to reveal more. When we reached my own flat, the doorway had been clamped over with a temporary heavy metal security door to stop squatters breaking in and taking it over.

'Not just squatters,' Jenny said, as she tried to sort out the right keys to the maze of locks on the outer door and the three locks on the inner door. 'It's the crack dealers who move in, set up in a flat and intimidate everyone else. But these doors don't keep them out. They use cutting machines and they just wrench the whole metal frame out.' I didn't like to ask what was to stop them doing that to the flimsy door underneath once the security doors were removed and a tenant moved in.

By now my expectations of this flat were zero. I feared the worst as Jenny finally pushed open the door and we stepped into a dark passageway.

I felt immediate relief. Once inside with the door shutting out the smell from the corridor, it wasn't bad, not bad at all. A good-sized sitting room, two bedrooms, a small kitchen and bathroom were all in cream-painted good condition. 'You want to remove the carpet?' Jenny asked. She wrinkled her nose at its uncertain spillages, dubious smears and brown sticky spots. I considered it, paced up and down, but thought whatever was underneath might be worse and I would have no money for anything else, so I said I'd keep it. I'd just keep my shoes and slippers on.

I stood at the window looking down on the scene below, noticing how people scuttled in and out of their blocks, hurrying to their own front door. I watched one woman in a bright red coat striding along, jaw jutted with a look of defiant determination. Everyone here walked fast and purposefully across no man's land. No one sauntered through these unwelcoming public spaces, no one looked much to right or left, avoiding eye-contact for fear of some unwelcome encounter. There were not even clumps of kids hanging about. The only place to be was inside the safe, familiar, private space of your own flat. That's how it felt; safe up here looking out, but with a desert down below to cross to get to the streets and bus stops of the outside world. Estates are curious places, locking the poor out of sight, their housing not arranged in ordinary streets like everyone else's. These were once architects' little utopias, designer fantasies of the good community life, fatally turned inwards upon themselves instead of outwards to join the bustling world beyond, little Alcatrazes remote from the swirling urban streets outside.

Agreeing the day I would move in, we stepped out into the hallway again. Jenny locked up the inner door and slammed shut the outer steel door with a mighty clang that echoed up and down the stairwell, but no one looked out to see what was up. Here no one ever did, however loud the noise.

I set off to walk home. It was not far and yet it was a world away. It takes ten minutes from the estate to my own front door, but it is a route I barely knew before, though now I know it well. On foot, it passes several other estates, though as these are not public places it feels like trespassing on other people's territory. As I walked I thought about Clapham where I have lived in the same fine old house for thirty years. I have watched some streets gentrify slowly, then suddenly boom in the last decade. Clapham High Street, recently tired and seedy, has been transformed beyond all recognition within the last eight years. Not long ago even the supermarkets had fled leaving one fly-blown Wimpy Bar and not much else. Now estate agents price flats by the proximity to 'the bars and restaurants of Clapham'; every other shop front is an estate agent or a bar spilling out the well-heeled young, money flowing, drinks at £4.00 each, Porsches in the side roads, property values soaring monthly to new breathtaking heights. This is Clapham's public face, the one that is featured in high-society gossip in the *Evening Standard* or in the property pages listing cool places to live. But the real Clapham where the great majority live is in the secret estates so cunningly hidden behind the façade of booming Clapham. Unseen, unnoticed by the new Porsche people, all the estates are still there and at this rate they will all be there until kingdom come, the underside no property boom can ever reach.

I chose to stay here on my own home turf to write this book because this is where best to draw a portrait of social justice in Britain. Poverty is not somewhere else, up north in Barrow or Jarrow, it is in the next street, intricately interwoven with wealth. It cleans the houses of the well-heeled, it serves them in shops and restaurants, it sweeps the streets and oils the works of all the public services they use. There is a far less deep North/South or regional wealth-gap than the great social divide to be found within each area, everywhere, including right here on my doorstep, rich and poor living in the same postal sectors.[1] In every big city rich and poor live cheek by jowl, close together yet far apart, managing to be almost unaware of each other in their parallel space. In places like Clapham the new conspicuous wealth of the last few years flaunts itself extravagantly in what remains London's poorest borough. So that is why I stayed right here to explore the widening gap between the top and bottom. In the course of writing I found myself crossing and re-crossing this social chasm, a culture shock each time I visited my family, my real home, my real life and then returned to this next-door yet foreign place where other neighbours live.

Do I exaggerate? When I wonder if I overdramatise this great fissure in a society that likes to think itself increasingly classless, I only have to tell friends or colleagues what I am doing and they are electrified, fascinated, full of questions, intrigued by how it feels, what it's like, how my accent was received. If I had said I had just been up the Amazon alone in a dugout they would have been far less interested in my traveller's tales. Sometimes I thought I was daring, in bed at night listening to footsteps and sounds on the staircase. Sometimes I thought this was all absurd since a third of the population live on housing estates and do low-paid jobs, so what's new? But when I see people from my own world look so astonished at the idea that one of us could for a while live like one of them, I know how wide the gap still is. Or I just think about the day I dropped back home from my cleaning job to find my own cleaner vacuuming my front room, which brings a laugh of wry recognition about the way we all live, we on the well-heeled left of centre, too.

The clock starts ticking. From the day when I was given the keys to my flat I started to live on the income of a single woman alone and looking for work. I had just £53.05 a week in Job Seeker's Allowance so I needed to find a job fast. But first I needed to furnish my flat. Where would I turn? The only place to go is to the state social fund. It is a strange and fickle beast, a flexible friend, dubious and duplicitous, as I was about to find out.

The main Lambeth benefits office in Blackfriars Road is an old-style monstrosity filled with rows of depressed or angry people gazing at a television set high on the wall, waiting for their number to be called. Security guards stroll up and down. Claimants coming away from frustrating interviews conducted through scratched Perspex screens sometimes curse under their breath as they go.

I had come to see Arthur Jones, a battle-hardened Lambeth officer with more than twenty years' service with the old DSS, now the Department of Work & Pensions. As he came down to greet me, he looked like a well-seasoned police officer in a short-sleeved white shirt with cotton epaulettes and grey hair cropped *en brosse*. As a social fund officer he had seen claimants by the thousand. He had heard every kind of entreaty and he had witnessed plenty of genuine hardship, he told me as he led the way to an upstairs interview room. I had arranged a hypothetical interview with him to find out what the social fund would give me if I was down on my luck arriving in an empty council flat with few possessions. I might be a woman fleeing a violent husband. I might be a refugee family. I might have had my home repossessed after losing my job and defaulting on my mortgage. These are common occurrences that Arthur sees all the time. In all these situations I would have been living in a temporary hostel or a bed and breakfast for a long while, so by the time people are finally rehoused in a permanent home they often have nothing much with them.

'How much can you give me to furnish my empty flat?' I begin.

'Nothing at all.'

'Nothing?'

'I can only loan you money.'

'Even if I am destitute?'

'Yes. That's all there is, loans.'

'OK, a loan then. How much can you loan me?'

'What's your income?'

'Right now I'm on Job Seeker's Allowance of £53.05 a week, but I hope to get a job soon that ought to bring in somewhere around £160 a week.'

'Well, how much do you want?'

'My flat is completely empty so I want whatever you can give me.'

'No, it doesn't go like that. You have to make a bid and I have to decide if it's reasonable. I judge you on how reasonable your demands are.'

'So if I make a lowish request I'm more likely to get it than if I start too high?'

'Perhaps. It certainly helps your credibility. Tell me what you need this loan for and I will tell you if I think it's reasonable.'

'First I need a bed.'

'Right. I'd agree a bed was essential.'

'How much will you give me for a bed?'

'£75 from Argos.'

'What else can I have?'

'We mostly reckon a cooker is essential, too, though some people don't cook.'

'OK, how much for a cooker?'

'£99.99 from Argos, page 474 in the catalogue.'

'So you always get a bed and a cooker?'

'Yes, though we get a lot of people coming in for replacement gas cookers, claiming theirs blew up.'

'Do you give it to them?'

'Not when it happens twice or three times in a year. After all, have you ever heard of a cooker blowing up? No, me neither. But in the end it all depends on whether they can afford another loan.'

'What about a table and chair?'

'I might say you could sit on the bed. Some officers would say that. But if I said yes to you, then I'd allow you £75 for a table and four chairs from Argos.'

'Curtains?'

'Only if you tell me you are overlooked and you need them for decent privacy. If so then it's £35 for those.'

After that he allows me £15 for crockery, £25 for pots and pans, £10 for cutlery and £50 for bedding. So, I ask, how much in all will he give me?

'That all depends on you,' he says enigmatically.

'How do you mean?' This conversation is beginning to seem surreal.

'How much can you afford to borrow, do you think?'

'That depends on how much you think I can afford. How much will you lend?'

'OK, £400 in your case,' he says. 'I think that's all you can afford. That will be £8 a week off your benefit, 15 per cent.'

'How long for? When do I have to pay it back by?'

'Fifty weeks.'

'Does it matter what I spend it on?'

'Not at all. Spend it on anything you like.'

'Thanks. Is that it then?'

'Just one other thing. How much I loan you also depends on how much I have in the fund on this particular day. We're very low at the moment.'

'Does that mean you might turn me away altogether?'

'No, it just means I'll trim the sum I give everyone. Maybe instead of £75 for that bed, it'll be £35.'

'I see. So where do I buy a bed for £35? Second-hand perhaps?'

'Yes, but we're not allowed to recommend second-hand. We only recommend new.'

'Is there anywhere else except Argos?'

'Sometimes I suggest Crazy George's in the Elephant and Castle. Try there. Although I'm not allowed to say second-hand, there's nothing to stop you choosing second-hand or anything else.'

'Although you are short of funds, will I still get my £400?'

'Yes, I think so this time, seeing as you have no debts and you haven't ever claimed before. Different if you'd claimed a lot before now; you'd come lower down the pecking order. One other thing. You didn't mention clothes. Are those clothes you're wearing the only ones you've got?'

'What if they are?'

'I'd give you money for a change of clothing, and if you tell me that coat is borrowed from a friend, I'd give you money for a winter coat too.'

'How much do you expect me to spend on my clothes? Marks and Spencer standard or not so much?'

'That's where my discretion comes into it, you see. You're unlucky because I buy my clothes cheap in the market so I'm not very sympathetic about clothes. This shirt, you see, I got for

£4.50 and it's very serviceable. But my colleague over there, he might reckon you can't get a wearable shirt for under £20.'

'OK, so I'd like some more loan to cover new clothes, please. How much?'

'No, sorry, I'm not going to lend you more than the £400 anyway because that's all you can reasonably pay back on your low income.'

'Couldn't I pay it back over two years instead of one and borrow twice as much?'

'No, sorry, we like to get the money back within the year.'

This has been a curious ramble around the many perversities of the social fund. I may be in a crisis but the state's response to my need depends on the mood and attitude of the officer, on the amount of money left in the pot and, above all, on my ability to repay. The poorer I am, the lower my income, the less loan I am entitled to. This mirrors everything that banks do – to those that have shall be lent, to those who don't really need money plenty more will be loaned. But for those who desperately need some right now, the doors are shut. 34 per cent of social fund Budgeting Loan applications were refused in 2001.

Before going I want to ask Arthur a few other questions about how to survive on social security. If I am on Job Seeker's Allowance of £53.05 and then I get a job, can I go on drawing it until I'm paid at the end of my first week in work? 'No,' he says. 'You must contact us by phone or in writing or come in as soon as you have a job. Immediately.'

So my social security will be cut off at once from day one in work?

'Yes. Though you could get a Job Grant of £100.'

'That sounds good. Just what I will need.'

'But you wouldn't qualify because you haven't been unemployed and drawing benefit for a year.'

'So what are you telling me? I should wait a year before making the difficult jump into a job? Can I get any other kind of help to tide me over that first week?'

'You could get a four-week Benefit Run-On when you are allowed to go on drawing benefit for a month to tide you over and make sure you are settled in your job before we cut your benefit.'

'Yes that's exactly what I need!'

'Sorry, that's only for single mothers.'

'Then how am I supposed to survive the first week in work? I'm already on such low benefit I couldn't possibly save enough to get me through a week without pay.'

'You could always ask your employer for an advance on your wages.'

'What? On my first day in a new job, ask for a loan? Of course he wouldn't, especially someone hiring low-paid, high-turnover workers. He'd worry I'd never come back and I'd be too embarrassed to dare ask. Do many employers agree?'

'Well, not many, but you could still ask.'

I do actually have a school-age son whom I have left out of this story. Had I included him in then I would have been eligible for more Job Seeker's benefit – £14.50 Family Premium for all families and £32.25 for my son, making a Job Seeker's total of £99.80. When I went to work I would also get Working Families' Tax Credit for him. Arthur said if I had counted in my son he would have given me a loan of £700.

'Is that because I'd need much more with my son in tow?'

'No, his needs have nothing to do with it. But your income would be higher so I would reckon you could pay back more, so I would lend you more.'

This feels more like a conversation with a loan shark than a benefits officer.

There are all kinds of reasons why I chose not to include my son in this venture, though he was keen to be counted in. I tried to imagine whether I would be richer or poorer with him and his extra benefit. What would he cost a week? Probably more than the £46.75 he would bring with him. He would need an £8.50 bus pass, £10 pocket money (£1.42 a day is no fortune) and that leaves £28.25 to feed and clothe him, buy school stationery, pay for school trips, save for holidays, replace his lost trainers and the coat nicked at school, and the glasses that he has lost, again. Since, like most teenagers, he would not be satisfied with a diet of rice and lentils when it came to the thin end of the week, I conclude he would cost me more than his social security would pay.

At the end of my bewildering interview with Arthur, I was uncertain whether his tone was entirely authentic. It was a bizarre encounter since his boss sat in on the meeting, keeping an eye on him. I could not decide if Arthur was being extra-tough in this interview: he had a touch of swagger about him, he was a man used to wielding the power of discretion over the desperate every day. Yet I suspected that underneath the tough exterior he was actually staging a kind of protest of his own, demonstrating to me the full injustice and absurdity of the system and the arbitrariness of his own adjudicating powers. (More than one-third of officers' decisions are reversed on appeal.) He was keen to make sure no claimants ever got one over on him, he knew every trick in the book if anyone tried to cheat him. On the other hand, before I left he made a point of saying, 'I am supposed to consider families "under pressure" but I would say every family I see is "under pressure". How am I supposed to interpret "under pressure"? The guidelines tell me to consider whether they are under the kind of pressure that could be alleviated by a loan or a grant. If the loan or grant will make no difference to their problems, then I am supposed to turn them away.' The way he said it implied – under the beady eye of his boss – that the system was rubbish but he had to do the best he could with it. His boss's quizzical expression suggested he more or less agreed with this evaluation and rather enjoyed Arthur's mischievous but deadly accurate exposition of this Byzantine corner of the social security system. It makes no more sense than the Mad Hatter's Tea Party.

Why was he obliged by the system to go through the elaborate charade of establishing my exact needs and what everything cost, since in the end the loan bore no relation to either? As with any loan shark only three things mattered – how much I could afford to borrow, how soon I could pay it back and how much money he had in his bag to lend out that day. The great advantage of borrowing from Arthur is that he would charge me no interest, unlike the crippling rates on offer to those without security or access to bank overdrafts. But there was also one big disadvantage in borrowing from Arthur: the money would be deducted at source from my benefit and I couldn't have the flexibility of deferring a repayment in some desperate week, hoping to catch up later. True, Arthur wouldn't come round and break my legs if I failed to pay but then he didn't need to. He just reached in and filched the money straight out of my purse every week.

Long ago, when Arthur first started working here, he used to administer the old Single Payments scheme. It was simple because it listed all the objects the state deemed that a destitute person needed to survive – bed, cooker, fridge, table, chair, cutlery, winter coat, working clothes and so on. It was relatively easy to administer because all he had to do was judge whether the person genuinely lacked any of the things on the list and hand out the money due, or sometimes furniture vouchers for each necessary item.

But Single Payments were abolished by the Tories in the late 1980s. They claimed the system was abused and that the case law built up over the years meant canny claimants knew exactly what to ask for. They always used the example of garden tools: one claimant successfully got a grant for garden tools so he could grow vegetables in his garden. Word spread around the claimant network and soon every benefits office was inundated with demands for money for garden tools as if some new Dig for Victory or Dig Your Way Out of Poverty enthusiasm had swept the land. Or so the story went. So the Tories swept away Single Payments and any notion that people had a definite entitlement to anything. Under the social fund, with a much smaller budget, the state would no longer promise equal treatment for all claimants according to need. Instead the state would pretend it was a charity, dispensing loans at whim according to how much there was left in the pot.

Nowadays, then, everything is left up to Arthur's personal discretion – so long as the money hasn't run out for that month. The fund gives out loans instead of grants; grants are only for children leaving care or people leaving mental hospital. While in opposition Labour rightly protested vehemently, but in power they have left this strange apparatus in place. Though they have doubled the size of the social fund, it is still minute. Recently the Commons Social Security Committee called for 'a complete overhaul' and warned that otherwise the government's own 'wider social policy objectives will be endangered'. But still loans are grinding down the incomes of the poorest, pushing those on social security to well below the lowest survival poverty threshold. After all, I was about to lose £8 off my meagre £53.05.

Even so, I thought I could just about manage and I would worry about debts later on. For now I was leaving the benefits office with a notional £400 in my pocket to furnish my flat. How far would it go?

Chapter 3

The Agency

I needed to get a job fast, but I had no idea how long it would take. I set off early in the morning on the first of many expeditions to the Job Centre. It was only fifteen minutes' walk from the flat to the nearest one off Brixton Hill, a place I had visited several times as a reporter to sit in on interviews in the early days of Labour's New Deal. I had sat watching, impressed at how the new personal advisers set about helping young people into jobs. Over the last four years I had dropped back in for a day now and then so I was worried that someone there might recognise me. But there was no need, the place was bustling with people coming and going.

It is a bright, carpeted and civilised office with a receptionist at the door, quite unlike the bad old-style benefits office where Arthur worked. Now these two agencies, benefits offices and Job Centres, are being brought together and all the joint centres will be designed to invite people in, not leave them waiting on bolted-down plastic chairs for interviews behind forbidding Perspex screens. In this open-plan space staff sit at computers interviewing their clients out in the open, far removed from the old labour exchanges I visited thirty years ago when writing my first book. As I crept in at the door, I worried the receptionist might stop me and ask what I wanted, but she was far too busy with others waiting their turn. There was a row of people waiting who would approach her desk one by one to complain about delayed social security cheques or delays getting new National Insurance numbers without which they could not work.

I sidled past the reception desk, glad that I knew exactly where to go. I headed for the bank of job-search computers which stand near the door for anyone to use, people on benefits or anyone like me just looking for a job. This is an excellent service for the nervous or for anyone who does not want nosy officialdom interfering. No one asks what you are doing, no one watches you. On these computers you can stand for hours and scroll through the jobs available. At a touch, the screen offers lists of options, from well-paid skilled jobs to the lowest manual work. At another touch it automatically prints out basic details of each job – pay, hours, qualifications required. However, the computer does not tell you exactly who the employer is or how to contact them directly. Before applying for a job, first you must be checked for suitability by Employment Service staff so that employers are not swamped with useless unqualified applicants. Job Centres try hard to attract employers to advertise their jobs here, though I discovered that large numbers of jobs are still only to be found in the local press. Since employers have to pay to put ads in the newspapers, while advertising at the Job Centre is free, this was a sign that some employers are still wary of anyone sent along by the Employment Service, assuming only the dross come here. The old labour exchange reputation dies hard. Later I came to realise that it might also mean some employers did not want their terms and conditions scrutinised by the Employment Service, if one way or another they were offering below the legal minimum wage.

After selecting a job you like the look of, you can either queue to see an adviser who will call up the employer for you, or if you prefer anonymity you can take the printouts home and call Employment Service Direct who will deal with your request over the telephone. This is much easier than a face-to-face confrontation. I was anyway at this point feeling extremely anxious: I had no useable work record, no trade qualifications, not one NVQ nor the six months' experience most jobs require, just a couple of fake references from members of my family that might not stand up to close scrutiny. I worried that I could be turned down flat by the Job Centre advisers before I even got as far as an interview with an employer. Maybe this whole project would fail right here at the first obstacle. There was also the problem of my age. I had read about people who can't get an interview once they admit they are over fifty, and with manual jobs, it might be even trickier. I could imagine employers looking me up and down and reckoning I didn't look like a good prospect, however hard I might protest I was strong and fit. Would I be able to lie about my age? I didn't know if that was possible.

After trawling through the computer for an hour, I printed out a sheaf of possible jobs and scuttled out of the Job Centre to ring Employment Service Direct from my flat, relieved at avoiding a meeting with an adviser who might give me a withering look. Later I discovered there was a bank of telephones in private booths inside the Job Centre itself where people afraid of approaching an adviser can call the service for free; clever psychology to encourage the shy.

Back home I summoned up the nerve to make my first call. The voice at the end of the telephone was reassuring: the woman sounded about my age, friendly, keen to help. First she asked for my name, which was OK: I am lucky that my official name on all documents is not the same as my professional name. My parents put down another name on my birth certificate but always called me Polly. My married name is a very common, unmemorable one, which I rarely use except on my passport, bank accounts and other official documents. This double identity now turned into a blessing.

The second thing the friendly voice asked was for my National Insurance number. As I read it out she typed it into her computer at the other end of the telephone and I held my breath. I did not know what kind of information about me that number might reveal. Would it give my employment record? (In which case it might show at once that I was a high earner, already in a job – though on sabbatical – and already paying top-rate National Insurance contributions.) Would she ask what I was doing looking for a minimum-wage job? Perhaps she would suspect I had stolen the identity of this person and was using a false NI number? There was a long silence and she asked for my date of birth again. 'I can't seem to find you with that National Insurance number,' she said.

I started to panic as if I really was doing something dishonest. But then suddenly she said, 'Ah! I've found you! So sorry, I typed in the number wrongly, silly me. Yes, here it is. Now, what can I do for you?' So whatever Big Brother information the state might hold on its citizens, it does not seem to be linked to National Insurance

numbers and I was saved. But this showed that there was no way I could ever fake either my name or my age, since all reputable employers demand a National Insurance number.

'So, do you have a job you want to enquire about?' she asked. The first choice I had picked out from the computer was a hospital domestic job, the location of the hospital unspecified beyond 'London area'. I gave her the job reference number. 'Oh yes, I've found the job on the computer,' she said. She was cheerily encouraging and asked no nosy questions about my past nor about my age. While I held on she telephoned the job advertiser and in a short time came back to me. 'It's an agency job, dear,' she said. 'Grange Executives in Shoreditch High Street. They say if you get down there Wednesday at eleven-thirty in the morning and ask for Samantha, they'll interview you. They say you must take a passport or birth certificate, National Insurance number, two passport photos, two references from previous jobs and your bank account number because the agency only pays through their computerised payment system. Is that OK?' I said yes, I'd be there. 'Come back to us if you have any other jobs you want to try for. Good luck!'

It took a long time to get to Shoreditch from Clapham by bus, but I already had my bus pass. I did have to spend £3 to get my two passport photos. I found the agency, a dingy shop front on a heavy traffic corner, and as I approached I could see a steady flow of people coming and going. I had no idea what to expect, but I had an interview and a cover story I was rehearsing over and over in my mind, trying to sound convincing. It was all about being a returner to work after my children had grown up.

As I stepped inside, the reception area was crammed so tight with people waiting and filling out forms that it was hard to find a place to stand. Eventually I pushed my way to the reception desk and before I could even say my name the young man behind the desk said, 'Passport please!' and I handed it over. Everyone who walked through the door had to surrender their passport before they even began to wait. The young man glanced at it and put it on a pile without saying a word. 'I've come for an interview with Samantha, for eleven-thirty,' I said. 'She's not here,' he answered brusquely. 'Just wait. We'll call your name. Fill out these forms while you're

waiting. Next!' I was quite wrong to have expected an interview at an appointed time. I soon learned that this was a concept from my other life. On this side of life everyone waits and queues and there are no times or appointments.

I watched the other applicants. Most of them were foreign; many seemed to understand barely a word of English. All were desperate for work, as each of them approached the young man at the reception desk, many with a friend to speak for them in equally halting English. The young man asked them a perfunctory question or two and if they didn't understand at all he sent them away, however hard they pleaded for work, but most were allowed to wait. Among this seething mass of labour were the eager, willing to take just about anything, and others with an air of weary resignation. In corners some were contorted with anxiety as they struggled with the sheaf of forms they had been given. As I looked on, the only strict rule that seemed to apply was that everyone must have a valid work permit or British citizenship before they even got a chance to fill out any forms. Immigration status was the one check that was rigorously carried out almost everywhere I went.

I set about completing the forms slowly and meticulously to help pass the time. I had come prepared for most of the questions and had planned what previous jobs and work history I would invent. Jobs I did thirty years ago were taken out and dusted down to look as if they were yesterday. I gave my mother as one reference ('carer for old person'; she is in fact fit as a fiddle and needs no care) and my daughter and son-in-law as the other ('domestic cleaner' or sometimes 'child minder' for my grandson). They had been well-briefed to say I was honest, reliable and a good cleaner/carer/child minder if anyone should take up my references. (Few ever did.)

I had plenty of time to study the small print of the forms I was about to sign, though the print is so small and dense I doubt many other applicants bother. The terms exposed in these tiny words explain why the NHS is using casual workers employed by agencies at pay and conditions it would never itself dare to offer in public. The Casual Work Agreement is an 'agreement to provide occasional services', in other words a zero-hours contract. One clause automatically opted me out of the 48-hour maximum working

week protection. 'The temporary worker hereby agrees that the working week limit shall not apply.' No sign no job.

That is perfectly legal. It is also precisely what the unions said would happen when the Labour government went to extraordinary lengths to block the 48-hour working time directive that every other EU country agreed to. Our 'flexible', 'lightly regulated' employment laws with low taxes and less onerous obligations for employers were too valuable to lose to a Brussels directive. Britain therefore insisted on an opt-out and any employee was allowed voluntarily to sign away their right to work no more than forty-eight hours. At the time the argument was all about enthusiastic high fliers in top jobs: were permanent secretaries, cabinet ministers, captains of industry, midnight-oil QCs or computer-programming whiz kids going to be obliged by law to stop working after forty-eight hours because of some pettifogging EU rule? But the effect – as predicted – has been that the opt-out clause is mainly imposed on the lowest paid who are obliged to sign the 'voluntary' declaration that I had just signed. Four million workers have 'voluntarily' opted out of the 48-hour law.

There were various other unsavoury clauses I had to sign up to: 'Uniform will be deducted from the following week's pay' and 'As a casual worker you will not be subject to the company's grievance and disciplinary procedures'. I would, as the law obliges, get four weeks' annual holiday but first I 'must do a continuous thirteen weeks work'. Since my time was to be at the complete disposal of the agency, in theory there was nothing to stop them making sure they interrupted my employment before I ever clocked up my thirteen weeks 'continuous'.

The next form I had to fill in was an 'Industrial test' – basic arithmetic, filing jumbled numbers in order of magnitude and filing names alphabetically. Looking around the room I could see that understanding these instructions had stumped many of the applicants, who tried to take away the paper to get help, but no one was allowed to leave with any of the forms or documents. This, I suspected later, was not to stop them cheating on the test: I was told some people got few right and it didn't really matter. It was probably designed to stop anyone taking the contracts home or to a trade union in order to challenge anything the agency did. Guessing I would not be given a copy, I took surreptitious notes of some of the wording. There was also a health form and a form giving consent for the agency to make a police check for any criminal record.

As time ticked by the staff disappeared for lunch. By 2 p.m. my name still hadn't been called. More people from every continent poured through the door, lining the walls, perching against counters until three o'clock struck, when the doors shut and any later-comers were sent away, however far they had travelled. Waiting, waiting, waiting, I considered how expensive job-hunting is in time and money. This had cost me not just £3 in the photo-me booth in Liverpool Street Station but precious time. What if this job didn't come to anything? As I was to discover, many job applications require travelling to far-flung corners of London to visit agencies and potential employers in person, to collect forms and return them with the requisite documents.

I sat there thinking how low value permeates everything about the lives of the poor. I had queued in the post office to pay the rent, trekked to the only shop that re-charges the electric meter and queued again. Everywhere I was kept waiting and yet my time was precious because, like all the people at the agencies, I needed to get a job quickly. But poor people's time is regarded as valueless. At £4.10 an hour, it is almost. Later I tried to apply for a cleaning job at King's College Hospital. When I rang, the domestic manager had sighed wearily, 'You come down here, go down to the services room in the basement, collect a form, fill it out, and bring it back.' I took the long bus ride but it turned out there were no jobs anyway and someone behind a desk just said, 'Come back for an application form next week.' At one point I was told that McDonald's would be interviewing at Balham Job Centre. If I wanted an interview I would have to get down there to collect a form, return it within two days and go back there again on the day to wait in line for an interview, no appointments. When I asked the Balham Job Centre if they could send me the form to save two journeys they said, 'No, sorry, the employer doesn't allow forms to be sent out.' The people with least resources, no cars, taxis or money for tubes, whose time and travel is the most precious are treated as if they were persons of leisure who could just drop by, no problem. If it made job-seeking difficult, it made job-swapping virtually impossible since all this always had to be done in person in the middle of the day.

Over time as I returned to the Job Centre computer, I acquired a more jaundiced eye. You learn quickly to expect that some of the jobs are already long-gone and many are non-existent, as agencies trawl aimlessly for low-paid people to put on their books with no particular job on offer or at least nothing like the one advertised, usually something worse. There were some jobs that stayed on the computer for months, such as one for a *pâtissière* in Dieppe which looked tempting but my cooking certainly did not run to *pâtisseries*. There were a couple permanently on display for work in Germany which neither I nor the Job Centre staff could understand as they were written in German, but they too stayed there for months, presumably a token EU gesture.

At the agency the waiting area had become impossibly packed and staff behind the desk more harassed by the time the clock ticked past three and the doors slammed shut to anyone else. At last my name was called out. My forms were taken and a young girl called Alana swept me into an interview cubicle. Alana was bubbly and friendly and she started by giving me the company spiel – be honest, be clean, be punctual. She glanced at my carefully manufactured CV but was not much interested. She asked cursorily about my referees, what I had been doing (cleaning), and had I ever worked in a hospital? (Yes, but she didn't ask when and I didn't tell her it was thirty years ago.) I handed over the photos, proof of address, proof of bank account and I got my passport back.

'Now,' she said. 'The job we've got for you is hospital porter. Is that OK?' I looked a bit dubious, having come here for a hospital cleaning job.

'Isn't that usually men's work?' I asked. She said she didn't know and went next door to consult a superior in charge of hospital jobs. I heard but didn't see this person, beyond a set of long bright fingernails waving in the air through a crack in the door. 'Oh no, it's fine, fine!' I heard her say and Alana came back in. 'She says it's fine for women too.'

I was not sure exactly what hospital portering involved. 'Is there a lot of heavy lifting?' I asked. 'No, no, nothing like that,' Alana said, though she obviously had no more idea than I. However, after such a long wait, a job seemed suddenly imminent, alarmingly easy with so few questions asked.

Alana then thrust into my hand a collection of papers with a big smile. The first page said 'Your application to join Grange Executives has been successful!!!!!!!' I was very pleased and Alana was bustling now. 'You start first thing tomorrow morning at the Chelsea and Westminster Hospital,' she said. 'OK?'

'Is that it, then?' I asked, somehow incredulous that there was nothing more to joining the NHS than this.

'Yep, that's it. Just turn up at the porter's lodge tomorrow and say you're from Grange Executives. Good luck!' She handed me a very official-looking identity card with one of my photos laminated inside, as if it were some kind of security pass. The next applicant was waiting so I hurried away.

So that was it. No police check; neither of my referees had been contacted, and I was setting off to work in a hospital. I could be just out of prison for serial unplugging of patients from life-support machines. I could have been released from a mental hospital with a peculiar taste for tormenting elderly patients. So much for security. Forget any idea of induction into the noble portals of the NHS. There could hardly be a more lackadaisical way of being dumped into it to turn a quick buck for an agency. Up in the realms where people like me debate about the NHS, its values, its need for reform (or not), its staff morale and the spirit of public service – that discourse inhabits another universe. Down here at Grange Executives it matters not at all what the job is or who it is for. By contracting out these services the NHS has abrogated all responsibility for hiring its ancillary staff, leaving its nether gateways guarded by agencies such as these which are now the main route into the lower ranks of the health service.

The bundle of papers Alana gave me were mainly instructions about what to do to get further jobs. 'We operate a waiting system, so come to the office daily to collect your bookings. Arrive in your correct uniform and ready for work.' The thought of getting down to Shoreditch and waiting every day was not appealing. As I left the agency, reading the papers as I went, I realised that it was not clear if my job was just for one day or longer. The most important instruction on the front page was in capital letters, 'NEVER give your personal telephone number to clients.' That was plainly not for our own protection but for the agency's, for fear they might lose their commission on future jobs. The uniform list for hospital porters was black trousers, white shirt, black shoes. There was another instruction: 'Always turn up to your booking 15 minutes early' which would add an hour and a quarter's unpaid time to the working week.

Other pages were filled with capital letter instructions: 'Take pride in your appearance. You not only represent yourself but also Grange Executives. BASIC Grange rule. NEVER LEAVE WORK WITH ANYTHING YOU DIDN'T ARRIVE WITH.' A page on Personal Hygiene and Conduct told me to take frequent baths or showers, use anti-perspirant and wear no nail varnish, with warnings about drugs, alcohol, eating and smoking. 'Never chew gum whilst working.'

Sure enough I had been given no copies of the forms I signed, so no chance to peruse the rights I signed away by becoming 'temporary' and 'casual'. Nor was there anything here to tell me how much of my wages Grange would take. All the same, walking back along Shoreditch High Street towards Liverpool Street, I felt elated. As my form said, I had been SUCCESSFUL!!!!! However humble the job, the process of getting it always cleverly confers on the applicant the sense that you have just won the lottery. You have been selected, passed a test, met with approval and you leave glowing with achievement even for winning a job at £4.35 an hour. However tight the labour market, the applicant is always the supplicant, the applicant is always the grateful one who says Thank You, never the employer. However desperate for staff – and many are these days – the employer never ever relinquishes the upper hand.

On the bus on the long trip back to Clapham, I was leafing through the papers again when I came upon one clause I had not noticed until now. Grange Executives only pays wages two weeks in arrears. I would have to work for two weeks before I saw a penny. That meant my debts would rise yet higher. How can anyone leave one job and take another, or leave benefit and take a job, if you have to starve for a fortnight before being paid? Later on, one or two jobs I did only paid out after a full month, as if they were paying an executive salary not rock-bottom wages to people living hand-to-mouth. I remembered Arthur's unlikely advice to ask an employer to pay money up front to cover the gap until pay-day. So when I got home I plucked up courage to call Alana. I didn't dare ask her for an advance but I did ask if they could pay me at the end of my first week, as I really needed the money. Her response was immediate as if she was often asked this: 'Absolutely not, we never do. Our payroll systems only operate after two weeks' work.' So that was that.

Chapter 4

Spending

Beside a railway line in Camberwell inside a large warehouse is the Shaftesbury Society furniture store. Here people with absolutely nothing come by appointment to choose the things they need to set up home. Most of them are families moving from temporary bed and breakfast hostels to flats they have long waited for. Arthur at the benefits office had told me nothing of the charities that can help out with furniture because he was not allowed to mention second-hand. It was a rule presumably designed to indemnify and guard the backs of civil servants by hiding the fact that the money isn't enough. But Jenny in the neighbourhood housing office had given me the printed list of second-hand furniture charities they handed out to all their new tenants. Without it many people could not possibly furnish their new homes with even the most basic items. My experience was not, of course, like that of many genuinely destitute people because I knew my way round the system, who to ask and how to ask for it. For me this was an interesting experiment, with none of the emotional desperation; I was not dragging small children along with me or unable to speak English. There was no way I could taste the crippling anxiety of teetering on the edge of an abyss, but at least I could test out how the system works.

My appointment was with Letticia Sabimana who had worked there many years. I had explained to the Shaftesbury headquarters what I was doing and why, and they were enthusiastic to help because they found themselves up against tidal waves of need that they could not possibly meet. They required more warehouse space, more staff, more money and they were eager to talk about the problems of people who came to them utterly destitute. The more publicity, maybe the more donations of furniture and cash. So the Shaftesbury agreed that I could come here to spend my notional social fund loan and they would deliver the stuff for free, as they do for needy people. In exchange I paid a donation of £500 and would hand back all the furniture when I left the flat.

Letticia was a middle-aged Mauritian, a warm and generous woman who at once put me right on some things I hadn't considered. 'So you think you got your social fund loan?' she asked. Yes, I said, the benefits officer had agreed a notional £400. 'Ah, but have you got the money in your hand? That we must ask first. Usually it takes weeks to come through; sometimes it can be a very long time.' But I thought it was lent for an immediate crisis? She gave a wry laugh. 'We have people who come here who have been turned out of their hostels the day they are given the key to their new flat by the council. By the time they get their appointment here, they may have lived with nothing for a while. Their flat is empty with nothing at all. They have no money to buy even bedding, let alone a bed.' The rules say that they cannot start to apply for their social fund loan until they already have the keys to their new flat, but as soon as they have the keys they are evicted from their hostels and must move into empty new accommodation at once.

What happens? 'They sleep on the floor in the cold with their children for many weeks. Maybe they have coats to cover themselves.' What can the Shaftesbury do? 'We can do very little until the money comes through. We do what we can.' But the charity is run on a shoestring and cannot afford to give out furniture without being paid first. Although their prices are very low, the money turning over keeps them in business. Without it, they would close at once. The Shaftesbury can't advance their impoverished clients the money before social fund cheques arrive because desperate people do not often come back to repay it once their money finally comes in: their need is so great they can't help spending it. To show how tight the charity's finances are, they have only a tiny sum – £20 a month called Mother Pat's Fund – which they can use to provide something for the most extreme cases who have no money for anything. Only £20 a month and they are seeing twenty families a day, turning many more away.

All families have to be referred by an official agency, a housing department, housing association or social services, to guarantee their bona fide destitution. 'Now, destitution, there is an important word,' Letticia said. 'If people go for a social fund loan and they do not know that word, they are often turned down. We can tell them they must use that word but if they go for their interview before we see them, they don't know that. If the social fund in their area is running low, officers can turn people away who do not know they must say, "We are destitute," in just those words.'

The Shaftesbury's furniture comes from people who call to donate unwanted items, getting rid of good but redundant furniture and usually paying a donation to the volunteer crew that comes to take it away. Shops sometimes donate old stock – Ikea had just sent a magnificent pile of free new bedding. The charity's drivers and some staff are paid but the men who do the heavy removals and most other workers are volunteers. Churches across London collect money and at Christmas several City companies' staff bring in one new toy or children's book each which the van drivers collect for the most needy families. 'Mothers sometimes cry when they see the toys because they had thought they could never afford anything for their children at Christmas and here they can get brand-new nice toys for maybe £1 each.'

Letticia explains that families coming to the warehouse get only half an hour each to select everything they need, so that the charity can serve their twenty families a day. Half an hour is not long. As I set off to make my selections, it was like participating in a version of the TV game show *Supermarket Sweep*, hurrying up and down the aisles picking out the crucial items in the allotted time. What is essential? A bed first. That day there were no double beds left so I took a single, thinking this condemned me to a lonelier life than I had intended: my partner had promised to spend some time with me in the flat. Next a cooker and a fridge. When these are donated, the charity must by law send them out to a fitter who reconditions them, giving them a safety check and a three-month guarantee. Reconditioning each appliance costs the Shaftesbury £50, so they charge £65 for a cooker and £45 for a small fridge with no freezer compartment. I hadn't thought out well enough exactly what I needed, and totting up the prices as I scuttled about the warehouse got confusing. I ended up buying a sofa for £15, two armchairs for £12, a table for £15 and chairs for £24. A bag full of old curtains from a hotel costs £8, essential on winter nights especially in the bedroom. A shabby old wardrobe was £10, two bedside tables £10 and an old dressing-table I really wanted because of the mirror attached was £20. A bundle of cutlery, a few plates, mugs and glasses, plus the only two saucepans left (both very thin and battered), a worn but useful plastic washing-up bowl and a £2 small hearth rug to cover the worst of the sitting-room carpet stains brought the total to £247. (I was bringing my own bedding, assuming that was one of the few personal things I already possessed.)

At the end of my half hour I felt I had been prudent and done well to get everything I needed for this sum, which showed how little I knew about being poor. I thought that leaving £153 of my social fund loan intact was a good safety margin, but I was quite wrong and Letticia knew this. She shook her head and said, 'You spent too much of your loan. You are furnishing the place the way you or I would, not the way a destitute family would. Bedside tables and a dressing table, yet! You will need more money than that £153.' She was right but she shrugged and let me learn my lesson the hard way. She arranged for one of her crews to deliver my furniture to the flat and I left her with many thanks. I could imagine the gratitude of the genuinely destitute.[1]

Now I still had to buy a television, the one truly essential item I could not live without: I would rather sleep on the floor or do without cooking. I found one for £49 in a local second-hand shop. It had an indoor aerial fixed to the top which I knew I would need as the flat had no external aerial socket. It worked well in the shop, but when I brought it back to the flat it didn't. I hadn't noticed that in the shop it had been plugged into an external aerial. I had to go back to the shop and buy another indoor aerial for £4. So now I had exactly £100 left.

Next I needed a heater. With no central heating, the flat was viciously cold in February and only the two small middle sections on the rickety old gas fire in my sitting-room lit up. I searched around cheap electrical stores locally for the best bargain and found a big convector heater for £24.99 that seemed to throw out a fair amount of warmth. I asked the man in the shop how good it was on electricity use. 'Well,' he said. 'It uses twice as much juice as that one over there, but that one costs £49.99.' Too much. Too bad about the electricity, I'd worry about that later. I bought the cheaper one, which left me with £75.01. The other essential was a telephone and it had to be a mobile as I was travelling around looking for jobs. The cheapest deal around was £49 and a pay-as-you-go rate that I estimated at a frugal £8 a week. Was that an outrageous extravagance? Most people in low-paid jobs I met did have cell phones and job-seeking these days would be very much more difficult without one. That left me with a grand total of £26.01.

I still really wanted a double bed, then my partner could stay sometimes and my son could use the single bed I had bought. Letticia had been depressed when I told her that Arthur would not and could not recommend second-hand furniture shops or even second-hand furniture charities, but she was outraged when I told her he had suggested I go down to Crazy George's to see what they could do for me. 'Crazy George!' she said. 'We have so many families getting into trouble from that place, deep in debt up to their necks. They will give credit to anyone on no security, especially to people who really can't afford it, at shocking interest rates.' I set off to explore what Crazy George might have to offer. After all, a lot of people would think advice from a social security officer must be worthwhile. Again I wondered if Arthur might not have sent me off deliberately to find the worst that can happen to destitute families, for Crazy George would certainly multiply their problems.

I found the store on the ground floor of the Elephant and Castle shopping centre, a lively place with a struggling run-down air surrounded by stalls and shops selling brands no well-off person ever heard of, full of shoppers hunting for bargains. Amid all this shabbiness, Crazy George's emporium stood out as a gleaming beacon filled with brand-new bright furniture and electrical goods, all bathed in golden glittering light. It is laid out like Argos with each item in the catalogue on show, but the customer must go to the desk to order from the stockroom the items they want. On the counter are the Crazy George catalogues with this message: 'Discover Affordable Shopping Made Easy!' Inside it promises, 'All our products are available with NO DEPOSIT AND NO CREDIT CHECKS.' Unlike discount stores such as Argos or Ikea, everything here is extraordinarily expensive, way beyond ordinary department-store prices for things that looked bright but shoddy. All the prices are quoted at the per-week hire-purchase price in bold letters. The total cash price is in small letters underneath, because people don't come here to pay cash. The cheapest double bed they offered, the 'Nicole', was a basic metal-barred number. It cost £4.99 a week for 156 weeks – three years. I was not convinced Nicole would last that long. Even smaller print said 'Mattress available separately', with no mention of what the mattress cost extra. The APR was 29.9 per cent. The small print underneath the picture said the Nicole cost an astounding £432.38 cash, without mattress. Checking around locally, I saw a bed that looked much the same in MFI in Clapham High Street for £189.00 with mattress. Other items in the catalogue were equally bad value: take the Accessory Package consisting of a small hearth rug and a small lamp with a matching coffee table. That also costs £4.99 for three years, or £432.38 cash.

But I could see why it was tempting to shop this way. However much better value it would be for me to buy the MFI bed from the remnants of my social fund loan, I just hadn't got £189 to buy it and I could not borrow that money from anywhere else. If I really needed a double bed, I could see how easy it would be to persuade myself that a mere £4.99 a week was more affordable, in my circumstances. Crazy George would give me the bed on production of nothing more than a payslip, a tenancy agreement and two IDs, even though I was penniless. Like most of the well-off I had never heard of Crazy George because the well-off never need credit at these usurious rates when every bank is tripping over itself to lend cash to the rich at good rates.

At the back of the catalogue there is the list of places with Crazy George branches, ninety-five of them in all, with more to open soon. The list reads like a roll call of the country's most deprived areas: Birkenhead, Bradford, Burnley, Byker, Corby, Doncaster, Easter-house, East Ham, Greenock, Hartlepool, Jarrow, Kirkby, Oldham, Paisley, Rotherham, Runcorn, South Shields and Wigan, to pick out a few. Wherever there is a Starbucks, a Waterstone's, a Jigsaw or a

Habitat you can bet there isn't a Crazy George's nearby. We who own cars can drive out to vast department stores like Ikea and pay cash for a houseful of good bargains. They who have no cars and no cash end up paying 29.9 per cent APR. Who knows what the repossession rate must be? Arthur should not be directing his social fund clients here.

By chance the very next week, as I scoured the pages of the *South London Press* early on Friday morning before all the best jobs had gone, I found this:

Are you persuasive, persistent, confident, tactful and able to deliver results? Do you want the opportunity to prove it? Crazy George's have a number of opportunities across London . . . You will be a central point of contact for clients in resolving all queries or issues relating to late payments. This will involve telephoning or visiting them at home. It will mean using your initiative and problem solving skills . . . We can offer fantastic career prospects and exceptional rewards – so act NOW!

I called the number. 'Yes,' said an enthusiastic voice. 'Crazy George's always has loads of jobs for debt collectors.' But it wasn't really the kind of work I was looking for. Another story, another day maybe.

Within a short time I had given up on the idea of acquiring a double bed or anything else. I would gladly have sold the bedside tables, wardrobe and dressing-table to anyone who offered anything for them. I could have done without my fridge too and saved myself £45 I desperately needed later: the flat was so cold I could have kept milk and eggs in a kitchen cupboard, no problem.

On moving-in day I sat on the floor of my flat in my coat in the cold on the none-too-nice stained red carpet, perched on my pile of bedding with my television and my heater beside me in the sitting-room. I leaned against the skirting board by the unlit gas fire, waiting for the furniture to be delivered and the gas and electricity men to do their connections. It was raining outside, the lift wasn't working and the stink from the rubbish chute on my floor was drifting in with particular pungence. Every time I opened the door the waft of rubbish flooded in and took time to disperse again. In a local bargain shop for 20p I did find an air freshener, Spring Flowers, to put by the door but when I got it home I found its sell-by date was 1994 and the scent had long since evaporated.

While I was sitting there waiting, I was yet again doing my accounts in a notebook thinking I must have got something wrong. I had already run into chronic trouble. This is how I was calculating my spending so far. Here I was in week one, in which I was moving into the flat, acquiring the basic furniture and looking for a job. I was counting on finding work immediately for next week. So for this first week I allowed myself £53.05 from social security for my Job Seeker's Allowance for a single person. I also still had £26.01 left of my social fund. If I prided myself on budgeting well, I was quite wrong. Without realising it, I was already deep in debt with worse to come.

Week One Fixed Outgoings:

No rent or council tax: paid by housing benefit as my income was as low as you can get.

Water rates	£2
Social fund repayment	£8
Gas and electric	£15
Bus pass	£8.50
Phone	£8
TV licence	£2
Total fixed spending =	£43.50

Before I had bought anything to eat, that left me with just £9.55 of my Job Seeker's Allowance plus the remaining £26.01 social fund, giving a total of £35.56. That sounded OK, but then I remembered that I wouldn't be paid on my first day at work, so even though I had got a job starting tomorrow, I would have to survive on this money for two weeks until I got my first pay cheque. Remember, Arthur had warned me there was no way I could still draw any benefit to cover my first week in work. I must declare I was working from day one and funds would be cut off immediately. If ever there was a disincentive to work, it might be the prospect of near-starvation plus debt in the first week in a job. In my second week I would also run up £43.50 in unavoidable fixed payments, so now I was in real trouble. Before buying a crust to eat I was minus £7.94.

No, it was even worse than that. I had miscalculated because I had forgotten that in my first week in work I would be counted as earning my first wage. Once I was no longer unemployed I would have to start paying rent. Rent on the flat was £59 a week. As I was a low earner, Lambeth housing benefit would give me a rent rebate of £17.56 making my total rent £41.44 a week. On top of that I would also now have to pay council tax of £12.65, which brought it back up to a total of £54.09 a week. (Council tax is deeply regressive as it hits the low-paid the hardest: the bottom fifth of households pay 8 per cent of their income while the richest fifth pay only 1 per cent.) So my debts rose sharply to £62.03 without even buying a packet of rice.

True, when pay-day came I would be able to pay this off. But in the meantime what would any pragmatic person do? First of all, decide not to pay the rent, council tax, water rates or TV licence for the first fortnight. I would certainly not bother to pay the social fund £8 back in the second week once I no longer had a benefit cheque from which they could seize it automatically. I would just hope to catch up with all these debts at some other time. So I did the sums again and found I could postpone £70.09. Even so, whichever way I looked at it, two weeks' of unavoidable spending items came to £71 and I only had £79.09. That meant I had just £8.09 cash in hand to last me for two weeks.

If all those figures are hard to follow, the final total I wrote down in my notebook book showed that for my first fortnight I had £4.04 a week to spend on everything I needed, with a £70.09 debt hanging over me. I was not a 'good manager' as the Edwardians used to talk about the better class of poor. Letticia at Shaftesbury had been quite right. As I mulled this over, I was ashamed to think about how many articles I had written about efforts to get the unemployed into work, without realising the huge financial quagmire people had to cross in getting themselves off benefits and into a job. I had no idea that anyone moving from one status to the other was bound to start working life in serious debt. Many nervous and debt-averse people might well think it safer to stay on the dole with their

rent fully paid – even at this pathetically low standard of living –
than take the risk. It is a perverse absurdity in the system that paying
no rent and bumping along the bottom on £53.05 could seem a
better bet than jumping into a job at a minimum wage of £164 a
week, if it meant running up debts. I was going to have to borrow
money since no one could live on £4.04 a week, certainly not for
two weeks in a row.

These calculations took me a long time, crossing out and starting
again several times, trying to think of ways of cutting back. Frankly,
I thought I had made a mistake but I have had these figures checked
and they are all too accurate. While I was puzzling over them, there
was a knock on the door and the furniture arrived from the
Shaftesbury, carried all the way up the stairs because yet again
the lift was broken. One of the volunteers was an electrician who
wired up my cooker, ready to go. I was deeply grateful and
apologetic about the lift but they were understanding because it
happened to them all the time on these estates. I didn't even have
any tea to offer them.

When they had left I manoeuvred the furniture into the best
places I could, an armchair each side of the gas fire, a sofa in front of
it with the small stained hearth rug that was only marginally better
than the sticky carpet underneath. I put the television on the table,
plugged in the new aerial and it worked. The small collection of
odd plates and cups went into the kitchen cupboards while the
knives, forks and spoons went into the kitchen drawer, with a tin
opener, a wooden spoon and a potato masher. I left one of the two
thin and dented saucepans on the stove to use for boiling water as I
had no kettle. I pushed the small single bed up against the wall in the
bedroom and shunted the dressing-table with the mirror into a
corner. Then came the bag of old hotel curtains. As I pulled them
out one by one they looked smart, but I found they matched in
pattern but not in lengths. They would look odd but that didn't
really matter as they were wide and long enough to cover the
bedroom and sitting-room windows to give enough privacy at
night.

What did matter and I had forgotten, was that there were no
curtain rails. I wondered vaguely what curtain rails cost, plus the

tools to put them up with. Could it be done at all without a drill and rawl plugs? The curtains were surprisingly heavy. At home I would have called a handyman in to fix good strong rails for me. But what could I do here? I suddenly remembered that at the bottom of my capacious and rarely emptied handbag, for a long time I had been carrying around a pair of extra-long laces that I had been meaning to give to my son to replace the frayed and knotted ones on his Converse boots. I dug them out and found that one each did stretch across the length of the bedroom and sitting-room windows and they felt strong enough to hold up the curtains. Later I went out to a small hardware shop, bought ten long nails for 20p and hammered them across the top of the windows with my shoe. The plaster crumbled a bit and the heels of my shoes took a lot of damage but the nails held, so I tied up the bootlaces across them. There was a moment's panic about hooks but I found the curtains still had most of their old hooks attached to them. I stood on a chair and hung them up gingerly, fearful the laces and nails wouldn't take the weight, but they did. The curtains sagged below the window-frame at the top, but they would do. I didn't dare to draw them for fear they would come crashing down, so I left them closed all the time, pinning them back with a few books in the daytime. Later, looking up at other people's windows, I noticed several had strange make-shift arrangements much like mine, presumably for the same reason. Curtain rails are expensive and hard to fix.

How did the flat look now? It looked like what it was, a collection of jumble. Anyone walking in would have reckoned this was some kind of homeless hostel, pretty bleak, not anyone's home. Maybe later warm touches could be added – a picture or two on the wall and some rugs or covers to brighten the worn, faded sofa and chairs. I had everything and more than I strictly needed and I would be comfortable enough, if desolate. All the same, standing at the window and looking out at the rain-sodden grass below, staring over towards the identical blocks on the other side, I could imagine utter despair at this moment if this really had been my life. Even though it was only my life for a very short time, it felt unbearably miserable and very cold. The cold was in the concrete of the walls and it blew in through the windows, whose warped metal frames no longer fitted and left wide gaps. It seeped up from the floor through the thin carpet. A concrete building that has never been heated has a deep and indigenous damp, a dank iciness in February that settles into the bones up through the shoes up into the soles of the feet. The cold never departs, even with my convector heater and the half gas fire. I could keep it at bay sitting close up to both heaters in the sitting-room with the door shut, curled up on an armchair, toasting my front at the fire while my back was draughty. I tried to imagine this was a country cottage and an open fire, the sort of cold that the well-off relish as part of the charm in weekend second homes. But whether psychological or physiological, concrete cold was not the same as cottage cold.

There was a small balcony outside my sitting-room but when I tried to open the door on to it the bent key didn't work and it had plainly been painted shut for years. Like many of the balconies in the White House, mine had been long abandoned and colonised by the pigeons. Upended in one corner there was an old broken child's bike, a rusted barbecue and some rubble, all of it covered in years of pigeon droppings. Two cracked pigeon's eggs had been left in one corner. Sheltering from the rain, wedged right up against the window panes on the outside ledge, was a row of the mangiest, most miserable-looking birds, sickly and balding. It was as if they too had found their social niche here in the White House, the bottom of the pecking order. I was revolted by the sight of them and banged on the window to make them fly off, but they were past budging and, wet-feathered, they barely shifted. This was their space and they occupied it all time I was there, adding to the general sense of dejection.

How things look matters only a little less than basic comforts. I was comfortable enough, but living here was deeply dispiriting. Even if inside my front door I had, like other families over the years, managed to make a warm and inviting home, that would not be enough. Tramping in across the estate, keeping a wary eye out round every corner, watching surreptitiously anyone coming and going, I always found the estate mildly threatening. Walking into it lowered the spirits. It wasn't just me, unused to it: long-time residents said the same. Instead of a lighter step and a lifting of the heart as you approached your own home from work, here was the opposite. The nearer you got, the worse it felt. Mild anxiety was only part of it, it was the visual assault on the eye even on a sunny day that made you hurry between the road outside and your own front door. It was the walk past the stinking bins, through the broken front door swinging on its hinges, up the smelly stairs, past the putrid rubbish chute, always on the alert for anything unexpected, aware of any other doors opening or shutting in the unseen corridors you passed on the way up. I never used the lift; after what Jenny had said, I was too afraid of getting stuck in it. By the time I reached my flat through this desert, there was no warm sense of homecoming, only relief at being able to shut out these sorry surroundings.

The curtain rails became a kind of symbol for everything I could not afford. Sitting now on a chair at my new table, I made a list of what I thought I needed, trying to work out what I might ever be able to afford eventually with extreme prudence. A bed, a hairdryer, an iron, an ironing board, a vacuum cleaner, an electric kettle, a toaster, above all lampshades for my bare bulbs – all these basic things I probably could acquire slowly, one at a time over a year or two. A new carpet might never be possible. A foreign holiday, or any holiday, was almost unimaginable. My list grew longer and longer, filled with all the things most of us take for granted, things someone in my new position might manage to obtain a few of, but never all of them at once, always juggling between choices. For now, I was thinking no further than food.

To start with, I realised I had no idea what most things cost. For example, there was not a single light bulb in the place and it would be dark soon. I had always bought a bundle of them, dumping them into my shopping trolley with no thought about their price. That is how I always shop. I go to Sainsbury's in Clapham High Street, park the car and fill it up with what I need. But I have only a hazy idea of what the total weekly bill usually comes to – about £100, I think, for myself and my family. But if I shop twice, it might be more, depending on family and social arrangements. I like to pretend to myself that I am not especially extravagant: I don't buy outrageously expensive things like fillet steak or Dover soles (except as a treat). I like bargains, priding myself on sometimes finding items close to their sell-by date with red Reduced stickers on them, which gives me an absurd sense of good housekeeping virtue. I often buy Three for the Price of Two bargains and feel pleased with myself without bothering to check if they are in fact expensive products and not a bargain at all. Or whether I really want three. I like products with 200 Extra Reward Points, without bothering to check if their price is higher than the worth of the extra rewards. I do know the price of a litre of milk and a standard loaf of bread, but I only make sure I always know that because it is a low trick I have occasionally used on politicians if they criticise the poor. Ask a male politician for the price of these essentials and most haven't a clue: it leaves them blushing. Well, I am blushing now, clueless about the cost of anything until I get down to the cheapest local cut-price super-market – Lidl on Acre Lane. Used mainly by the hard-up, it is ten minutes' walk from the estate and a bus ride back with the shopping.

So, in the afternoon, it is shopping. What can you get for £8.09 to last a fortnight? I take a notebook and wander around Lidl's, noting prices carefully before I choose. The trouble with shops like this is that everything cheap is big and I can only afford small amounts. I assemble:

One 7 kg sack of potatoes	£1.79
1 litre of milk	45p
1 pack of yellow split peas	40p
1 pack of spaghetti	39p
1,000 g pack of rice, reduced	55p
1 pack of garlic bulbs	39p
1 tin of tomatoes (I never knew peeled were cheaper than chopped)	11p
160 teabags	£1.49
salt	15p
washing-up liquid (bargain!)	15p
3 light bulbs @ 19p each	57p
large white cabbage	62p
8 oranges	99p

I add it up and it totals £8.05! How clever! I feel like one of those smug people who sometimes send me letters responding to pieces I have written about poverty, boasting about how they brought up a family of six on lentils and home-made bread – and jolly good it was for them too. I have had to cut out things I originally included. Out goes bread, cooking oil, curry powder, instant coffee, cheese, pepper, sunflower spread, baked beans, tomato paste, one light bulb, onions. How do you choose between garlic to make very dull food bearable and a light in the toilet?

As I pace up and down the aisles taking notes and working out my sums, a manager stares at me and my notebook, clearly thinking I am an inspector or a spy from a competitor store. In the end I fill my trolley with the above items, calculating that I could survive, just, on this for a fortnight, and it would no doubt do me good to lose a lot of weight. But living like this is unbearable, and I will, of course, borrow and get into worse debt as most poor people do.

It takes a long time to shop this way. It was an interesting experiment to do this once, but being as careful as this will get a great deal more dispiriting every week that goes by. Although I have added it to the above list, Lidl did not sell any dried beans or lentils to make a long-lasting soup, so I walked the ten minutes down to Sainsbury's, crossing the line back into my old life, another social zone from Lidl's. I had thought of lentils as the cheapest most wholesome food, but I found they cost twice as much as yellow split peas. I bought just one 40p pack at the express till, looking round at the stacks of food I would usually buy, noticing their prices for the first time.

This was a sobering experience. After taking the bus home, carrying all my bags, I unpacked this prudent shopping into my kitchen cupboard. It was a dismal array of food. Nourishing, solid, this was a sustainable diet of pea soup, rice, potatoes and pasta, with just garlic and salt for flavour, but without any pleasure. Oranges were the only treat. But of course this was not prudent at all. I had 4p left in my pocket, and there was no way I could manage to buy nothing else at all for a fortnight. Thinking about borrowing and the way the poor cripple themselves with debt, I could see why once you had no money, borrowing no longer seemed much of a problem. There is no further to fall, so why not? If you are living hand-to-mouth anyway, debt does not seem to aggravate matters much. With 4p in your pocket and £70 of rent and other arrears already, nothing could be worse, so why not?

Chapter 5

Portering

It was an unexpected coincidence that the agency sent me to the Chelsea and Westminster Hospital. Only eight years old, it is a gleaming piece of modernity, vast, bright and airy, with rows of high-level walkways crossing an atrium up to the sky where three banks of glass-windowed lifts shoot up and down all day. Its walls are decked with works of modern art; the place prides itself on using the arts in medicine to cheer the eye and often the ear as bands play and music belts out frequently at lunchtime, resounding through every corner. There could be no greater contrast to St Stephen's, the hospital that stood on this site when I worked as a ward orderly more than thirty years ago.

In *A Working Life* I described the deep ingrained filth of the old Victorian redbrick building, the kitchen in the maternity ward where I worked encrusted with grime and grease. The food I served the patients was unspeakable: thin grey mince and tapioca pudding, slimy breakfasts cooked the night before with fried eggs left to simmer in fat on trolleys overnight, bread buttered the day before curled and hard. Overworked nurses had no time for the new young mothers who stayed a compulsory two weeks after the birth, inducing its own kind of post-natal depression in those dismal surroundings. It was a place where only the poor had their babies: the local middle classes headed straight for London's many teaching hospitals. Dirty, unkind, bleak and neglected, it deserved to be pulled down and amalgamated with the high-status Westminster teaching hospital, an improvement beyond imagining back then. Now the Chelsea and Westminster had become the hospital of choice for a large middle-class clientele from everywhere south of Hyde Park.

But some things had not changed, or had changed for the worse. Then as now the pay was bad and in those full employment times there was the same hectic turnover of staff, the same wasteful stream of low-paid labour, stop-gap workers on the look-out for something better, treated badly. Then many ancilliaries were Maltese, Italian or Spanish; now many were West Indian, Asian or East European. I can't claim that being directly employed by that hospital in those days engendered great emotional loyalty to the NHS because, then as now, the low-paid were treated as cheap and expendable labour. There was no miraculous St Stephen's Hospital ethos among the exploited ancillary workers. But at least back then all employees were interviewed and employed by the hospital, by the supervisor who would be responsible for them and their work. I knew who had employed me, what I was supposed to do and whom I was answerable to. Now, arriving as an agency worker, I belonged to no one, no one was responsible for me nor me to them. The supervisors I would work to in the new hospital had not hired me and did not pay me. I was casual, temporary and entirely detached from the greater life of the institution. I did not even work for the contractor.

What really startled me was this: my wages as a ward orderly in 1970 were £12.50 a week. Now, as a porter in the new hospital, they were £4.35 an hour or £174.00 a week. How does that compare? The Institute for Fiscal Studies made this calculation: if my pay had kept pace with general earnings, that £12.50 a week should now be £210. So I had actually fallen behind in the last thirty years, a story repeated all too frequently across the public sector. While the country as a whole saw its GDP double, while national income became twice what it was in 1970 – 30 per cent more in the last decade alone – the real value of my low-level hospital job had fallen by £36 a week. For these people there has been no progress, only a falling-behind. True, there was now a fine new hospital and a far better working environment but the pay and conditions were worse. My work was not only relatively lower paid than thirty years ago, it was also entirely insecure, day-to-day agency employment. Back then at least I had the security of joining the staff of the NHS from day one: it was a safe job for life if I wanted it, but now everything is shifting sands for the low-paid. It is called 'flexibility', and in the name of 'flexibility' the hospital had shed or 'outsourced' all its ancillary workers. I was about to learn the full meaning of contracting out.

I arrived at the hospital, hoping my makeshift second-hand uniform would do, exactly a quarter of an hour early for the shift, as required. That extra unpaid hour and quarter a week was something demanded in every job I did. In each job I always had to be ready in uniform in some distant part of the building well before the official paid start of the shift. I found the porters' room in the basement at the back of the hospital in a far underground recess, a tiny cramped space where two controllers were sitting in front of computers and telephones. They were taking orders from all the wards and clinics in the building, logging the jobs on to computer worksheets and then assigning them to porters in rotation through their radios.

'Is this the porters' lodge?' I asked a thin, grey-haired Asian man, as he put down the telephone and looked me up and down.

'What can I do for you?' he asked politely.

'I'm the new porter, from Grange Executives.'

'You!' he said. I panicked at once – wrong age, wrong clothes, wrong demeanour, something wrong altogether?

'You weren't expecting me?' I asked.

'We never know what to expect from agencies,' he said with a deep sigh. Then he put his head back and laughed. The other controller looked at me and laughed too. I felt terrible. 'Whatever next!' he said and I thought they might send me away. Seeing my embarrassment, he leaned forward and patted my arm kindly. 'No offence. We just had your surname but we were not expecting a lady. We never had a lady porter before.'

'That's what I said at the agency. I asked if this wasn't a man's job, but they said no. Is it very heavy lifting? Is it something a woman can't do?'

The controller was at once contrite and friendly. 'Not at all, not at all! Of course there's no reason why you can't. We shall be very pleased. It just took us by surprise, you see?'

Mr Patel, known as Mr P, turned out to be a gentle man, quietly elegant and courteous, a porter for twenty-eight years, first in the old hospital, now in the new one.

'No, no, we give you a very big welcome and of course I am sure you can do the job very well. But people will be a little bit surprised to see a lady porter, you see? But no problem, no problem at all!'

After that, he was unfailingly kind. Everyone liked him.

Next door was the small porters' rest-room with chairs and a table grouped round the television alongside a microwave, a fridge and a hot-water urn. Mr P introduced me to the men getting ready for their shift and jaws dropped with a bit of sniggering banter about a woman porter. But soon most were friendly enough. My age was not the problem I thought it would be – some of them were older than me. One night porter I met had retired and then unretired again at seventy, finding himself too short of money. As for my general demeanour, I don't know what they thought but I soon discovered that a curious array of people from all kinds of back-grounds fetch up here and in most low-paid jobs, for any number of reasons. This I found time and again: there is a conspiratorial democracy in minimum-wage jobs, everyone levelled down by the lowness of the wage that binds people together. A middle-class accent is an irrelevance down in the fraternity of low pay.

Here many of the porters saw themselves as either on the way up or having fallen down: few regarded these jobs as their natural lot in life. Many had stories they were eager to tell of more prosperous days, of having tumbled down to this level from better lives in the past. Others, the younger ones, lived with their dreams of what was still to come, of somehow working their way up. But most were family men, just earning a living as best they could, working as many shifts as they could manage, some with second jobs elsewhere. I fitted in well enough, once they got used to a woman.

Most porters were dressed in smart white shirts with plum-coloured company ties and navy V-necks emblazoned with Car-illion, the logo of the company that employs all the non-medical staff. Whatever else, private companies are good at eye-catching uniforms, branding their employees all over, offering a reassuring appearance of confidence and affluence whatever the reality beneath the logos. In the hospital now everyone below the rank of nurse – all the cleaning, catering, portering, technical and other non-medical staff – work for Carillion not the NHS. Or at least they work for Carillion in principle but in practice, as I soon discovered, many of those wearing the Carillion colours were, like me, employed by agencies, working for the proliferating array of agencies around the fringes of London. I was working not at one but at two removes from the national health service, lower paid and more insecure than even the Carillion workers, who were themselves lower paid and more insecure with worse pensions than thirty years ago.

Hanging my coat on a corner peg, I was put with Samuel for the morning. Samuel was a Jamaican in his forties who had worked in the hospital since he arrived in England some years ago. Like many of the others, he said he was not planning to stay much longer, eager to get back to Kingston, Jamaica and set up his own taxi firm again. His 'useless' brother had driven the last one into the ground. In his head he was not a hospital porter at all but a small businessman. He had two children in school in London, and he worried about them. Would they get on, do well, pass exams? He worked exceptionally long shifts to pay for his family, while his wife worked as a cook. 'You can't survive, not with a family, unless you do the long, long hours, unless you both work all the hours there are,' he said. He was concerned about his children being left alone too long, because of the combined working hours of him and his wife. I witnessed this frequently: good parents who earn so little they are reluctantly forced to become bad parents by working overlong hours to make ends meet. Many said they would work shorter hours if they could find higher-paid jobs.

One porter had been a high-earning, self-employed electrician on building sites until he had a heart attack and had to take a less stressful job. 'The walking all day here is very good for me, the doctor says. But my standard of living fell through the floor since I got sick.' There was an accountant from Russia whose English was execrable: he read the encyclopaedia every night in his bedsit to try to improve it, hoping to be able to move up into an accounting department of the hospital one day. But there was no ladder up, no encouragement. In some hospitals the union, Unison, runs English language courses for foreign staff. It would not cost much for the NHS or for the contractors to run on-site basic literacy and numeracy classes everywhere. Another porter, Olly, ran an elaborate and incomprehensible Irish social security scam from his farm in Ireland, with its sixty sheep and twenty-four cows. It somehow concerned the fact he looked exactly like his brother. There was Francisco from the Philippines who had been an embassy butler for twenty years, until he took to the bottle. Anyway, he said, the money in butlering was just as bad and the hours far worse: he was full of horror stories of how badly he had been treated, working from dawn until the small hours with no overtime pay. Most people had their own private explanations for why they had ended up in a dead-end job: desire to work in the health service for the greater good of public service was not at the top of their list. But then no one had ever suggested to them that they were an integral and valued part of the institution or that they could contribute more.

Samuel was a good explainer and guide, for at first this huge place was a daunting maze. Maybe it was a test, but during my time at the hospital the only heavy lifting job I was given was the first one that morning. We were sent to collect hefty tables from the Hospital Friends Library to set up in the main atrium for a sale of toys and books the Friends held every day to raise money. An old lady Friend who ran the library gave us each a Kit Kat. 'She always does that,' Samuel said. 'That's why we are desirous to do this particular job in the mornings.' He had that West Indian-educated use of a wide and flowery vocabulary from a good old-fashioned schooling, spoken in a strong accent.

I had to learn not just the names and locations of thirty-two wards spread across the top four floors (which, confusingly, were not numbered but named), but also myriad clinics, X-ray departments, CT, MRI, haematology, pathology, various out-patient departments, the many mansions within A & E and all the specialist labs with their own acronyms and abbreviations. It needed a taxi-driver's brain to absorb maybe a hundred locations. Messages would come through on the radio; 'Samuel and Olly, go to Adele Dixon and take Kamal Abdullah on a bed to OP3.' Moving patients in beds was a two-porter job and Samuel showed me how to fix the bed's brakes, pump up the height, watch out for the weights if patients were in traction and trundle them down the long walkways to the lifts, find the right clinic, park them in the passage and hand in their notes at the clinic desk. This we did all morning, wheeling beds up and down and in and out of clinics and wards, the old, the young, the unconscious and the snoring, patients with drips and oxygen, patients who moaned, others who were embarrassed at these very public bed-journeys in nightdresses and hospital gowns, naked down the back.

By the afternoon I was given a radio, a map and a list of locations to find my own way around. There were too few leather pouches for carrying the heavy radios so porters hoarded them jealously, hiding them in secret places for their next shift. That meant I had to carry mine in my hand all the time while pushing people in wheelchairs. Next day I brought in a black leather belt-bag from home that just about fitted the radio, plus an essential notebook ready to take down the details of each job. In my second-hand black trousers, jumper and white polo shirt (of which more later), I did not look as smart as the men with their neat leather pouches and Carillion ties, but the belt-bag worked and left both hands free for wheeling. How important small irritations are at work, when repeated all day long. Enough radio pouches for all porters was just the kind of niggling request Carillion ignored. 'We ask, we keep asking, nothing happens,' Samuel said with a shrug. 'It is always the same thing.'

Once alone, I was often lost, wheeling people up and down, in and out, and sometimes round and round hoping they didn't notice us passing the same spot twice looking for the George Watts Dermatology Clinic or the Physio Gym. The radio messages were hard to hear. The various controllers all had their own accents, some so strong the porters often asked to have messages repeated. Porters from all nationalities, some speaking little English, were trying to understand English spoken in a variety of ways, from Mr P's Indian accent to another's Filipino, to thick Scots and other less identifiable accents all calling out names of wards and patients over the crackling airwaves. It meant much guesswork, writing down the sounds and hoping for the best. As you arrived in a ward with a half-heard, half-guessed genderless name of a patient, the nastier nurses would often give a snort and say tartly, 'No, no one here of that name!' In several wards there were running battles between porters and nurses who liked to chide and sneer at us. Sometimes you would stand at the nursing desk for five minutes waiting for one of them to deign to break off to speak to you. In other wards, kindly nurses went out of their way to avoid wasting your time.

Then there was the wheelchair problem: there were never enough of them. Often I spent twenty minutes searching every ward and corridor, hunting through out-patient departments and occasionally finding a secret trove piled up on the ground floor at the patient transport exit. Fifteen minutes was assigned to every wheelchair job, twenty minutes to a bed journey, so failing to find chairs was a cause for anxiety. Sometimes porters would try to hide a spare one in a back lift area or behind a door, but usually another porter would find it and whisk it away. The wheelchair hunt was a constant source of irritation among porters, another of those petty meannesses that cost a great deal of time. Worse, some of the wheelchairs had wheels as bad as broken supermarket trolleys, some had jammed brakes, so that dragging a patient backwards was the only way to go. Complaints had been made many times, but to no avail.

On the notice board in the porters' rest-room minutes of the last Carillion Staff Forum registered yet another complaint about wheelchair shortages that nothing had been done about. These minutes were revealing of what was happening in other departments, too. A cleaner had raised the issues of mops: 'Mops were being shared and the same mop was being used to clean the toilets and wards. She (the complainant) added that she even had to buy a dustpan and brush from her own money.' Another complaint came from the staff on the front desk who 'raised the issue that there were still no seats on reception and that the heated floor was causing them to go home with swollen ankles. Questioning why the staff couldn't sit down, the reply was that they were not allowed to sit behind the counter.' Another complaint was of 'a general lack of equipment in the hospital in both the portering and estates department'. All these and more complaints were handled within Carillion between managers and workers of the company, nothing to do with the NHS management who had effectively lost control. These were not, after all, NHS staff any longer.

If it wasn't for the miserable pay, however, this could have been a good and satisfying job. Although it meant walking all day on an eight-hour shift with only a half-hour break for lunch, it was a pleasing building and a purposeful job. Trundling along, waiting for lifts, patients liked to chat and tell their operation stories, worrying about what was happening next, confiding about their families or the doctors and nurses they liked or feared. The porters seemed like the life-blood of the place or perhaps like the engine oil that greased the system, fetching and carrying, finding out everything that was happening, well-conversant with the pleasant and unpleasant staff in different locations. We knew the snappy receptionists in some clinics, the downright rude nurses in some wards, the very friendly ones elsewhere, the places where nurses would let you stop for a quick coffee, other kitchens where you would be chased away. An arrogant male staff nurse was the worst, 'You, porter person, come here!' he snapped at me my first day with deep disdain, as if he hadn't also crossed a traditional gender line. Nurses complained porters were bone idle, porters complained nurses did nothing all day but chat. Neither was often true. It was ever thus, the notch above in the hierarchy is always the class in any workplace that gives you a hard time, the kulaks, the foremen.

This was hospital life from the underside, where the passing doctors belonged in another universe, even the young medical students. (They never held the door open for a porter with a patient, letting it swing without acknowledgement.) The nurses straddled the two worlds, snooty ones pointedly placing themselves beyond communication with porters or cleaners, the nice ones helpful and welcoming. You could bet those who were nice to porters were nice to patients too. But there was no predicting, no useful stereotype – neither age, gender, race nor nationality predisposed good or bad nature. There were friendly Africans and surly angry ones, cheerful Australians and grudging ones, older nurses who might be abrupt or warmly helpful.

One thing became clear: people are recognised more by their status than by their face. I was now a porter first, myself second. Passing by in the corridors and in the wards, I saw several consultants I had interviewed in the past; one whom I knew quite well had treated both my daughter and myself. Once I saw a patient I knew. But porters are part of the invisible below-stairs world, the great unnoticed. No one ever recognised me.

Desperately anxious to please in my first days, I worried about being late or lost or having no wheelchair for a job. So I scuttled furiously from place to place, eager to radio in the moment a job was done, with a breathless 'Job completed!' like a kind of Joyce Grenfell on speed. The number of jobs each of us completed per day was listed on the computer worksheets and I feared falling behind the others. As the only woman porter, I had something to prove. But on the second day Samuel said to me, 'Cool it, chill out, man.' He tugged me into the back area by the service lifts where several porters were leaning against the wall for a few minutes' rest where they couldn't be seen by Big John, the boss, if he happened to pass by on the prowl. I didn't meet Big John for days but watched out warily for anyone who might be him, well warned by the others. We perched on an old upturned shelf behind the door near out-patients, eking out any spare time, making sure each job was checked in at fifteen minutes, never less.

Some jobs took longer because a patient was not ready or took time to shift into a chair. Sometimes a patient would be surrounded by a doctor and his entourage and we had to wait at a respectful distance. Sometimes a patient was still very slowly eating lunch, not to be rushed. Some patients were just bloody-minded and refused to move. There was the mountainous woman with terrible sores on her legs, a job everyone dreaded because she was bossy and bad-tempered, obviously in great pain. She needed the Fat Boy, a special extra-wide wheelchair that had to be collected from the basement, and she took a long time to manoeuvre into it. Jobs took longer when a lift was out of order: waiting for lifts wasted as much time as hunting for wheelchairs. So jobs could take longer than their allotted time but the porters' private code said a job should never, ever, take less than fifteen minutes. 'Why are you scurrying around like a mad rabbit?' Samuel said. 'Wait a bit. Take it easy, pace yourself.' It was good advice. I realised that in my anxiety I had got ahead of the others in jobs checked into the computer.

When the hospital services were first privatised, Carillion (then called Tarmac) had the first contract and cut back many jobs, including porters. 'How else do you think they were going to make their money?' Samuel said. Later Carillion cut staff numbers again. Mr P described how they had started with sixteen porters before privatisation but were now cut down to eleven, although the numbers of jobs grew all the time with an ever-faster through-put of patients. 'They promised no cuts when they privatised but of course we could all see this would happen, and it did. Now they are talking of cutting two more. How, I ask you, are we to get the work done?' That Saturday, there had been just one porter on duty who had complained vigorously that the workload was impossible. That pattern, I later discovered, exactly mirrored what happened every-where after contracting-out began. Every report and study records how pay and conditions were cut and work was made harsher as staff were shed. It goes on still, this paring down to the bone, cutting right into the bone at times.

So if we lingered by the lifts to ensure no job was ever done in under fifteen minutes, there was a purpose. These men had learned through experience to give no inch because, every time they did, it was taken advantage of. If the time-and-motion men studying our computer printouts saw that some jobs were done faster, they would never understand why other jobs took so much longer. They would assume we could work all the time at the speed of the fastest jobs. They would never take account of the mountainous lady with the seeping legs or the old woman who cried for ten minutes about her dog before I could coax her into the wheelchair, or the time I stayed with a frightened woman gripping my hand while she waited for her X-ray when I should have been off calling back to base.

Being nice to patients was not designed into the job; quite the contrary. Samuel explained, 'Never touch a patient. That is the company rule. Touching patients, helping them into wheelchairs, is

nurses' work, not ours. We have been told never to touch a patient
even just on the arm because if they fall they might sue Carillion.'
By then I had heaved countless patients in and out of wheelchairs
when there was no nurse in sight to help. Very frail old people
slowly edging out of their chairs at risk of tumbling and breaking
bones needed an arm. I had thought portering meant, well,
portering, carrying things and especially people if need be. That
was certainly the case thirty years ago when the porters always
helped the nurses to carry patients. But since the work has been
contracted out, that kindly part of the job appears to have been
written out of the contract specification altogether. Whatever is not
specified in cold contractual print does not happen.

'We are not trained in lifting so the company tell us never to lift
people,' another porter said, too. This was lunchtime, sitting round
in the porters' room, and the others joined in. Yes, definitely,
absolutely, only nurses were allowed to touch patients. Yes, they
agreed, as a result diminutive nurses heaved about hulking great
patients while porters had to stand by with their arms crossed
because that is what Carillion declared. The nurses were not
Carillion and they were covered by NHS hospital insurance if
they harmed themselves or a patient sued, so it was OK for them.
Insurance matters more than anything, never mind the nonsense of
able-bodied porters standing there watching nurses struggle un-
aided.

That was just another unintended consequence of privatisation.
Most of the porters were decent people, not really jobsworths, and I
saw them lending a hand more often than not. I often saw them
help out with patients in ways that were not in their job description.
But they said they could be disciplined if found physically aiding
patients, though yes, many of them said, of course it should be part
of their job. Osman, a suave Iranian porter, said a patient had fallen
yesterday when she stood up to get into his wheelchair. He did lift
her up because he couldn't just leave her lying there, whatever
Carillion said. 'But maybe the company could be sued.' The effect
of the litigation mentality that now poisons many aspects of NHS
life is exacerbated by private companies' over-anxiety to protect
themselves.

Worse was the lack of any idea that we should play a part in caring for the patients. We would park them in corridors and out-patient queues, many of them old, confused, frightened and needing a friend. Although mostly the system worked well and they didn't wait too long before being taken back to the wards, there were plenty of days when people in distress or pain, lost and dumped, begged me to take them back to their wards. 'You brought me down, can't you just take me back?' they would cry out as I hurried by.

One woman was in tears because her friend was waiting for her upstairs and, although her X-ray had been done two hours ago, she was still waiting to be wheeled back again. It would not have taken long, I wanted to do it for her, but no, I could not, it was more than my job was worth. I did, nervously, ask the particularly brusque ward clerk in X-ray if he could call my controller and request a porter, then I might be assigned the job to take her back. The ward clerk barked out an unsympathetic answer, rightly taking it as a personal criticism that he had left a plainly distressed woman sitting there in front of his nose for so long. All the same, out of his earshot I also called my controller to ask if I could take her, but he said firmly the job had to wait to come up in its turn. So I had to leave her there. No initiative was permitted, no extra kindness nor any chance to step in and put right something that had gone wrong. Just follow instructions, that was all the company required. In the end that lack of initiative is what makes any job unbearable.

Big John was a powerful man. I felt his unseen hand long before I came across him, for he set the rota and said yea or nay to requests for shift changes. (His answer to my request for a shift change had been relayed back as a nay.) He was short and rotund, black, with the officious air of managerial importance that came with his Carillion blazer. 'So you are the new woman porter?' he said to me suddenly one day as I was walking out of A & E. 'How do you like the job?'

I said I liked it fine.

'You think you will stay?'

I said I was thinking about it. The job was fine – which it was – but the problem was the pay.

'Maybe you will become permanent when you have worked out your time with the agency,' he said. Maybe, I replied, but the money would still be a problem. 'You would move up to £4.85 an hour then,' he said. He was having difficulty with the high turnover of staff which the other porters said was getting worse month by month, with more agency workers and more people passing through for a short time.

Now I had the chance, I asked what the prospects were for some kind of training to get a better job later on? He thought about it and suggested, 'You could do training in restraint and calming methods. That gives you a certificate so you could work in security.' A security job would be no better paid with no better prospects than portering. Otherwise it seemed that Carillion was offering no inducements with any vision of a path upwards to a better career in the hospital some time in the future. Growing and developing staff was probably not high on Carillion's agenda for staff at the bottom. Big John looked at his watch and said, 'I hope you decide to stay,' which was gratifying, and he glided away on his rounds.

I had my doubts about how long it would be before I might be made permanent if I did stay on. In theory, after three months I would be free of the agency and allowed to apply for an interview to be taken on by Carillion with all the rights and conditions of a member of their staff. It seemed to make sense that Carillion should want to take on any agency workers as soon as possible. After all, they were paying some £7–8 an hour to these agencies to employ people who only received £4.35 of that. Why shouldn't the company want to end this waste as soon as possible? But it didn't work that way, either deliberately or out of managerial inefficiency.

A good example came from Winston, an earnest young black porter who talked about his working conditions while we were waiting together for a patient outside A & E. Although he was wearing the smart Carillion uniform, he said he was still trapped working with his agency in Catford after a year of portering in the hospital. He was given the Carillion uniform because his working life was so complicated he often couldn't get home to change his clothes. He lived in Edmonton, took a course in IT in central London and often did double shifts to cut down on his travelling time. His journey from home to the hospital took him two hours by train and two buses and cost him £74 a month. 'I have filled out the application form to be taken on by Carillion so I can move up to the £4.85 rate. I keep asking for an interview with Big John but they keep putting it off. They say yes, I will get an interview, then nothing happens. I keep asking, but I just get excuses. I don't know what else to do now. One porter filled out the Carillion application three times; they kept doing nothing about it and then he started to get angry. He started coming in late and answering back, then they told him to go. I know how he felt.'

It would make a big difference to Winston's pay. It was not just the job security and the extra rights; it was not just the extra 50p an hour. If he was taken on to the staff, he explained, he would get time and half for his overtime and double time for Sundays. As I knew, because I had signed the same terms and conditions, any overtime for agency staff was paid at the regular flat rate. 'I worked twenty-one hours in a row last week,' he said. 'That would be a lot of overtime money if I was staff. But they just won't give me that interview. It costs them too much.' There were other staff perks too. One of the older porters who had stayed on from the old hospital told me the Carillion staff got a £180 a month Inner London weighting allowance, plus a £180 a month bonus. This was on top of a £4.55 an hour pay rate, plus overtime. Why £4.55? He didn't know.

The pay structure was Byzantine because everyone I asked (they were all quite happy to discuss their payslips) came up with slightly different sums per hour or different bonuses for reasons they could not really explain. £4.85 was the highest hourly rate I encountered, while the bonus had no clarity about it, either in who got it or what exactly it was a bonus for. (Later a union official explained why employers prefer adding bonuses: if they raise the base rate it would also raise the time-and-a-half overtime rates.) Porters who rotated at the controllers' desk, operating the telephones and computers, were paid a little more for those shifts, but not enough for many of them to strive for that job. Many preferred the freedom of walking the hospital to sitting in this poky underground dungeon all day with the added anxiety in busy times of hot pressure when nurses and clinics were shouting for porters and couldn't get through on the telephones. Often by the time they did get through they were already angry at the shortage of porters.

Winston blamed Big John personally for refusing to give him the interview to transfer him from the agency on to the Carillion books but it was far more likely to be company policy higher up the line. Big John, for all his airs, was only a small jump up from the rest of the porters. Winston was particularly gloomy that day: 'You can try really hard at this job, like I do, but you just get nowhere. I work and work, I never hang about, I try to get noticed so they will transfer me. But in the end I can see I will get like some of the old ones, the ones who keep telling you to slow down all the time. That's the way it is, no reward for hard work here.' If he could only pass his IT qualifications, he would be off and away but he said his hard working life with its gruelling and expensive travelling made getting to his IT classes increasingly difficult and he wasn't sure he would make it to the end of the course. He wanted to get married, but life was just too hard at the moment.

Later that day Winston and I were talking to Steve, a dapper porter in his thirties with a grey-streaked quiff. 'You ask Steve,' Winston said. 'He's in the same position as me.' Steve nodded and said, 'I don't know if it's something I do or if maybe they don't like my face, my face don't fit or something, you know what I mean? Why is it I fill out the Carillion application form three times and three times I ask for an interview, but they will not give me it. I cannot get this transfer from the agency to the company. I wait, wait, wait, but nothing happens.' His wife was a cleaner in the hospital, and they worked alternate shifts so they could take it in turns to be home for their children. The result was that they rarely saw one another.

Winston was right about one or two of the older ones who were not paragons of porterly virtue. Irish Olly was the most adamant member of the 'slow-down' faction. He was as idle as he could manage, skulking about, stirring up trouble wherever he could. He picked arguments, teased and bullied in surreptitious ways but, when I turned on him once, he just waved his hands in the air and said, 'No harm meant. Just joking! You've got to have a laugh, haven't you now?' in a thicker than usual Irish brogue, as if blarney would always get him out of it, but he lacked charm. You had to watch out for him as he picked on newcomers to torment. He would mock and mimic foreign accents or small things people got wrong, as when I reported through my radio 'Job finished' on my first day and he made fun of me for not saying 'Job completed, over and out', like the others. Once I saw him hold on to the back of the Hospital Friends' trolley so that the elderly volunteer wheeling along her array of Lucozade, knitting wools, newpapers, sweets and Kleenex tugged and pulled but couldn't understand why the thing wouldn't budge.

He had strong dislikes and deliberately got me into trouble on my first day with another porter who was his old enemy. A Malaysian porter had stopped to talk to someone in one room, foolishly leaving his empty wheelchair outside in the corridor. 'Take that one!' Olly hissed at me. In all innocence I did as he said and he told me to hurry, hurry away with it to the lift. By the time the Malaysian came out I was wheeling it down the walkway and he shook a very angry but safely distant fist at me, cursing under his breath, giving me black looks thereafter. Olly, of course, had nipped out of sight, leaving me to take the blame. Dull jobs breed petty rows and rivalries that reminded me of school. Olly was keen to confide in me, tell me the wheezes and ways round things but I avoided being taken under his wing.

Winston and Olly were from opposite ends of the public-service spectrum. I saw them as the two distant poles, North and South, that represented political perceptions of the public sector and its workers. If Tony Blair and most of his ministers are ambivalent about public servants, it is because they have both Winston and Olly in mind. One day there will be fulsome political praise for the hard work, devotion, enthusiasm and determination to get trained and move up of a Winston. Thinking of the Winstons ministers will talk of the need for more money, more training, more support and even more pay for public-sector workers. Then in the same breath they will spoil it all by remembering the Ollys and talk threateningly of the need for 'reform' to go hand in hand with any extra money. The code is well-understood. It means no more money for the

Ollys unless they show better spirit, harder work with more motivation, more flexibility in working practices and willingness to take on other tasks. Fair enough – but this carrot-and-stick language is desperately wrong-headed. To be sure, every workplace has its Olly quota of shirkers and grumblers but in this hospital, among the porters, nurses and clinic staff, the enthusiastic, well-motivated Winstons I came across outnumbered the Ollys ten to one.

The policy question is how do you grow and keep more Winstons and improve the Ollys? Under the present system the NHS is losing too many Winstons as anyone with initiative and enterprise leaves these low-level portering and cleaning jobs as soon as they can, their potential wasted. The Ollys stay and fester for life, sour and disaffected. With a private company responsible for all the support workers, everything was quick-fix day-to-day solutions, whatever was cheapest and fastest, with no thought for building a workforce that was content, fulfilled and on a clear ladder upwards with something to work for. For as long as agencies kept shovelling any old labour through the back door at the bottom of the heap, as long as the staff looked respectable enough (and uniforms could ensure they did, even if they were not entitled to wear the Carillion logo), no one seemed to mind how much of that same labour leaked out again at the same time. To Carillion, agency labour appeared to be preferable to employing people direct, with its added costs.

I left the hospital with regret. There was a warm camaraderie among the porters that I liked and I liked the job itself. I liked scurrying about fetching and carrying and talking to patients. I liked the beautiful brightness of the place that had sprung up on the site of what was anything but beautiful before. But the job could and should have been better organised; porters could be more useful and better used. However, now that the work was privatised and divided off from the rest of the hospital management, no one could use the untapped potential in the porters because everything was precisely prescribed in ironclad contracts. If union deals were rigid and hard to renegotiate in the old days, they were nothing like as non-negotiable as trying to open up a whole contract between hospital and Carillion, respecifying exactly what porters should do. No one could now devise imaginative ways to cross boundaries and use them better, enhance their talents or set them up on training ladders that might develop their motivation and their prospects. I only now realised the full destruction caused to the NHS by this atomisation of functions, destroying the chance for good management to create a modern teamwork approach that includes all strata, breaking down hierarchies. Flexibility had been sacrificed to the rigidity of contracts.

It so happened that on the day I left Tony Blair was making an important speech about public services. It was another of his ambivalent muddled messages. He praised public-service workers but then called for more 'reform' and 'flexibility', which from the ground floor felt like a threat. The government always speaks with several agendas, and they are often contradictory. The low-paid public workers consist of the working poor, the deserving poor, most of them women and mothers, the very people the Working Families' Tax Credits are designed to help. These are the very families whose poverty the government has pledged to abolish. But that springs from the part of the government's brain labelled 'poverty targets'. It is the contrary part of its brain that calls for higher productivity and more 'flexibility' in the public sector, making sure pay doesn't rise too much, squeezing every last penny of efficiency out of each worker, whatever the human cost to them and their children. For the government the great advantage of privatisation and PFI deals is that they can get the Carillions to do the Gradgrind work for them on the one hand, while still worrying about how to overcome poverty with the other hand.

Yet if the government wants to reach its poverty targets, it will find the biggest single group of the poor right here under its nose, hard at work in its own schools, local authorities and hospitals. Raising their wages would help hit the poverty targets. Screwing down pay and conditions may make productivity look good on paper, but it simply keeps the poor down and produces a worse service at the same time. I worked hard, walking most of the eight-hour day with just a half-hour break. It was an essential job: the hospital would grind to a halt without porters if already scarce nurses had to waste hours away from the wards. But I was paid just £174.

After tax deductions I took home only £150.67. In other words, I was not even getting that pathetic sum of £4.10 an hour. After taxes, I was only paid £3.76 an hour. If you add in my council tax of £12.65, that left just £3.45 an hour. What might that buy? An hour's work buys me a slab of cheap cheddar, a quarter of a taxi ride between my home and my office, a pack of washing powder, a bottle of wine, half a cinema ticket. It would take me eight hours to buy a pair of modest but comfortable working shoes, nine hours to buy a West End theatre ticket, two days' work to buy a cheap pair of new spectacles and another two days' work to buy one return saver fare on a train to see relatives in Manchester.

No one this poor can afford to pay £35.98 a week taxes, not if the government is trying to redistribute towards the poor. But I think that is the wrong way to look at it. Every working citizen ought to be able to afford to pay taxes, since it is one of the key elements of citizenship, conferring genuine inclusion with rights and responsibilities in using a vote to decide how those taxes should be spent. Removing the poor from taxation (or from the TV licence) is sometimes suggested as one way to alleviate poverty, but that is only another kind of undercover government subsidy to employers instead of paying people a fair living wage for the hard work they do.

From time to time while wheeling people up and down the airy walkways of the hospital I would think about the money I so easily earn and so enjoyably spend in my usual life. If I compared it to the value placed on me and my work here, I could make no sense of it at all. There just is no explanation I could give if a child asked me why. There is no explanation.

How many people now work in the public sector? How big is the state? Government figures give a swift reply: 5 million out of a national workforce of 28 million, down from 7.4 million in 1979. But how many people work more loosely in the public sector, doing the same jobs as in 1979 but now contracted out? I worked in two NHS hospitals, a primary school and a government nursery and all these would be regarded by most people as essentially public-service jobs. But now that they are contracted out they are no longer counted, although the state still pays these workers indirectly. I tried but never succeeded in finding a job actually working for the state.

I asked the Office of National Statistics. No, they said, they had no idea how many people are working within the public services, even if contracted out. They publish labour-force figures on how many people do what work and at what pay, but with no definition of how many jobs are broadly doing public work. They said try the Cabinet Office which is in charge of the civil service. I did, but the Cabinet Office said they did not keep any such figures either. Try the Treasury, they said, so I did. The Treasury said they had no figures but they would find out if anyone had done any surveys or research or estimates. No one had. I asked academics and researchers in the field, but no one knew. Thirty years ago we knew exactly how many people worked in the public sector, so we knew exactly the size of the state. Now no one has the slightest idea. It has all been contracted out and conveniently obfuscated.

It matters greatly how many there are because the state has direct control over not just its own 5 million employees but over all those millions who work for its contractors. If it wanted to improve the working lives of a very large slice of the population, it could do so at a stroke by demanding higher minimum pay and conditions for the ship of state and all who sail in her. With public spending now rising fast after the decades of drought, the numbers of people who would be covered by such an edict is growing rapidly too. A rule fixing a living wage minimum would transform the going rate in the entire low-paid sector.

The words are 'outsourcing', 'subcontracting', 'market testing', 'best value', 'externalisation' – for people working on the bottom rungs of the public sector, all these words have meant just one thing: lower pay, worse conditions, less security. It has reduced the idea of public service to a cheap and expendable commodity. The public ethos of these private companies is negligible: profit and avoiding litigation is everything. There is no loyalty to the staff they hire, nor any expected from them. The surprise is that the staff give so much anyway.

Living in Lambeth for over thirty years, I saw the worst of the time when public services often seemed to be run for the benefit of the producers and not for the consumers. Lambeth in its militant red days was probably the worst-run council in the land, dysfunctional from the top right down through its service departments, delivering bad services under non-existent management, led by perverse politics. The unions and the political leadership were a cartel combined against the interests of the voters and the consumers. It needed cauterisation. Management needed to reassert control, politics had to return to providing what people needed, the unions had to return to representing their members not running the council. Lambeth was always held up as the wicked reason why all public services had to be privatised, the unions broken and private contractors called in to take over. Nicholas Ridley, Secretary of State for the Environment, publicly proclaimed the purpose of compulsory contracting-out: 'The root cause of rotten local services lies in the grip which local government unions have over those services in many parts of the country . . . Our competitive tendering provisions will smash that grip once and for all.'

But even in its red heyday, Lambeth's collusion between politicians and union bosses never resulted in the poor bloody infantry getting any of the benefit. The cleaners, caterers and gardeners were low-paid then, as they are now. They had job security, but they were still at the bottom of the scale. Something did have to be done about cases like Lambeth and Liverpool: managers had to regain control over chaos. But these were famous extremes and not representative of the state of public services in general. The purgative medicine Mrs Thatcher prescribed was worse than the original disease and it has left NHS and local-government managers with even less control: not only are their workforces contracted out, but so is much of their own managerial authority.

As the Thatcher government rolled out compulsory competitive tendering (CCT), using Lambeth and others as their battle-cry, NHS catering, cleaning and laundry were opened up to competition and all local authorities were forced to tender out their services. The Conservatives had then (and still have now) an ideal of the small 'enabling' state as purchaser not provider. Small government is the cry of the right everywhere and the Tories are once more attacking the NHS as a 'monolith', 'soviet-style command and control', 'the biggest employer in Europe' as if the size of a public body were proof of its ineffectiveness, though size in the merger-obsessed business world is seen as a sign of vigour and virility.

Did their perfect model of competition between bidders work? There has been less genuine competition between the companies bidding for contracts and it is shrinking. Only a handful of large, experienced, mainly international companies are deemed capable of handling these big local-government contracts, so the work gets carved up between the few, who swap places every few years – less hot contest than a gentle game of musical chairs.

Profits were made at once by shedding 40 per cent of NHS ancillary jobs. Everywhere there were cuts in refuse collectors, street-cleaning and maintenance, cut by up to two-thirds in some councils. Public squalor descended on hospital wards and the streets of Britain. The impact on the remaining workers was drastic. Between 1980 and 1985, hospital porters, cooks, cleaners and kitchen staff suffered real pay cuts. Their pay grew slightly later but significantly below equivalent groups in the entirely private sector. Women were the big losers since the majority of services selected for competitive tendering were women's jobs, forming some 70 per cent of the workers contracted out: the gender pay gap grew by 3 per cent as a direct result of this. There was a 66.6 per cent increase in the use of temporary workers in public administration and a similar increase in the NHS. Twice as many local authority workers were now on temporary contracts: by 1998 it was one in eight, mostly women, allowing employers the 'flexibility' to hire and fire without cumbersome redundancy procedures.[1]

In 1983 the Conservatives abolished the Fair Wages Resolution, which until then had obliged any company contracting with a public authority to give the same national pay and conditions. Then they abolished the Wages Councils that set a minimum threshold in each occupation, protecting the weak in non-unionised industries. How quaint those old workers' rights sound now. It was transparently clear that squeezing employees' pay was the main path to profit. Even the Department of Environment's own study reported in 1993 that in 51 per cent of councils, manual workers had suffered cuts in basic wages, bonuses, hours, holidays and sick pay due to contracting-out. It concluded that contracted-out services 'are labour-intensive and the only way that savings are likely to be made is by one or other aspects of staffing'. They noted that 'Manual staff, in particular, have borne the brunt of the changes that have been made in working methods, pay and conditions'.[2]

The public sector has traditionally been a better employer than the private sector. Three times more public workers are given family-friendly hours, extra maternity leave, nursery places, career breaks, paternity leave and parental leave. But instead of celebrating that tradition and making it a benchmark for all employers, during the last two decades the state simply shed all its most vulnerable workers. Only 7 per cent of public-sector workplaces now have any low-paid employees left, so it is hardly surprising that I failed to find one of those few jobs myself. 'The public sector has managed to effectively transfer low-paid jobs into the private sector', one report concludes.[3]

When staff are transferred from public to private sector, they are now protected by TUPE – Transfer of Undertakings (Protection of Employment) – to prevent cuts in their pay and conditions. But none of that applies to new staff taken on, as I found at the Chelsea and Westminster where there was an array of different pay and conditions among people working together doing the same job. TUPE protects the old employees for a while, but over the years their pay tends to fall back. There is, after all, no one left in the public sector for them to compare themselves with. A nearby hospital, St Mary's, has changed contractors seven times, which has left them with rafts of workers doing the same jobs on six different historic pay rates from previous contracts. Since February 2001 new legislation allows councils for the first time to take pay and conditions of workers into account when they assess rival bids for contracts: this was forbidden before. It is still unclear if this will improve matters. A new 'Code of Practice' for contractors is also promised.

A 2002 national survey by the public-services union, Unison, among contracted-out workforces showed the contrast in pay and conditions between the old original workforce protected by TUPE and unprotected new starters. The findings on this two-tier work-force were stark: 62 per cent of new starters were paid less; 44 per cent had more unsocial working hours; 58 per cent had worse sick pay; 73 per cent had less holiday; 51 per cent had worse pensions; 44 per cent had worse job security. Of the 1.5 million staff most affected, 71 per cent are women. These figures not only prove that things were better for public-service workers before and that new workers are being hired at worse rates, they show how in future as the old better-paid workforce retires and is replaced by more new starters there will be yet more lowest-paid workers. Contracting-out has been an act of national vandalism.

By coincidence, while I was researching all this Unison went on strike for a day across London in pursuit of their claim for a £4,000 London weighting allowance. I only discovered this because, to my indignation, my local Lambeth library was locked with a strike notice on the door. It catapulted me back all too forcibly to the bad old strike-ridden days no one wants to return to. To be fair, Unison in London had not been on strike since the 1980s and this time they had a just cause: they deserve the allowance since the police get £6,000 plus free travel while many Unison workers get little or nothing to compensate for the high London cost of living. I never got a penny in any of the jobs I did, yet it is the norm for workers higher up the scale. Employers are paying agencies high rates for stop-gap temps like me instead of paying a London allowance that would bring in permanent staff at decent pay.

But however justified the cause, the strike weapon no longer finds much popular resonance. Though when there was a full national one-day strike of public-sector workers in July 2002, an ICM opinion poll showed strong public support for the dinner ladies, cleaners and the rest of the mainly female workforce who came out demanding a £5 per hour minimum.

Even so, often when I talk to people about the damage con-tracting-out has done to the workforce, one common response is, 'But it did stop the strikes, didn't it?' The fear of bringing the workforce back under direct state employment is that the unions will get a grip again with all their old immobilism, rigidity and bloody-mindedness. They will take us back to the bad old 1970s when battling Granny Brookstone, an old communist shop steward for NUPE (now Unison), brought the Charing Cross Hospital to its knees by building barricades to keep out the patients.

What is to stop it happening again if we don't keep the workers well-battened-down by contracting private companies to sit on the hatches? The answer is that we now have employment laws designed for more harmony than conflict. Margaret Thatcher forced democratisation on the unions (as Barbara Castle had tried to do before her), and Labour has now given every workplace the right to trade-union recognition for the first time.

Modern trade unionism has evolved into seeking win–win deals with management, instead of the old politically motivated confrontation. They have negotiated good workplace education and flexible-working deals. They held back in Labour's first term – with remarkable self-restraint – from demanding to catch up on two decades of falling pay. But growing impatience at sub-survivable wages has caused the election of more strident leaders in some unions.

However, unions are pitifully weak, with only 65 per cent membership in the public sector and a pathetic 19 per cent in the private sector (which includes the contracted-out workers who need it most). The low-paid, isolated in their kitchens and care homes, desperately need unions to protect them but they are rarely organised. Also, in recent years the quality of public-service management has changed out of all recognition since those days when the managers lost control: bringing them back into the public sector would not mean a return to reckless 1970s union militancy. Contracting-out was too drastic a punishment meted out to both public-service workers and managers.

Has privatisation delivered better and cheaper services for the public? There is no evidence that it has, unless you count as a 'saving' the cuts in pay of the workers already at rock-bottom. Cost can be measured, but quality is harder. How do you measure the value of the way porters in a hospital behave to patients? The 1998 *Workplace Employee Relations Survey* asked managers in both public and private sectors about the effect of having contracted out services to other companies: 42 per cent said cost savings had been realised, but another 31 per cent said they were now paying more, while the rest reported no change. What about management? Is the private sector better at it these days? I saw no sign of it. Within the NHS there is a growing cadre of highly experienced, talented and enthusiastic managers for whom the idea that Carillion or the rest attract better managerial talent is a gross insult. Public-sector management everywhere is now brimming with enthusiasts who want to deliver this government's better services. Tom Bremner, Housing Manager in Clapham Park, is a typical dynamic young example of the genre, but he finds himself hamstrung by the tangled legacy of a spider's web of contracts over which he has too little direct control.

Under Labour contracting-out is still galloping ahead as PPP and PFI schemes absorb public investment, hiring new staff mainly into the private not the public sector. Where do its cost savings come from? The IPPR's *Commission on Public Private Partnerships* (2001) found 'Approximately two thirds of the total labour cost savings appear to represent a reduction in the aggregate pay, benefits and conditions of the workforce'. The NHS Confederation, representing trusts and health authorities, comes to the same conclusion about PPP/PFI deals: 'The schemes are not . . . necessarily better value for money . . . or they achieve that by reducing the terms of working conditions of staff involved.'

Yet there are now well over 400 major PFI deals worth nearly £20 billion in progress under Labour, including major hospital projects as well as prisons and local education authorities. The contracts for most of these have very little to say about the pay and conditions of their staff, equal pay or family-friendly working. What is written between the lines, unspoken yet eloquent in its silence, is the understanding between both sides of these contracts that pay and conditions of the lowest grades of workers is where profit margins lie.

The government has conceded there is a problem, so there will be three pilot schemes in which staff remain NHS employees while being seconded to work in new privately run PFI hospitals. It was revealing that when this was announced, Sir Steve Robson, former

Treasury architect of much privatisation and PFI policy under the
Tories, now chief executive of Mowlem, itself a big government
contractor, immediately protested in the *Financial Times*: 'The
danger is that the private sector contractor might be told the terms
and conditions under which he could employ staff. He might be
invited to manage a service on the basis that some of the staff
remained public sector employees.' Exactly so. Here the grand
panjandrum of privatisation himself admits that the chief purpose
always was to bear down hard on the poorest workers.[4]

What now? The government could reverse this dismal trend. It
could legislate for a new Fair Wages clause to be inserted in every
contract between state and private company. Every contractor
could be obliged to pay the same rate as public employees and
offer the same conditions. It would stop companies competing for
contracts by vying over which of them could treat their workers the
worst.

Public pay has finally been rising faster than private pay in the last
couple of years – but it still lags far behind equivalent private-sector
jobs. As I found, it often falls behind 1970 rates of pay, which is a
national disgrace. The nurse who trains for three years gets less than
the estate agent starting out with no training. The teacher with the
post-graduate diploma gets less than the middle manager without a
degree in a middling firm. However, although people tell pollsters
that they want to see public-sector pay rise (opinion polls support
rises for teachers and nurses), there is a curious fear that the
ancillaries might creep upwards too. It is as if this troglodyte
below-stairs army might break out of the earth beneath the feet
of schools and hospitals and gobble up all the resources put there for
patients or schoolchildren. It would be 'inflationary' to pay them
more, despite the years of deliberate hardship inflicted on them. It is
always the pay at the bottom that is said to threaten inflation, never
at the top. The same mentality pervades the public sector. It is good
value to pay doctors, teachers or nurses more, but it always feels like
money thrown away to pay more to those beneath them.

That attitude leads to the wastage of a strong resource. Intelligent,
capable, experienced people are misused and undervalued: the
fragmentation caused by privatisation has made it worse. Much

nonsense is talked about the lack of skills in the British workforce but it would take very little workplace training to make better use of the untapped talent I kept finding. Most of the people I worked with were forced down into jobs well beneath their capability by outdated hierarchies. They need to be integrated into a more holistic vision of their workplace. They should be seen not as the bottom floor of a hierarchical pyramid but as equally valued bricks within seamless arches: in all these key public institutions, the failure of any one brick causes the collapse of the entire edifice. If these undervalued assets were well-rewarded they would soon be well-used. Once employers had to spend more on the low-paid, they would stop using them as cheap disposable dross and find ways to make more creative and productive use of them. The best intentions of modern progressive managers to create workplaces that use and enhance all the talents of all the workforce cannot be developed within the present shape of the public sector: contracting-out rules it out. As I went from job to job, it became depressingly plainer every step of the way.

Chapter 6

Job-hunting

It was too difficult to move seamlessly from one job to another with no unpaid gap between. I doubt anyone manages it without financial hardship. I was heavily in debt by the time my first pay cheque arrived, so no one in my position would choose to change jobs until that debt had been paid off and that would take time. Then they would need to save spare cash to tide them over while they precariously walked the financial tightrope from one job to finding a better one, almost impossible to do while employed. Clocking up debts, I was discovering the true cost of moving from benefit into a new job, and from job to job.

These were the direct costs of going out to work: before arriving at the Chelsea and Westminster I had to acquire suitable uniform working clothes. I found a smart, white short-sleeved polo shirt with a neat collar for £3.99 at Bargainwear in the parade of shops along the west side of Clapham Park. Even better, I found a similar one in the Save the Children shop in Clapham High Street for £1. I had black trousers but they were dry-clean only, which would cost £3.50 a time. At that price there was no point in taking with me any clothes that needed dry-cleaning, another item I had forgotten to count in. Instead I found a pair of washable Marks and Spencer trousers in the Age Concern shop for £5, along with a washable plain black V-neck sweater for £3.25.

Then I made a bad mistake. I didn't have any flat black walking shoes, so I was pleased with myself when I found a pair that looked fine for £12.99 in a local bargain shoe shop. But they were not fine, not at all, and this was money wasted. By the end of my first day at the hospital my feet were in agony. Since the job demanded seven and a half hours a day on the hoof, I needed efficient hoofs. I bought some sticking plasters – £2.00 were the cheapest in the expensive chemist by the hospital – and I gave the shoes a second day to break in but after an hour I knew I could not walk in them any further. They rubbed and pinched on every side, made with a rock-hard sole that had no suppleness. Stubbornly, they would give not an inch in any direction and they smelled terrible too. I was hobbling along the ground floor, hanging on to a wheelchair for support, when there, by a miracle, was a sale of shoes by the hospital Friends. Clarks shoes were available at knock-down prices and nurses were swarming around in search of foot comfort. There they were, my size, flat, black, lace-up, bendy, soft, easeful. When I slipped my feet into them it was like walking on clouds and I bounced away in them, spring-heeled and happy. Cinderella in her slippers never felt this good. These kindly shoes lasted me well through all the jobs I did thereafter, but even at sale price they cost £25. So my frugal mainly second-hand uniform, including both the good and the bad shoes and the £3 Photo-Me photos for the agency had cost me £54.23, the true price of starting out in a new job.

After my first three weeks, I now owed £144.18 in back rent, council tax, water and TV licence fees. I was exceedingly frugal. I had to spend £31.50 on the third week's fixed unavoidables (bus pass, gas and electric, and pay-as-you-go telephone), so I was left with just £14.22 from my first pay-cheque for food and anything else. Although I had been careful, I was not prudent enough and I did now have to borrow.

There are so many unexpected extras in life. One day at work I had a bad headache and in the lunchbreak went into the expensive chemist again. I never thought what Nurofen cost, but it was £3.00, which was a shock. Then there was the weekly launderette at £2 a wash, £1 to dry. I set aside £5 for my share of Sunday lunch which I went back to cook for my family each week – and £5 any other time I had a meal with family or friends. I know this was cheating, but by counting in the notional cost I could at least keep track of my actual spending. My original meagre shopping included no toiletries – no shampoo, soap, toothpaste or toilet paper. I started

out with half a tube of toothpaste, a small bar of soap and one roll of
toilet paper, on the assumption that I had a few possessions. I know
a trick with shampoo from an article I wrote about detergents years
ago: there is virtually no difference in the chemicals used in
washing-up liquid and in shampoo, so I used a little diluted
washing-up liquid. But I needed more toiletries within a short
time, which added to my debts. I will not bother to list every penny
I spent in my first three weeks, but I allowed myself a few small
extravagances. I did go to the movies, £6.50 at the Streatham
Odeon, which was a wicked, unaffordable luxury. I reckoned I
would just about be able to afford a cinema ticket every other week,
once I was on an even keel, but even-keeling would be months
away at the rate I was going. I did buy a few other things to eat: a bit
of cheese, bread and spread. I did once buy a bottle of wine at Lidl
for £2.50, and so on. I did not live within my wretched budget for
those weeks because it would have been insufferable. I did what
anyone would do if they could in those circumstances, I chose to
borrow and worry about the consequences later when my finances
gradually improved once a weekly pay-cheque was coming in.

Where do you borrow money from if you have no capital, no
collateral? The local paper was full of ads for loans, but they were
only for home-owners. 'Sorry, no tenants' they had written at the
bottom in small print. Anyway, they all offered loans of a minimum
of £1,000, far more than I could afford. No bank was likely to lend
me £200 without security. Only a loan shark would do it. 'Shark'
may be unfair because if there is nowhere else to turn when you are
plainly a bad risk, anyone who will lend you money feels like a
friend. I called Provident Personal Credit Ltd, one of the leading
personal loan companies. What rate would they charge me for
£200? The clerk on the telephone said the money would have to
be paid back at £6 a week for fifty-four weeks. She punctiliously
gave me the official warning that this was an APR of 170 per cent.
However, that seemed to me possible. At that stage, with nothing,
the prospect of paying £6 a week into the distant future seemed a
lot more desirable than living off nothing now, already in deep rent
arrears. But working it out, over that fifty-four weeks I would be
paying back £324. This is the reason why Arthur's social fund

should be uncapped, so that people in real need can borrow from there without ever falling into the clutches of companies such as these. It is a reason there should be grants for people moving into work, so they don't start working life in deep debt.

At least I have never had any romantic illusions about the simple life or the joys of downsizing. I was never one of those who pine for some better golden era before 'consumerism'. I have always liked consumerism, but think this pleasure should be more fairly shared between people. I like shopping, which is the nation's pastime. (Those who worry about the domination of global brands and logos should try shopping in cheap places where there are only weird and suspect-looking packs of food and toiletries, no reassuringly familiar brands to guarantee consistent quality.) I like eating out, going to movies and theatres, cooking and dining with friends, wine, clothes, holidays and the pleasure of flying off to some foreign city for a long weekend. I do not wring my hands at the wickedness of modern society and its materialism. Humans were always materialistic, hence the striving for progress absent from animals' thinking. I have no problem with acquisitiveness. Apart from concern about things that may damage the planet, I have no moral abhorrence of the comfortable life, absolutely no *nostalgie de la boue* or fond notions that the life of the poor of the earth is in some way morally superior or closer to nature than that of the well-off.

Re-reading *The Road to Wigan Pier* by George Orwell, I found I had forgotten his self-loathing, his casual contempt for a middle-class education and bourgeois way of life that his 'happy workers' went on to seize with glee whenever they got the chance. It reads oddly these days, when the mass working class has moved up into the home-owning middle class. These days it has become clear that there is no good reason why the last third could not follow them upwards, if future growth were shared out better. I came across this passage in which he eulogises the simple pleasures and essential happiness of the securely employed working man in his home:

> I should say that a manual worker, if he is in steady work and drawing good wages – an 'if' that gets bigger and bigger – has a better chance of being happy than an 'educated' man. His home

life seems to fall more naturally into a sane and comely shape. I have often been struck by the peculiar easy completeness, the perfect symmetry as it were, of a working-class interior at its best. Especially on winter evenings after tea, when the fire glows in the open range and dances mirrored in the steel fender, when Father, in shirt-sleeves, sits in the rocking chair at one side of the fire reading the racing finals, and Mother sits on the other with her sewing, and the children are happy with a pennorth of mint humbugs, and the dog lolls roasting himself on the rag mat.

He mocks 'education' as a useless obstacle to happiness and celebrates the homely virtues of manual labour. I am not with him here. If the low-paid had some secret answer to the getting of happiness, the well-off would have grabbed it long ago. Formal education may not be quite the only escape route from a life of drudgery – there are always those seductive dreams of football or pop stardom – but almost every other route upwards is now closed off to those without qualifications. Wherever there is more choice, life is more fulfilled. Wherever choice is narrowed, either in what can be afforded, places that can be visited or opportunities and horizons that can be reached, life is worse. Wealth may not guarantee happiness but the relative poverty of those who are surrounded by affluence and yet are denied any of it themselves is even less conducive to contentment. 'Relative' poverty is ultimately the only measure. Living in a world where the norm has become much richer, families at the bottom cannot help but compare themselves and their possessions with everything that the surrounding culture tells them they too should have. That they are paid relatively less than they were in 1970 shows how much more detached they have become from mainstream Britain.

There is a long tradition of well-educated people looking on with longing at the deceptive 'simplicity' of the lives of people who have fewer things, fewer difficult choices. In the workplaces I saw, I found people – most of them women – with very little choice, not even the choice to shift a short distance away to a similar but slightly better-paid job. They had no choice over where they lived: a housing estate was the only option; they were lucky to get it. Their fears were all for the choices of their children for whom they wanted the whole wide world of opportunity they had never had.

For the purposes of this book, I had to jump from job to job in a way that is simply not economically possible for the truly low-paid. I decided to award myself for the rest of Lent the £150 a week I would have continued to earn after tax had I stayed on in the portering job at the Chelsea and Westminster. (That is, remember, higher than the minimum wage.) To keep an honest and accurate account, I took that £150 as my benchmark and spent £43.50 a week of it on fixed outgoings, plus £54.09 on rent and council tax. That left me £52.41 a week. Then I had to take off the usurious £6 a week I owed to Provident, which left £46.41. I did not know how soon I would start to get demanding letters for the rent, water and TV licence arrears, but I hoped I could get them to give me twenty weeks to pay it off and that would cost me another £7.30 a week. That left me with a disposable income of just £39.11 for food and everything else. So all this time I worked very hard at tiring jobs for a disposable income of under £1 an hour.

From now on, that is the sum I will allow myself each week, plus a bit in hand for emergencies from the £200 Provident loan because of course there always are extras. (My brother and his wife had their first baby: that required a decent present – £35 from my loan.) However, so long as there were no disasters, nothing broken, nothing stolen, I could manage for the short period of Lent, and so I shall write no more about it because that is not the point of this book. The point of the experiment was to find out what happens and to work out the sums. £39.11 is not starvation, quite, but it is a miserable sum financing a life without pleasures and without many necessities. (I never afforded paper lampshades for my bare bulbs.) A washing-machine was for ever out of the question.

That sum went down to £34.41 a week because one luxury I insisted on was a newspaper: the *Guardian* every day with the *Observer* on Sunday cost me £4.70 a week. The low-paid do not get the free newspapers that are thrust at the more affluent because their custom is worthless to advertisers. London's free daily paper, the *Metro*, is only available each morning inside tube stations, never at the bus stops, presumably because the bus clientele is too poor to bother advertising to. Nor does anyone trouble to deliver the *South London Guardian* to the Clapham Park Estate, the weekly free local paper put through the letterbox of my real home each week.

Even when I paid off all my debts in fifty-four weeks' time, I would still only have £52.41 a week. It would be pretty unendurable, yet people do endure it. They work on in schools and hospitals and local authorities, in restaurants, bars and kitchens, doing jobs society depends on for less than a living wage. Their reward is shockingly little. Back in my real life, without even thinking about it, I spend more on one restaurant meal, more on getting my hair cut, on buying some small pleasure which takes my fancy, than I have earned in a week at these jobs.

Once I dropped back into my old life to appear on 'Head to Head', a BBC debate programme I do from time to time with Kenneth Clarke, former Conservative Chancellor. For half an hour's enjoyable conversation in the studio I was paid two full weeks' take-home wages worth eighty hours of portering at the Chelsea and Westminster. In crossing the line back into my old life, I was suddenly earning 160 times more per hour. The precise relative value of journalism/entertainment versus keeping a hospital's wheels running is imponderable, but the sheer scale of this gulf in reward between the two is beyond justification.

In case anyone worries that I cheated Lambeth council by failing to pay my rent, I ran two parallel economies. In the real world, I paid all my outgoings on time. I did not, of course, claim Job Seeker's Allowance illegally in the first week, nor housing benefit nor draw a social fund loan. Nor did I borrow from Provident after discovering their rates: I borrowed from myself. I paid the Shaftesbury £500 for their time and trouble. I just kept paper accounts of what I had to live on had I been genuinely dependent on these funds, and then I lived on the sum as calculated above for the period of Lent.

How realistic is any of this? Not very. I was probably more cavalier about getting into debt than a prudent person with no cash, fearful of the future. It was impossible for me to simulate fear or any sense of insecurity. On the other hand, by setting up home from scratch, I put myself in the position of someone *in extremis*, a homeless woman who had lost everything she ever had. It happens all the time, the Shaftesbury said, and they are only one of many charities besieged by people in crisis every day. But this is not typical of most low-paid people most of the time. My simulated life had no family and no friends able to give me help and support or lend me a bit of cash, though research shows that the poor only get by with support from family networks. Another thought: my mental arithmetic is not brilliant, but working out these sums has taken me hours, filled notebooks, and some sharp eye will probably find mistakes. To survive at all the low-paid have to keep these accounts scrupulously or risk catastrophe.

When it came to choosing jobs, pay and working conditions I deliberately avoided the worst. I could have spiced up the misery of low-paid work by taking the late-night kitchen portering and washing-up jobs in some of the seedier kitchen hells of West End hotels and restaurants. Agencies are always clamouring for that labour. There were always plenty of meat-packing jobs or 'cleansing rangers' (which turned out to be public toilet attendants). I did not, for example, go for one of the worst jobs I saw advertised in the *South London Press*: gutting fish in Wandsworth on a shift that started at 3.15 in the morning and paid just £4.10 an hour. I was looking for ordinary and routine jobs, most of them in the public sector or at least what was once the public sector.

I did try hard to get one bad job, but without success. In 1970 the NHS had its own laundries, but now that work had been put out to private companies. In Acre Lane, near Lidl and a convenient walking distance from Clapham Park, the Sunlight Laundry takes in NHS work from several hospitals. It is a strange 1930s factory building with a tall chimney that billows out steam night and day. At shift changes a great flood of workers pours out into the steamy night air, like a scene from a Lowry painting. For years passing by I had been curious to know what went on inside.

I found the entrance round the side where a battered old sign gave times of the week when applicants would be interviewed. High turnover was obviously endemic. Inside there was a narrow reception hall with a long hard bench where people could sit and wait. The first time I went in two middle-aged women were sitting staring into space, hoping something might turn up. I was reassured to see women about my age and took my place beside them. A bored young security guard sat there all day staring at the CCTV screens in front of him which showed views of the lorry park behind the building. He explained there was no system for getting a job here except first-come-first-served. You could not phone up to see if there was vacancy; you could not leave your number in case one turned up; you just had to turn up on the off-chance every day. 'The work is hard. People leave all the time,' he confided. The two women were not deterred, one of them explaining to me that a job here was within walking distance and she could fit in an evening shift with her day job in a kitchen. The guard would pick up the phone and try to get through to a manager to see if there were any jobs available. It always took a long while for him to get an answer so I would sit and wait, usually alone, sometimes with one or two others. 'No, nothing today,' he always said, though once or twice he told me I had just missed a job by an hour or so. The two women I met on the first day were lucky, or maybe more persistent, as he told me they did get jobs in the end.

I came to know the young guard quite well, as I would drop in several days a week on my way to or from work, getting off a stop early. In the end I had to stop going there because he took pity on me and kept imploring me to look for work anywhere else but here. 'You could be a receptionist, £6 an hour easy! Easier work than this!' He was not directly employed by Sunlight but came from an agency across the road, which he pointed to with disgust. 'I hate them,' he would say. 'I get £4.10, they get £7 for my work, parasites! But you could go over there and get a much easier job.' He nodded in the direction of the swing doors into the laundry where I was left to imagine what lay beyond. The more he begged me to seek other work, the more intensely curious I was to find out about life inside the laundry. But I never got to see beyond the swing doors. His kindness became an insuperable obstacle, for he was right that cleaning jobs were easy to come by locally and I could think of no good excuse to keep coming back here. 'Then why do people work here?' I asked. 'It has many shifts here that can fit other jobs,' he replied. 'Some people here can have up to three jobs, if they can work the shift system right. Night workers here have maybe an office job in the early morning, then a full day job, then an evening shift at Sunlight. I don't know how they do it, I don't.' But after that, I could not face going back there day after day, lacking a plausible enough reason.

There were other jobs I tried for but didn't get. The *South London Press* had an ad for general catering assistant in the House of Commons for 'a brand new cafe and souvenir shop in Westminster Hall. Are you a team player? Do you enjoy working in a busy modern environment?' I pondered over whether the House of Commons could be called a modern environment, but I thought it would be good to test the invisibility of below-stairs staff to its limit, as I would be bound to see many people I knew. I thought my manufactured CV was impressive, together with my clean police check, but months later back came rejection: 'It is with great regret that I must advise you we will not be pursuing your application further on this occasion. I wish you every success for the future.' It was a disappointment. So was my rejection as bar staff for the Dulwich and Sydenham Golf Club, also without even getting an interview, which I thought my CV deserved.

More puzzling and alarming was my failure to get an early-morning office-cleaning job with the Strand agency in Forest Hill. The ad in the *South London Press* offered government office-cleaning in the Vauxhall area from 6–8 a.m. I thought I could fit it in neatly before another day job so I applied, only to be told it would require a full government security clearance. When I told them I already had a police check certificate, they were very enthusiastic as they needed someone quickly and police checks can take forty days. (Knowing I might need one, I had taken the precaution of getting one before I embarked on this project.) I went all the way to Forest Hill and filled out elaborate and daunting security forms, with details of my parents' dates and places of birth, my marriage, my partner's details, pages and pages of it including swearing neither I nor those close to me had never belonged to a banned organisation. But oddly, it did not ask for an employment history so I did not have to reveal I was a journalist.

Elaine at Strand explained that the original job they had

advertised was office-cleaning in the green and cream MI6 building on the Thames at Vauxhall Cross, but that one had just gone. However, an even better one was on offer: I would be cleaning the palatial house belonging to the Foreign Secretary in Carlton House Terrace. I was even more delighted at this prospect. That is where Robin Cook still lives on the top floor, while Jack Straw works and holds receptions in the rest of the house. I had been there before many times to interview foreign secretaries. I could see myself in Strand overalls cleaning the drawing-rooms, stairs and corridors, wondering if either Robin Cook or Jack Straw might pass me by.

But it was not to be. Strand warned me that the security services could be very slow in issuing clearances. A month or so later they came back to me with a query: why was my passport in my official Christian name but signed Polly? As I had to give my father's name, Philip Toynbee, they might have put two and two together, but then my name might mean nothing to a security-clearance officer. Perhaps my father's name flashed up as an old Communist? He was a Communist president of the Oxford Union in the 1930s and he recruited Denis Healey. Although he left after the Hitler–Stalin pact, he was for a while refused admittance to America in the 1950s. I called a few times to try to find out, but Strand just said they had never heard back. It happens sometimes, they said vaguely. When pushed, eventually a formal letter arrived revealing they had detected who I was: the secret service proved its efficacy.

Later my editor was summoned for a briefing with the head of MI6 and his team. At the end of the session he was surprised to be admonished for the crude and blatant attempt by a member of his staff to infiltrate the secret service – as if I had been on the hunt for secrets.

Chapter 7

Dinner Lady – Always Happy, Never Sad

Now here was a job that looked enticing, an easy one. When I found it on the Job Centre computer I rushed to apply, knowing anyone else who saw it would try to get there first: 'Room Attendant. £5 an hour. Permanent. Must have good customer care skills, cash handling experience and waiting experience. Will be delivering tea/coffee to rooms in the Town Hall.' I could put together a CV from long-ago waitressing jobs – the Golden Egg, the Wimpy and the Pepper Mill coffee bar in Notting Hill plus a spurious one from a friend of my daughter's who has a bar. It would only take a little economy with the truth over the dates, but what's three decades when no one checks anyway?

I could imagine myself wheeling a tea trolley through the corridors of Lambeth's Town Hall; as a working environment it sounded like job heaven compared to many. I hoped that, at £5 an hour, it might even be a rare job in the direct employ of the council, instead of through an agency or a contractor. It would be interesting because I know some of the councillors, though they might not know me in an overall. I have known Lambeth's Chief Executive, Faith Boardman, ever since her tough time as head of the Child Support Agency. I had taken her out for a Chinese dinner near the Town Hall to find out what was going on in Lambeth shortly before embarking on this project and I liked the idea of startling her by serving her coffee at her desk. Though maybe as in other jobs I would turn out to be invisible here, too.

Yes, said a warm-sounding woman called Sally when the Employment Service put me through to her about the job. The post was certainly available; I sounded suitable, and would I come for an interview at the ServiceTeam offices on Thursday? So it was not a directly employed council job after all but another privatised contractor. ServiceTeam is the company that runs all Lambeth services: rubbish, catering, gardening, security, cleaning and transport. So yet again this was a job working for the state at one remove, not technically a public-sector job. Most of Lambeth's manual staff are now employed by ServiceTeam, which runs Birmingham, Sheffield, Portsmouth, Greenwich and Camden, among others. Knowing how contractors underbid one another by squeezing wages and conditions, I kept searching for genuine civil service jobs at the Job Centre, but they always turned out to be agencies or contracting companies, never direct government employment.

It was raining hard and the wind was blowing up a gale. My umbrella had turned inside out so many times that day that three spokes had broken and the thing was a miserable crumpled joke. After a bus to Herne Hill it was a fifteen-minute walk to Shake-speare Road, where ServiceTeam has its Lambeth headquarters. I was a neat five minutes early, furling up what was left of my umbrella as I stepped into the security entrance beside a goods yard full of ServiceTeam trucks.

'Who you for?' asked a surly security guard.

'Sally Hampton,' I said.

'She don't work here.'

'Yes she does. She called me for an interview today.'

'I SAID, she don't work here no more.'

'But I talked to her only two days ago!'

'That was then. This is now. She has left the company and that's that.' He went back to reading his paper. I stamped my foot and swore.

'I've come miles to see her. I was told to see her. I want to see someone else. About a job that was advertised!' I don't usually talk this way, but I was tired and wet and very angry.

'Ain't nobody here. You mean a catering job?'

'Yes, in the Town Hall.'

'I don't know nothing about it. All I know is all yesterday and all today there were loads, I mean loads, of folks coming here asking for Sally Hampton and they all been sent away. She left, for good. No interviews today.'

'Is there anyone else?'

'Nope, they've all gone home now.' When I insisted, he reluctantly gave me a name and number I could call the next day. But this is how it goes with these jobs. No employers bother to cancel interviews when jobs are gone or things change. Poor people travel miles they cannot afford chasing jobs that come and go on the unexplained whim of unseen people they never meet. All those people lining up in agencies, leaning against walls, waiting, waiting, filling forms and waiting again in grim and shabby lobbies all over the city are inured to it, unnaturally patient with no expectation of good treatment and no disappointment or surprise when things turn out badly. They are well-used to having their time and shoe leather wasted, employers so careless about them without even thinking about it. Cheap labour is treated as if it were water from a leaky tap. I was only angry because I was not used to it.

Next morning I called the name the security man had given me. The voice on the phone was brusque to the point of rudeness. 'Sally Hampton has left this company.'

'What about her interviews? I came yesterday. Is someone else doing them?'

'No. There will be no interviews. She reconfigured a lot of jobs and advertised them but we decided it was the wrong thing to do, so now she has gone.' In my mind the disappeared Sally Hampton had become a heroine of the working class, trying to hire people at better rates for better jobs, but who knows?

'What about the room attendant job in Lambeth Town Hall?'

'That job is no longer happening.'

'Is there anything else?'

'Catering assistants is all there is. You can come Monday morning 9 a.m. for interviews and induction then.' He slammed down the phone, and that was that. The dream permanent £5 an hour easy tea-trolley job had vanished, too good to be true.

So on Monday morning there was another trek back to ServiceTeam headquarters where Maria, one of the area catering managers, handed out a wad of application forms to the seven women and one man who had turned up for catering jobs, half of us white, half black, all neat in interview wear. The single man was wearing the now-familiar universal polo shirt, in bright red with another company logo on it, plainly already working somewhere else.

The ServiceTeam jobs on offer turned out to be the most miserable I had found yet. £4.12 an hour as catering assistants in Lambeth school kitchens for only three hours a day – a lot of travelling for terrible pay for just fifteen hours a week. Maria, who sounded East European, said the pay rises to £4.50 after six months worked, but there was no pay during holidays. Our pay would be spread out thinly over the whole year to keep the cheques coming in evenly, she said kindly, as if that were for our benefit, though it also meant that ServiceTeam could hold back sizeable sums instead of paying it out directly. What's more, we would only be paid at the end of the month: a four-week wait before we got a penny. Spread out across the year, this plunges far below the minimum wage to £3.75 an hour, but technically it is within the law.

Maria's talk was all about the company and avoiding being sued. 'You are out there as ambassadors for Team Lambeth' (the name the company gives itself in this borough). 'No one is to hear any sounds of any rows coming from the kitchen, ever.' We will, she says, fulfil the company's contracts, come what may – so even if children never eat it, we will serve up two hot vegetables a day if that is what the client contract says. When there are inset days when schools are closed for teachers' staff training, we will not be employed or paid, nor on bank holidays. I sign a personal Colleague Commitment contract promising 'Customer care is my responsibility'; 'Work quality is my responsibility'; and 'I'm dedicated to public service', though nothing much has been said about public service. We are not given copies of any of the forms we have signed, nor any evidence of our contract of employment. There is nothing in this contract about how responsible or dedicated my employer is or isn't to me. We sign that we have received this morning's induction and training in health, safety and food hygiene (though there has been no mention of children or nutrition); there will be a full day's food hygiene course in a few months' time we must also attend. Some mothers protested they couldn't manage that without a crèche.

Maria took us through colour-coding rules in the kitchen, so that raw meat and fish never meet cooked food. I took notes that salad is green knives and cutting boards, cold meat is yellow, raw meat red, fish blue, veg brown, and dairy and bread is white. It sounded complicated. We were told that bacteria doubles every ten minutes in warm food. We were taught knife-handling and instructed that the only language ever to be used in the kitchen is English, and then we signed statements that we had been taught these things.

There was a low groan round the room when we were told that there were no dishwashing machines in any of the Lambeth school kitchens and that catering assistants would be doing it all by hand. There was to be no coughing or spitting, no jewellery, watches or nail varnish. There would be no sick pay in the first six months. She said no kitchen shoes would be issued either in the first six months. 'With out high turnover in the kitchens, we'd be out of shoes in no time!' she said as if this were a joke but no one laughed. The high turnover came as no surprise. Everywhere this is the excuse for treating people badly – why bother, they never stay? No management course seems to have considered that keeping people by paying and treating them better might even turn out to be profitable.

Maria drifted out of the room from time to time and we talked. Trisha, who was sitting next to me, was desperate. 'I need sixteen hours, not fifteen,' she says. 'If I do sixteen hours I qualify for WFTC and childcare tax credits, but I can't find any job that fits school hours yet takes me over fifteen hours. I'll have to take this for now.' Judy, whom I'd sat with to fill out forms earlier in reception, was about forty-five and worked evenings in a canteen. She needed another job she could combine with her children's school hours. Her husband had just been made redundant as a technical manager in Morden. But after a virus last year he had been left with serious heart trouble, keeping him off work frequently. 'He'll never get another job now,' she said. 'Today he's gone to the doctor to see if he can get invalidity, but I don't know if they'll give it to him. I need another job but this isn't much, is it?' Everyone was complaining about the pay but because of children no one here had any choice but to take it. That is why ServiceTeam gets away with paying this wage, despite London prices. The people who need it most are least likely to get any London weighting allowance. These employers know mothers are trapped in the low-pay cycle by their children. Because they are low-paid they can never afford any child care that might let them get a job or training to lift them out of poverty. Childcare tax credits are available to low-paid mothers, but at a maximum £70 a week they don't cover half the real cost nationwide, let alone in London. If there were no minimum wage, ServiceTeam could probably offer these jobs at even lower pay and still find women desperate enough to take them.

Schools were handed out to us according to postcode, but none was close to my flat. Clement Atlee Primary was to be my school, two bus rides away. One bus and the tube would have been twice as quick, but the two stops on the tube would have cost me £2 a day off my preciously slender £12.50 a day pay. My allotted hours were not good either: 11 a.m.–2.30 p.m., with a half-hour lunch break that would not be paid. I asked if I had to take a lunch break when I would be working such short hours? Yes, Maria said, that is the way the job goes at that school because there is a natural break in the work between finishing the school meal and other tasks (as yet unspecified).

It did not sound good but I balanced that against the general image of dinner ladies we all have from schooldays. As seen by schoolchildren, they seem to lounge around at the school hatch, doling out dollops of sludgy food while chatting cheerily. It didn't look too bad, the sort of job cosy mums did for a bit of extra pin money. Dinner ladies are a national joke: there was even a group named The Dinner Ladies not long ago and the recent television sitcom of the same name showed them having fun, sitting about telling jokes and gossiping all day in a friendly school atmosphere doing very little work, certainly nothing gruelling.

Clement Atlee Primary is in the middle of a sea of old LCC-built housing estates, a single-floor school complex with a big play-ground. The children are of a multitude of ethnic origins. In the league tables the school scores only a little below the national average and, like other Lambeth primaries, it has been improving each year. Walking down to it on the first day, I considered the school's namesake. How would the members of that 1945 government view the working conditions of 2002? Considering the futuristic optimism of the Festival of Britain with its Skylon, I imagine they would be disappointed to find that fifty years later a third of the British workforce is still paid below the EU decency threshold.

I pressed the bell at the school gates, said 'catering assistant' into the entry phone and was let in by an unseen voice. Once I was inside, someone pointed me to the kitchens through a door behind three shut hatches in a corridor and I entered anxiously. This is the worst part of new jobs: arriving, knowing nothing and feeling a useless fool. This is another reason why workers don't shop around for new jobs as much as they should to seek out better pay and conditions. Finding the job is bad enough – going through the interviews, inductions and generally alarming humiliations – but arriving at a new job clueless about what to do is a real deterrent to job mobility. People tend to stick with the friends, routines and procedures they are familiar with because there might be worse out there. Economists' models for the mobility of labour suggest people will move around following the wages market as easily as capital flashes around the world from a City dealer's desk. But then economists have never had to walk into an unknown kitchen to announce themselves to a group of workers probably less than thrilled at the arrival of yet another inexperienced gormless-looking temporary catering assistant.

As I entered the kitchen, a small, round, wrinkled cook in a less than immaculate white overall and a blue hairnet peered at me from behind a rack of baking tins. 'You the new one?' she asked, looking me up and down. At least she was expecting me and knew my name. Then she beamed out of her big bright pink face and I felt better. She was about fifty but looked much older, wrinkled and plump, with sleeves rolled up exposing ruddy arms roughened by years of hard work. 'Now,' she said, bustling up to me, 'I'm Maggie and this is Wilma. She's my right arm, my big support and I couldn't do without her!' She flung an arm round Wilma, a solid Ghanaian woman who smiled at me too. There were five of us to do the work of ten men, Maggie said with a kind of laugh, as she introduced me to the other two kitchen workers, both young black men – Morris who was permanent and had been there a while, and Eddie who was another temporary newcomer employed by the Blue Arrow agency, though he wore a different agency identity tag on a chain round his neck reading The Work Exchange.

'Got a uniform?' Maggie asked. 'No, of course they wouldn't think to give you one, would they?' She took me into the small changing-room with lockers where a radio was left on all day pumping out mega-loud music. After rummaging about she found an outfit discarded by a succession of other temps. There was an old ServiceTeam orange polo shirt, the universal company uniform with its big blue T. There was a blue tabard-shaped overall with an orange ServiceTeam logo on the front, a plastic apron and a baseball cap, also with a big orange T. It was a rough approximation of a McDonald's uniform. She couldn't find any company trousers so I wore my own with my Clarks shoes. Later she found a blue hairnet somewhere and gave me that, too. Does anything look worse than a blue hairnet and a baseball cap? Looking your worst in company uniforms is another dispiriting part of these jobs. I try to imagine the *Guardian* office if we all had to wear luminous *Guardian* polo shirts and baseball caps.

The running of this kitchen was fast and furious, efficient but, to a newcomer, dauntingly incomprehensible. It bore no recognisable relation to the induction we had been given but presumably the company covered itself legally by telling us how it should be done, making us sign to say we knew the rules and then turning a blind eye when every cook ran their kitchen in their own way. That way if anything went wrong it would always be the employees' fault: our signatures would prove it. For example, we were told that if ever there was a wet patch or a mopped patch on the kitchen floor, we must immediately put up a big yellow Danger sign, then if anyone slipped the company could not be sued. But if I had followed that rule the entire kitchen would have been an impassable sea of yellow signs as the floor was wet and slippery most of the time – not dirty, but always awash and constantly mopped.

Maggie took me over to a notice on the inside of a door where a complicated rota with several charts had been written out in pencil by some manager. It listed the series of jobs for each of five staff performed in rotation on a weekly basis. I was to take the jobs assigned on the list to 'Sharon' for week four on the rotation. Sharon was some long-departed catering assistant the others remembered vaguely as talking too much. Maggie couldn't read the rota – wrong glasses, small writing – so I read it out for her. The first job was Clean Brown Cupboard. 'Oh yes,' she said vaguely. 'You'd better do that then.' The brown cupboard was filled with dusty herbs, spices, half-empty sugar packets, cake cases, chocolate sprinkles, odds and ends that hadn't been touched for a while. New and anxious to please, I carefully took everything out and scoured each shelf, replacing it all in neat lines, taking much too long.

Wilma looked at me, shrugged and then mercifully took me under her wing. She had a stern aspect that suddenly burst into reassuring smiles. She was the one who organised the rest of us, leaving Maggie the cook to do the cooking while we did everything else under Wilma's command. First she told me to clean the two giant stoves and I hunted about for scouring pads, bucket and detergent. I set to work scraping and scrubbing, carefully lifting off every metal plate and crumb-catcher, chipping away at what might or might not have been age-old burned-on indelible marks. The cookers looked 1950s or earlier to me, as did some of the burn-marks, Clement Atlee's date, maybe. But as I hadn't seen the stoves before they were used that day, I had no idea how clean they were supposed to be. Eventually Maggie and Wilma stopped and stared at my excavations with their hands on their hips and told me to just give the cookers a wipe down, which was a relief.

Next came the washing of the giant pans and utensils Maggie had used to cook the dinners, including the vast heavy mixing bowl of the Horton mixer and its whisk, still half-filled with glued-on mashed potato. This was hard work but, compared with what was to come, it was the calmest period of the day, a deceptive start to what turned into a punishing finish. With only fifteen minutes before lunch, we hurried into the school hall as soon as it was empty and at a run hoisted great stacks of small but heavy tables and chairs out of a cupboard on to trolleys, wheeled them into place and set them out in neat lines, six to a table, laying them with cutlery and plastic beakers.

Then it was lunchtime and the big hatch doors were lifted open as we took the tins of food out of the ovens and laid them on the hotplates. Morris took out an electronic thermometer to test the heat of the meat dishes and record them on a chart, collecting a tiny sample from each dish to keep in case of any legal action for food poisoning. There was a salad bar with bread and butter alongside a good array of hot food – chilli mince which virtually no children chose, baked potatoes with melted cheese, lamb burgers, and a vegetarian bake. I was on the vegetables, with a scooper for mashed potato and two big tins of peas and sweetcorn. Suddenly the stream of children arrived, keen-eyed, bouncing, jostling, chatting, some polite, some intensely anxious about what might or might not be put on their plate: this was the best part of the job, but it didn't last long.

I was not told the rule that every child must have at least a small portion of one vegetable and some were sent back to me for a dollop. 'Fussy, they are so fussy!' Wilma said. She was serving the steamed currant pudding and custard, with a bowl of yoghurt poured out of a mammoth plastic bag as the second option. Most of the children's utter horror at even a shred of green veg on their plate suggested that maybe nature has not designed children to eat cabbage or peas, the dislike is so intense and almost universal. They screwed up their small faces and said it made them sick, even the thoughtfully minuscule portions I gave them. Wilma and Morris knew many of the children's names and their individual fads and habits. Some were so shy they could hardly speak to say what they wanted, others were bustling and demanding. Watching them pass by it was hard to know whether to be worried by the ones who piled their plates as high as possible with everything (were they too hungry?) or those who reluctantly accepted the absolute minimum on their plates and were left in the dining-hall with a stern classroom assistant until they ate at least something. There was one tiny frail girl who looked perhaps Ethiopian, who would not even murmur what she wanted though Wilma got her to use a few whispered words. She would not eat anything, sitting all alone long after the other children had left. She looked as if she really needed to eat, but she wouldn't.

When the children were gone, a mountain of food was left and Maggie gave the signal for us all to take a plateful and push it into the hotplate for later. The others piled their plates to overflowing as this was their main meal of the day and an important perk of the job. Wilma brought out two big take-away tin-foil containers with lids and filled them with chilli mince to take home for her children's supper, which suggested real need: how many children would be thrilled by their mother bringing home a dish of old school dinner in the evening? She urged me to do the same or it would all just go to waste. Indeed, next we scraped away vast trays of food into the bins, some hardly touched, waste on a scale that took some getting used to.

While we were emptying out the serving-tins, Eddie and Wilma began talking about the imminent Zimbabwe elections and the wickedness of Robert Mugabe. Neither of them came from Zimbabwe but they followed African politics with keen interest. Eddie was a part-time student at a scheme in Brixton called The Biz. He took classes in computer graphic design, hoping to become a designer of video covers some day. But he said it wasn't going too well, partly because of his patchwork days of agency jobs, and he was starting to lose heart.

It was now that the tempo of the shift moved from hard and fast work to a controlled frenzy of washing-up. Conversation came to an end. We were, I suppose, cheaper than industrial dishwashing machines but we imitated them quite well. First we put all the cutlery into great wire trays and lowered them into a large sink of piping-hot detergent and water, then with a big old wooden brush with mangled bristles we reached in and scrubbed them all in a general sort of way. Next we shook and joggled the steaming heavy trays, swooshing them up and down, before lifting them into an even hotter sink of clean water with more swooshing and joggling. There was no time to leave them to dry, so they had to be wiped down fast and put back on to the cutlery trolley, all facing the same way. After that came mountains of plastic plates and the plastic trays used by the youngest children: trays like airline dishes with indentations for different kinds of foods. All these were also dunked and scrubbed and stacked at high speed. The steam from the sinks billowed up; the water was lobster-boiling hot if you dropped anything in. Rubber gloves were available but no one used them as it slowed up the work. Last came dozens of big serving-tins, pans and lids to scrub at an electrifying speed I found hard to keep up with. Putting them all away on precisely the right racks, doing it on the run while trying to match up remarkably similar but subtly different shapes which didn't fit together if you matched them wrongly, was heavy work done with incredible speed and dexterity that took me time to learn.

I was puzzled by the way they worked. Why so hard and fast, non-stop, harder than seemed necessary with time to spare and no obvious supervisory whips at our back? It was Wilma who set the frenetic pace and everyone had to keep up with her. It was she who directed who should do what job. Finally it was done and the kitchen was suddenly calm, the floors mopped, every tin, bowl, pan, whisk and ladle in its right place. The cloths were hung up and there was a moment of peace while everyone stretched their backs and sighed. We were all tired.

Maggie said we could take our lunch now, so we retrieved our plates of food from the hotplate and hurried into the locker room, where there were a few chairs. Everyone ate very fast. Ceremonially we each praised and thanked Maggie for her cooking because it was the only recognition she ever got. I still hadn't understood why we were in such a rush, why we were all bolting down our food when the kitchen was now clear and clean, all the pans done, the fryer and stoves wiped down. Maggie and Wilma were used to so many new catering assistants passing through this kitchen that they didn't bother to explain anything to me except as it happened, tired of giving elaborate explanations, too tired altogether. So I just took instructions one by one and picked it up as best I could.

After about four minutes Wilma glanced out of the window. 'Here they come,' she said with a deep sigh. Everyone got up at once, scraped their plates and hurried back into the kitchen. Drivers dressed in fluorescent ambulancemen's jackets were unloading about fifty huge yellow plastic containers on to trolleys and wheel-

did eventually arrive there, saying his bus had been stuck in traffic. 'You just worry, worry, worry all the time. There's so much bad stuff around here, you don't know how to protect them. And there's the drugs and all that.' She talked bitterly about hard-working families trying to make ends meet for their children, only to have their kids so easily go to the bad in a bad area like this. But how could they ever afford to move?

For herself, she would like to have trained as a cook, but since cooks start so early she couldn't as she needed to be there to see her children off to school in the mornings in case they didn't go. Here was an intelligent, hard-working woman who should have had the chance to do something better, but no other chances had come her way. How could she have worked so long and so well for the company, without anyone recognising her potential for promotion? She didn't expect it; she didn't expect much except to hold on to her own strong personal sense of dignity in a hard world. Part of that dignity came from the knowledge she did a very tough job very well and maybe no one else could do it as well as she did in the allotted time.

This instinctive sense of pride in hard labour has always been traded on by employers. I saw it among the coal miners thirty years before, watching them underground on their knees bent double as they hacked out coal with dangerous power tools in seams three foot high. Among the miners there was less indignation at being required to do it than pride that they could and did do what to outsiders looked impossible. The danger and the hardness of it bred a solidarity between them that bound them together and bound them to the work. But it never seemed noble to me, just a psychological way of holding on to some pride while doing a terrible job there was no avoiding. The big difference for them was that at least they knew they were kings among manual workers, the highest paid, the strongest organised, and the country was obliged to acknowledge that its economic survival depended on the energy they mined. But a primary school kitchen? It lacks all that heroic glamour, especially the money and the respect. It is just mothers' work at mothers' pay.

One morning Ali the repairman arrived with a big step ladder to mend broken strip lights over the hotplate. He was a short, jolly, foul-mouthed old Turk, a familiar friend to Maggie and Wilma, but today he was spitting with anger. 'They redunding me!' he exploded. 'I only got a year and half to go to my pension. I never get another job now! I'm sixty-three and they now say they redund me because I cost too much. Because I am long-time, many years Lambeth council worker from before this ServiceTeam shit. That means I get more pay than the others, the most out of all the workers, they say. So that's it. They don't want me no more. They say they reorganise my job so it don't exist no more, which is a fucking lie. Fucking, fucking lie! I know the man they give my job to, this work still must get done. My job is no redunding, they give it to someone they pay a lot less!' He was going to fight it all the way, he said.

'You been to the union?' Maggie asked. He said he had: 'You have to give the union guys a big kicking or they do nothing for you. But now they take my case. Maybe I get early retirement, a bit better, but I no get my job back.' It was getting close to serving-time but Ali lingered, fuming, watching us lift out the dinner tins on to the hotplates. He began a long political diatribe while we prepared to serve. 'Unions once were strong. I am old and I remember the miners see off Ted Heath government good and strong, but then Margaret Thatcher, she destroy the miners and all the unions. Now the bosses do what they like to us! They privatise everything, no unions much now, everything fucked for us workers!' Wilma, Maggie and Eddie agreed heartily, but the children were lining up and Ali stamped off with his ladder.

On Friday Eddie didn't turn up which left three of us to do the early work without him. Wilma fumed that he was always late on Fridays with some excuse or other. Maggie said this time she was marking it on his time-sheet, losing him an hour and a half's money. Then he arrived just in time for serving the children, saying something about being burgled, to which Wilma just harrumphed. Later, Eddie and I had a brief dust-up over the tin-washing at the sinks. I was talking about agencies and he misunderstood what I said. I was complaining about the way agencies charge employers

£7 or £8 an hour while only paying workers the minimum wage. He was edgy because he knew he was in the wrong about being late and he thought I had said something rude about agency workers. It took a while to soothe him and explain that, although I wasn't agency on this job but working direct for ServiceTeam, I had worked for an agency before and I was not complaining about the quality of agency workers. He was mollified; he smiled. But later Wilma grumbled quietly to me about agency staff, saying they were never reliable, never helped out when they had done their particular job, never pulled their weight. Eddie was touchy because wherever he went agency workers were resented by the permanents. Everyone needs someone to look down on and he didn't like being that someone.

Leaving the kitchen was difficult. I felt so bad about it that I didn't tell Wilma and Maggie I was going at the end of the Friday shift. I had said goodbye at the hospital when I left, but here, shamefully, I funked it. They had both said kindly that they really hoped I would be a rare one who stayed, which was gratifying: the only praise anyone got in this place was praise we gave one another. But I said nothing and bit my lip, ashamed to tell them I too was going. Temps leaving all the time created extra work for them, training up new staff time and again. More than that, though, the high turnover of temps departing every week was deeply unsettling for those who stayed behind and I found this everywhere I went. When people quit they were rejecting the jobs Maggie and Wilma chose to stay in. The implication was that the jobs were rubbish and even that their offered friendship was rubbish, too. By walking away, temps were rejecting Maggie and Wilma's hard labour and rejecting them as people. It made their conscientiousness, their expertise and their dedication feel worthless.

I did call the catering manager to warn her I wouldn't be going back, to make sure they got a replacement for Monday, and I went out of my way to tell her forcefully why everyone left that job – grossly overworked and grossly underpaid. 'I'm sorry, my dear, but that IS scheduled as a three-hour job and that means the work CAN be done in three hours!' she said crossly. Clearly she had never tried it herself. I felt ashamed at going and even more sorry at not explaining to Maggie and Wilma why it was time for me to move on. I missed their warmth and comradeship as soon as I walked out of the door. It shows how even a truly bad job can hold on to you, and I felt like a rat.

Chapter 8

Nursery

On the Job Centre computer the post sounded inviting because it asked for no qualifications, while most wanted NNEB nursery nursing or NVQ2 exams. It had a rare welcoming tone in among the mainly chill and peremptory demands for hard work, punctuality and cleanliness in most job ads.

> Nursery Assistant, £5 an hour. Temporary. Childcare experience helpful but not essential as life skills are valued. You will be required to interact with children in a busy nursery and helping to supervise play and activities, accompanying on trips and helping with lunches and snacks. Full and part time position available. This is a temporary post.

As usual I chose not to approach the desks in the Job Centre which seem daunting, and instead went home and telephoned Employment Service Direct, quoting the job reference number. As ever, the voice on the other end was friendly, prompt and immediately put me on to the advertiser.

It turned out to be Acorn Nursery inside the Ministry of Defence in Northumberland Avenue, which delighted me as I never expected anything so grand. When I telephoned a voice called Caroline said No, they had no vacancies at the moment, but their new nursery just opened at the Foreign Office did. That sounded even better. Another telephone call and I was summoned for an interview the very next day. Arriving at the Foreign Office in Whitehall was nerve-racking. I had been there often enough to see ministers and officials. Signing in at the security desk under my official name, I was left waiting in the fine pillared portico of the front vestibule, burying my head in a paper and hoping I saw no one I knew.

Shirley appeared smiling in a bright blue uniform polo shirt emblazoned with the Kinderquest logo and she shook my hand with friendly enthusiasm. She took me out past the security guards with my day pass, round the building to the side entrance in King Charles Street. She smiled warmly, an energetic, welcoming woman with none of the managerial airs and graces of some supervisors. She chatted away about the new nursery for Foreign Office staff that had opened only a few months ago. Kinderquest runs forty-eight nurseries. They don't run any independently for the general public; all of them are exclusively set up for government departments or big blue-chip companies around the country on their premises for their employees only. As we walked along she said, 'You do realise this is temporary? I hope that will be OK?' I said I did, although at the time I didn't fully appreciate the significance of this. I could not possibly have taken this job had I been genuinely dependent on the income.

Past another set of security guards and up in a lift, we arrived inside the most beautiful nursery I have ever seen, breathtaking in the lavishness of all its fittings, the tall airiness of its rooms, the array of gleaming new toys and books, a bank of small children's computers, slides, climbing frames, games and easels with pristine paints. This infant paradise simply could not be bettered. Everything was brand-new, made in the best wood; there were little gates and bright carpets; it was as unlike an institution as possible. Any parent would gasp in delight at the sight of this baby splendour.

In her room looking out on to the main play area, Shirley explained a little nervously that she wasn't used to interviewing and wasn't quite sure what to ask. I filled out the usual application form – no crimes, no illnesses – giving false references and false previous jobs. She consulted a printed list of questions and I gave my prepared answers. I was a childminder (for my grandson) and, although she didn't ask for it, I handed over the glowing reference I had written myself and made my son-in-law sign, which read: 'We will be very sad to lose her but we understand she wants to move on to work in a nursery . . .' and so on. Shirley, who looked about forty and had worked in the company for years, explained they had a positive policy on employing the over-forties (which given I was the over-fifties was generous).

We trotted through the printed questions with no difficulty and she explained she was desperate for someone, so could I start in two days' time? I could. But then she explained what 'temporary' meant. The job was just to fill in whenever she needed someone for odd shifts at a day or two's notice. So it would be just one shift this week, three shifts the next week and being on call whenever necessary. I said that was OK, but of course this kind of zero-hours contract is virtually useless because it could never be combined with any other job to build up to a living wage, as you would never know what hours you might be needed. It could never guarantee a fixed income. 'I don't know what the pay is,' Shirley said vaguely. She called up head office and asked if she could pay me £6 an hour. This was a bonus, since it was advertised at £5, but then I realised that being temporary, hanging loose and waiting for her call should command a lot more money than full-time guaranteed hours. An extra pound was not nearly enough. One shift this week – eight hours with an unpaid one-hour lunch-break – amounted to only £42: some shifts might be shorter, she said, in which case it could be less. She was offering me three shifts next week which would come to £126; it was not enough, and with uncertain future hours there would be no way of signing up for an extra job elsewhere. I asked if there might be a permanent job. Well, she said, not at the moment but I would be in a good position to hear about any permanent posts in the company that might come up in future and I could apply. Later I learned that the company was planning to take on quite a few more temporary assistants for now, rather than permanent posts.

Perhaps the security question did not matter, though the Foreign Office was on Black Alert at the time due to the 'war on terrorism'. Perhaps it didn't matter that I had no references, no experience, no checks (except the police check, which I handed over even though Shirley seemed not to expect it and had not asked for it). Any mother anxiously employing nannies or inspecting nurseries knows that in the end it all comes down to trust and instinct: is someone going to be kind, gentle and responsible? Any number of bona fide references and years of experience don't tell you that. (The only really bad-tempered nanny I ever employed was also the most experienced and fully qualified. She hit my child so hard his nursery alerted me to a bruise marking a handprint on his bottom. She said he fell over; the nursery said they knew a handprint when they saw one. Yet she had an NNEB and fulsome references which I had checked thoroughly.) Long after they had already employed me, Kinderquest did write to one of my referees and did start the process of getting a police check on me (as if they never registered the one I handed them), but not until long after I had already started working with their children.

However, this nursery was so well-run and well-supervised it would have been impossible for anyone to treat a child badly. It was all open-plan, and everyone kept an eye on everyone else. Above all, the prevailing ethos was one of extraordinary affection for the children, awareness of their smallest individual idiosyncrasies, much hugging and joggling about of any baby at all distressed, much personal play and attention all day long, a model of how things should be. The care was every bit as good as the luxurious surroundings and equipment; no secrets here to worry any parents.

When I arrived for work two days later, I was given my bright purple Kinderquest-imprinted polo shirt, the standard issue for most low-paid work – crisp, bright short-sleeved shirts with collars, embroidered with the firm's logo. Easy to wash and iron, smart and bright, they confer a cheerful, classless, convenient, smart yet clearly uniform air. I was given a locker to put away my outdoor shoes, since hygiene rules here required a strict outdoor and indoor footwear code to keep the carpets babies crawled on as germless as possible. This was going to be a nice job. Everyone here smiled all the time.

I was put in the baby room with Leanne. The two of us had to be in that room with eight babies without fail every second of the day, although Shirley or her equally likeable deputy, Natalie, were always in and out of there as well. The room was a large sectioned-off part of the nursery with a low half-door so everything that went on in the place could be seen from all around. At the far end was the babies' sleeping-room, with rows of immaculate, identical, expensive wooden cots. The babies were tumbling about, crawling or lolling, reaching out for the multitudinous stimulating and tasteful toys. With my own grandson just two and four children of my own, I felt reasonably at ease in this pleasing sea of infants.

Each day had a fixed routine, strictly adhered to down to the last minute so the children would know exactly what to expect. Each time of day had its designated activity so they were never bored. I was handed a printed sheet headed 'Sunrays Daily Routine' (the babies were called Sunrays; the over-twos were Moonbeams). It explained my duties for the official Kinderquest day: '8 a.m. Breakfast. Nappy change. Freeplay. 9 a.m. Breakfast finishes, tables and high chairs cleaned. Freeplay, cuddles, socialising and exploration. 9.30 a.m. Getting ready for morning walk. Bathroom to be cleaned. 9.45 a.m. Morning walk, making sure that all babies have the appropriate equipment for the walk', and so on. At the end of the day Leanne showed me how to fill in big bright report charts shaped like teddy bears to give to each of the parents, detailing what each child had eaten, how long they had slept, what toys they had played with or anything interesting they had done. This was five-star care such as I had never seen before – and probably never delivered to my own children, either.

The walk was by far the most difficult operation of the day, requiring the efficiency and planning of a military expedition. On a cold February morning each baby had to have its nappy changed and then be wrapped up warm in its snowsuit with complicated arrangements of gloves on elastic, socks and shoes, all done as fast as possible so the first ones were not left sweltering in all their wrappings for too long while the last ones were done. In carefully organised detachments, four of us went up and down in the lifts collecting babies and buggies in strict rotation. Eventually we were ready to set out, a flotilla of triple buggies, with the good walkers holding on to the buggies on either side while firmly attached to us by reins round their wrists tied to our wrists. We made slow progress out of the Foreign Office side entrance, past the security checkpoint, down King Charles Street, turning into Whitehall towards Downing Street.

This was the part I really dreaded. In my usual life I walk down here many times a week. I visit departments, see special advisers and ministers, go to press conferences, hopping in and out of government buildings for one journalistic purpose or another. I rarely walk along Whitehall without bumping into another journalist, an MP or someone I know. I visit Downing Street quite often, usually in the early morning for seminars at Number 11 given by the Smith Institute, sometimes to Number 10, too, to see advisers or policy people. The police at the gates of Downing Street are well-trained to recognise thousands of faces and they usually know me when they tick my name off at the door. So the process of passing those great gates at snail's pace with the police taking a bemused friendly interest was excruciating. We were quite a spectacle and people stopped and stared and smiled as our outing made its stately progress towards St James's Park, not unlike dog-walkers with our cluster of little children on leads. There I was in my purple Kinderquest uniform, pushing a big triple buggy with another child attached to my wrist, part of an eye-catching procession and my heart pounding with anxiety. What would I say to some fellow political journalist, some MP? I need not have worried. Women pushing buggies are unnoticed in Whitehall, part of the women's world that doesn't count. A middle-aged nursery assistant pram-pushing along with a row of others was an absolutely invisible non-person out there.

Except once. As we were turning into Whitehall a posse of neat-suited men stepped out of a doorway and bustled down the street in fast and purposeful group formation towards us. Of all the people in the world I would least like to encounter, this was he – Peter Mandelson, whom I have known for many years. There he was, the ever-elegant, sharp-suited paragon of style who carries with him the aura of a man who is where it's at, whatever the indefinable 'it' or 'at' may be. He misses little, his sharp eyes sweeping up and down whatever street or room he enters, taking everything in. So it was that he glanced at me, glanced again, gave half a nod, even a trace of a smile then looked away. His expression said that he thought he knew me, might know me, but how or why he could not place. I blushed and prayed he would not suddenly remember. Behind him in his fast-moving retinue was Philip Gould, the Prime Minister's pollster and general doom-watcher, who despite his morbid pessimism about all human nature is good company and I have had several breakfasts with him at his favourite table at the Savoy. He looked straight at me and at our procession but did not recognise me at all.

We push on, my heart pounding for fear of further encounters. If challenged what would I say? What would the other staff say? How would I explain myself to both at once? But it didn't happen. We turned into Horse Guards, the children pleased at the sight of the Household Cavalry, their shining breastplates, red cloaks, tufted helmets and above all their horses. We crossed the great parade ground and entered St James's Park, filled with early spring crocuses, pansies and daffodils. London's best-kept park, with its fountains, pelicans, swans and landscaped flower beds could not have been a better place for the babies' daily walk. We let the Moonbeams loose to run about on the grass, Leanne chasing them around to intense giggles, Lara making them laugh with her terror of the geese that approached in menacing battalions.

Back from the walk, rosy-cheeked from the cold, we undertook the elaborate ceremony of unwrapping each baby and carefully storing each pair of wellingtons, every glove and sock in the right cubby-holes. We kept precisely to the prescribed schedule: '11 a.m. Return from morning walk, babies nappies to be changed. Circle time.' All accomplished. '11.30 a.m. Lunchtime. This is a very social experience and gives the babies a wonderful time to socialise with each other and their Key worker.'

Being new I was given just two children to feed, one baby in a high chair, one eighteen-month-old in a little chair at a little table. Dinner was fish-cakes, chips and baked beans, all cooked by Winnie the cook on the premises. My baby had cheeks the size of footballs and ate voraciously, waving his hands about for more between each mashed-up mouthful. The little boy, Alexander, was skinny and ate nothing at all, shaking his head over and over with great emphasis. He pointed at the pudding trolley, but when it came to bread and butter pudding with custard, he wouldn't eat that either. Finally he settled on a bowl of cooked bananas and custard. No one got agitated about this. 'We let them eat as they like. No point in fussing,' Natalie said wisely. 'We find the less we fuss them about eating, in the end the more they eat.' This was a sensible place, with its rules and routine laid down in minute detail, tried and proven practices, all mirrored exactly across the company's forty-eight nurseries, with the same things happening at exactly the same time in each one: they do it well.

On one particular day – it would happen by bad luck to be when I was there – we were told there would be a visit from the Foreign Office's Permanent Under-Secretary, Sir Michael Jay, and his wife. Lunch was delayed and the sacred routine was broken so that he would arrive to see baby lunchtime and not a less appealing nappy-changing or sleep time. But even as we·delayed lunch the message came through that the PUS was 'running late'. We held on as long as we could, but we had to start serving meals. I was sitting in my uniform on a tiny chair, spooning mash and beans into the round-cheeked baby, while Alexander was shaking his head and saying, 'No, no, no,' when the visitors swept in. I know Sir Michael, not well, but well enough to recognise him. When his tall elegant wife swept down upon my table I thought she had recognised me and the game was up. But she just said, 'What lovely children!' and I mumbled, 'Yes, aren't they!' She picked up Alexander's spoon but with no more success than I, as he shook his head ever more vigorously. I kept my head down and looked neither of them in the face, speaking when I had to, very quietly. (I often found it was the style and timbre of voice not the accent that is noticeable. Just talk quietly and more hesitantly and you fit in anywhere.)

Sir Michael, it had to be said, looked as if he would rather face a Taliban Sharia court than have to inspect babies. Tall, etiolated, grinning with hideous embarrassment, he had that distinctive Foreign Office gawkiness and gaucheness, big brains no doubt but all long legs in stiff dark suit and hands flapping about awkwardly like Prince Charles. He approached my table gingerly but couldn't think of anything to say, except what sounded like a kind of 'Awfully, yes, well, jolly, my goodness me' sort of noise delivered from behind clenched teeth and stiff smile. And then, mercifully, they swept away. Again, in my uniform, I was invisible.

Leanne, who had been in the baby room all day with me, was from Tottenham, had been a childminder and was now working towards her NVQ3 which would eventually make her a qualified nursery nurse. She was clever, sassy, lively and adored every one of her babies, captivated by everything they did, talking about all their little ways and the pleasure of watching them develop and learn. But she was not well-rewarded for her diligence and enthusiasm. As a permanent nursery assistant she was earning £10,000 a year, she told me – £192 a week. That is half of median male earnings. Luckily she had a husband who worked, so they managed. When she was qualified she would earn more but even here in this highest of the top echelons of the nursery world, the Foreign Office relied on very cheap labour to carry out a job that probably mattered as much or more to those parents than their own. Who doesn't worry how their children are cared for while they are at work? Nurseries, childminders, nannies and the worry of strangers looking after your children are the perennial anxious conversation of all parents of young children wherever they are.

But of course Kinderquest pay-rates were nothing to do with the Foreign Office. As ever, the state manages to avoid implication in low pay by outsourcing these functions. I am sure Sir Michael did not know – or want to know – the rates of pay of the staff hired here because they belonged not to the government but to Kinderquest or, like me, to the nursery's own agency, Staffquest, which hired me. Sir Michael could shuffle his awkward way through here, admiring his staff's babies, their surroundings and the excellent care they received without asking himself whether the staff were well-enough rewarded for their skill, or whether they could live on the pay. According to the Day Care Trust, there are over 100,000 childcare workers, 95 per cent of them women on average pay of less than £11,000 a year, with a manager paid around £13,000. Typically, national pay-rates are lower than cleaning or gardening, so not surprisingly there are acute recruitment problems that yet again, curiously, do not seem to lead to the labour market adjusting and raising the pay. Certainly no woman who works in childcare could ever afford to have her own child minded while she worked, which is an irony. Here is an impossible cycle of women's low pay leading to women unable to work because they cannot afford child-care, and therefore a shortage of women to work in childcare because so many who would like to are trapped at home looking after their own.

Parents here at the Foreign Office were exceedingly lucky. They were spending £120 a week to have their babies cared for in the best possible way. But this was heavily subsidised as the Foreign office not only gives these spacious premises rent-free, it had also paid for the place to be set up in this grand style with all its magnificent fixtures and equipment. According to Laing and Buisson, the care sector analysts, the average cost of a standard crèche place in inner London is £151 a week and for a private nursery as beautiful as this in central London it rises to £250 a week. Naturally such nurseries or any others are far beyond the reach of most mothers.

As I left the Foreign Office, I considered what a monumental difference it would make to the fortunes of poor children if they too had access to nurseries like these. Imagine a Children's Centre in every area, as much a part of the welfare state as the local primary school or the GP's surgery. Imagine each centre with a breakfast club to accommodate mothers who start work early, as well as a tea and supper shift for late workers. It would include after-school clubs and homework clubs for primary school children whose mothers could not be at the school gates at 3.30 p.m. It would incorporate help for struggling or depressed mothers with medical and psy-chological support, with self-help groups to get them on their feet right from the start. It would be a place with clinics and health visitors for all mothers to turn to with any worry. Children's Centres would be a universal resource for all children in the area, rich and poor, since desperation about the cost and the lack of childcare places affects women high up the earnings scale too. Parents would pay according to their means, some a lot, others very little. It would tempt in reluctant, isolated parents by including training facilities for adults, keep-fit classes and a gym, literacy, numeracy, IT and English language lessons, classes for pleasure and classes for work, while their children were well-cared-for.

It would offer deprived children the early education that is of greater value than anything that tries to compensate later in life. In the US the Peri High Scope scheme so often quoted now, part of Lyndon Johnson's Great Society programme, was a phenomenal and proven success: the children who had been through two years intensive pre-school education did markedly better in later life. Thirty years later a very high proportion of them had a college education, better jobs, owned their own homes, had never drawn social security or committed an offence, compared with a control group of children from the same impoverished backgrounds who had no such early-years teaching. Every dollar spent on the programme saved the state seven dollars in the children's later lives. It was inspiration from that research which led Labour to set up Sure Start in some of the poorest areas to offer special help and support to families and early education to babies and toddlers. But it is still a thinly scattered scheme that covers only some of the poorest children. Although the government promises a million more child-care places by 2004 – a tremendous boost – it will still not be a universal programme, reaching only one-third of poor children.

The reason why fewer single mothers in Britain work than anywhere else in Europe is entirely because there is much less state-sponsored childcare. While it has been a solid part of other countries' welfare state provision for years, the Conservative government refused to accept that childcare was a proper function of the state. But like health, it is something most individuals cannot pay for on their own. The Tories cloaked their parsimony in sermonising to mothers, telling them to stay home. Now Labour has a National Childcare Strategy which accepts the principle of the state's role, but it still has a long way to catch up on the lost years. The government has added a Childcare Tax Credit to the Working Families Tax Credit for working mothers, but even at around £90 a week, if a mother still has to find another £50 on top of that, it is impossible for her to work. As a result there has a been much lower take-up of these tax credits than expected. UK parents pay 75 per cent of childcare costs, while the rest of Europe pays only 30 per cent. There are many more childcare schemes now with Neigh-bourhood Nurseries, 100 Early Excellence Centres and various Sure

Start schemes that may or may not include some childcare, but there is still only one place for every seven children under the age of eight.

Apart from money in their pockets and fair wages for their work, what most low-paid women need to transform their lives is good childcare. The lack of it is what often traps them in these bad jobs, making them unable to travel far or choose their hours. If the aim is to help them move upwards, then good reliable childcare would be worth far more to them than any kind of training. At the same time since the government is concerned to break cycles of deprivation with speedy intervention where families are in trouble, nothing could do it better than universal Children's Centres. The Day Care Trust which is campaigning for this estimates that it would require 10,000 centres, one for every primary school in the land, and that they would cost the state £2.5 billion a year.

How much is that? Not very much. For example, if the personal allowance were to be restricted to the basic rate of income tax, it would bring in another £2.6 billion a year from higher earners, without harming those on basic-rate tax. It would iron out an anomaly in the tax system that benefits the better-off and it would deliver the sum required in the fairest way. That is just one option but there are countless others, such as raising the higher rate of income tax directly or again raising National Insurance, though that is the less progressive option. To give an idea of what a small sum would be required to fund Children's Centres, every extra 1 penny on National Insurance brings in £3 billion. After the US findings on the long-term cost-effectiveness of nursery education for deprived children, the money would be a prudent investment, saving much future social spending on children in trouble. It would also buy every mother's vote (and grandmother's too) not just among the poor but among the middle and the quite affluent too, all of whom struggle to find childcare they can afford.

As I walked back into Clapham Park from the Foreign Office, I could imagine a gleaming Children's Centre here as beautiful as that one in Whitehall, rising up out of some of the unused open land. It would be a children's palace to take in every child on the estate and there would be a teenagers' palace next door with every kind of activity – sport, art, music and drama. I wondered whether the New

Deal might not do better to spend every penny it had on these, before anything else. But turning into my staircase, it was hard to believe anything as glorious as the Foreign Office nursery would ever come to a place like this, even though it needs it so much more.

Chapter 9

Clapham Park Neighbours

The Clapham Park Estate may or may not be the worst in Lambeth – other estates later indignantly protested they were far worse. But in bidding to become the borough's New Deal for Communities project, earning it £56 million to spend over ten years, it had put up a pretty good case. It is a vast rambling clump of linked estates built at different dates, some in old red brick reaching back to the 1920s and 1930s. In all, around 7,300 people live here. Among its many misfortunes, the South Circular rushes through it, while another major road bisects it arbitrarily into east and west opposing camps. Young people from one side will not cross the road to join activities organised at a community centre on the opposite side, suspicious because they do not know each other. This whole area is a drive-through zone with the estate set back from these expressways by grass verges that are a no man's land. For years I have driven fast past here daily while taking children to and from school, barely noticing it. I never gave much thought to what lay behind the blocks and the grass, a place no outsider has any reason to venture, a dead zone to the outside world.

What persuaded the powers-that-be that this is Lambeth's worst estate? In its New Deal bid it collected some hair-raising evidence. There was the parade of mainly crack-addicted prostitutes along New Park Road at one end; the estate has seven times the national average for prostitution-related offences. There were the many crack-houses that spring up as fast as the police shut them down, with drug-dealing in the alleyways and bus shelters. Violent crime here is double the national average. 90 per cent of local businesses had been the victims of crime in the last year. Since most residents want to get out, it is hardly surprising the population is deeply unstable with a 50 per cent turnover every four years. As in all the poorest places, there are above the average number of elderly people, more children and more single mothers than even Lambeth's high rate. A third of residents are from ethnic minorities, a high proportion of them non-English-speaking new arrivals. Local school results are below the national average (though now rising), people are sicker here and 78 per cent of residents said they were scared to walk outside after dark.

In order to win their £56 million, Clapham Park was obliged by the government to sign up to promises that take the breath away. Every time I read the pledges they made I am both impressed and incredulous. 100 per cent of the housing must reach official 'decent standard' – that is the easiest target by far. Crime must be cut to the national average (not just the Lambeth average). The residents' fear of crime must be reduced by two-thirds. Sickness must be cut by a third, creating fewer visits to GP surgeries. GCSE grades must reach the national average and, even harder, so must the qualifications of all working-age adults. The next target is almost unimaginable: the market value of the flats on the estate must rise to equal prices in the surrounding area. As surrounding property prices soar each year, can that ever happen? These very clever targets were devised by eighteen separate task forces set up by Downing Street to examine every aspect of what is wrong with problem estates; admirable research but terrible edicts to implement.

Everything on the estate must improve to such a degree that three-quarters of the residents can report that they 'feel involved' in their local community and 85 per cent can say they are 'satisfied with the area'. This target for community involvement struck me as an impertinence. 75 per cent of the people must feel involved with this community? How and why? It is strange that it is always the people with fewest resources, struggling the hardest against the odds, who are the ones who are expected to galvanise themselves into heroic acts of citizenship. Most people most of the time just wish the civil servants or the politicians would get on with delivering the things they are paid to deliver. Since no one ever demands the residents of Mayfair get involved with their street lighting or pavements, why should these people, whose difficult lives and lack of money make it harder? There is a curiously Victorian notion that 'community' activity is a good of its own, or at least that it is good for the poor on council estates.

I went to my tenants' association AGM for the 3,500 people living on the west side of the estate and only a handful of residents turned up – too few to make a quorum and elect a committee for the next year. Despite the publicity, despite the £56 million to be spent, most people have not the time or inclination to get involved. Admirable though it would be if the residents took an active role, the best-functioning communities may well be those where everything is run so smoothly by officials that there is no need for residents to band together in Neighbourhood Watches or protest groups. The biggest public meeting while I was living on the estate was in response to a sudden announcement that a Sainsbury's Local was moving into a street at one end of the estate – good news for the residents but very bad news for the small shops scraping out an already marginal living in the area. The shopkeepers turned out in vociferous force, packing the hall with people who had never bothered to show up to any other meeting. Community action is usually a protest against something some people object to, not necessarily a sign of community harmony.

These are eye-wateringly difficult targets, a social revolution in just ten years. All this has to be achieved by the Clapham Park Project board of directors, half of whom are local residents learning everything as they go along, struggling with spreadsheets, appraisal forms and Treasury systems that are often monstrously obstructive. The same smallish handful of energetic people keep this whole programme going, running the sub-committees, attending several meetings a week each. The rest of the board are the professionals from the council, including Lambeth's Chief Executive, the police chief, the Housing Manager and others, all strong enthusiasts who give admirable amounts of their spare time to evening meetings. Everyone here knows how much now depends on the success of these first New Deal plans: if the programme fails this may be the last time any government commits so much money and zeal to failed estates. Such places would be written off in future as beyond hope. Can Clapham Park perform this miracle?

But that is another story that will unfold over the coming years. I am here to consider the lives of the working poor at home. On the estate 40 per cent of people live on less than £200 a week. Unemployment is 13 per cent, phenomenally high now the national total is under a million and falling. But the rest of the residents of working age have jobs. They work hard, they earn little with little chance of escaping life on this estate. The respectable majority are pulled down by relatively few bad people. I am only intending to live here for a short time, only to calculate the true cost of living on low wages. But every day as I come and go, criss-crossing between my rich life and my artificially poor life, I become more indignant at the skewed values that pay these people less than a living wage for doing essential work, while condemning them to live in places that are perilous for their children's future success.

I wondered how it would have been to bring my own children up here, and how they would be now. An adult can feel quite safe here – I was never threatened in any way and the longer I stayed the less nervous I became. But it is different for teenagers. I would be alarmed at bringing up a child here because teenagers have to navigate a dangerous social structure of their own. My son has been robbed four times in the posh end of Clapham. That sounds worse than it is: while crime has gone down, street robberies – or 'muggings' as the emotive press calls them – have risen sharply, especially in Lambeth. But the great majority of these crimes are committed by teenagers upon other teenagers, snatching mobile phones and money with menaces. My son has been shaken down, and once he was pinned up against a wall and had his money taken off him, but this is all about young boys. It is closer to nasty playground bullying than heavy violent crime. It is about boys' faces that don't fit, maybe about class difference, some-times about race, dress codes, fashions, the ins and outs of group cultures. What happens out there in Clapham High Street in the open is just a hazard of boys' urban life that my son has learned to minimise, taking evasive action, keeping his head down, he and his friends not drawing attention to themselves when other groups of boys are around.

But if I had brought him up as a child on Clapham Park so he knew these other boys well, he might have to make stark decisions about whose side he was on, whom he might have to placate and appease with what gestures of mutual vandalism or crime. The risks would be great. Many of the parents I met were fraught with worry about their children and the frightening influence of a few bullies in the estate. I could, at a pinch, imagine myself living on the estate permanently if I had to. But I would do anything to avoid bringing up children here. It doesn't take many bad families or many bad children to destroy the social fabric of the place. That is how many families here feel and that's the reason they get out if they ever have the chance, creating this high turnover and churn of tenancies. But while hard-working families are cast down into perpetual low pay, most can never hope to buy their way out of the estate and into the home-ownership that would help secure their present and their future. The low-pay culture that decrees care assistants and hospital porters are worth so little traps them in places like this.

A good example of this is Tina, who has lived in one of the better, older redbrick blocks at the opposite end of Clapham Park all her life. It is one of the blocks that has acquired real architectural charm over the years, with little balconies and an old-world solidity that would make it a prime target for estate agents. Tina is part of the old aristocracy of the estate, brought up living with her grandmother in the flat beneath the one she occupies now, a family stretching right back to the early days of the oldest parts of the estate. Now she lives with her partner (both of them working), an eleven-year-old son and a one-year-old baby. 'This was a lovely block, a lovely staircase,' she says. 'We used to take it in turns to clean the steps, wash the walls and keep the flowers on the balconies. We all knew each other, looked out for each other's children, who grew up together.' Her older son's best friend was a Nigerian boy who lived upstairs. Born almost on the same day, they were brought up closely together. 'They'd sleep over every night together at one house or the other,' Tina says. 'Lovely family.' But sadly that family moved away recently and everything changed when new tenants moved in. A chaotic family with six out-of-control children now occupies the upstairs flat. Their bath has overrun twenty-two times, flooding Tina's flat below. They leave rubbish on the stairway, including open dirty nappies. They make loud noise all night: music, feet stamping, doors slamming and shouting. The new children forget their keys and smash the entry-phone to get in; it has happened so many times the housing office now refuses to mend it. In any case, Tina points out wryly, what is the point of an entry-phone if the sort of people you want to lock out actually live in the block, letting in all kinds of riffraff friends? This is not a race issue: although Tina is white, most of her friends who are the other respectable staircase tenants are black.

Many in the block have protested to the housing office, who told Tina to keep a nuisance diary, which she did, to no effect. The family's arrival had led to a breakdown in the delicate social order that worked so well before. No one tends flowers any more or cleans the steps or washes the walls made dirty by a dysfunctional family that ignores their community ethos. Why should everyone else clean up after them? People have retreated behind their front doors again, abandoning the communal space they had once tended. Tom Bremner, the Housing Manager, knows all about the staircase but what can he do? 'You need extraordinary evidence to go to court to get a family evicted. The judge would throw this case out. He would ask for witnesses and no one would dare give evidence. Even if they did, the judge would say that making a noise and leaving rubbish on the stairs were not sufficient to justify an eviction. There is no crime committed and judges take evictions very seriously. Ideally I could try to move this difficult family to a bigger ground-floor flat where their noise would cause less trouble with no one beneath them. But I don't have any suitable ground-floor flats available and they might not agree to move. My hands are tied unless they do something much worse than just being anti-social.' If these estate targets are to be met, there may need to be a more draconian approach to bad neighbours.

One Saturday morning I found water pouring down the bedroom wall. The back of my bed was soaked and I pulled it away from the wall to find the carpet below it sodden. The hall had turned into a swamp, the carpet squelched a couple of inches deep. Water was dripping down the front door, which had swelled and was almost impossible to open. I thought I might be trapped but, putting my hand through the letter-box and tugging hard for a few minutes, it juddered open. I reported this waterfall to the neighbourhood housing out-of-hours number who called out an emergency crew, but they said there was nothing they could do. The upstairs tank in the roof was broken and the whole system needed draining.

By Monday morning several other people had reported it. I went off to work but it was still cascading down the walls when I came back. By now my front door had swelled so much I had to kick hard on it for several minutes, running at it and banging, kicking and thumping, to get it open. The noise echoed down the concrete corridor and stairway and I wondered if someone would come out of a flat to see who was breaking down a door, but no one came. People don't. They stay inside their flats and keep out of any trouble. Once inside I was afraid to shut the door completely as the warp was worse and I might not be able to get it open again. I asked myself whether it was worse to risk being trapped inside or to leave the door slightly open so that anyone straying into the building and up the stairs would see at once that my flat could be entered with a hefty push. I chose being trapped.

But the waterfall did have one positive advantage. It gave me an excuse to knock on neighbours' doors on this floor, above and below, to find out if they were flooded too and whether they had also complained to the housing office. So far I had met no one in this block and I had been wondering how to make approaches. If I saw anyone they were always scuttling fast, looking neither left nor right, certainly not about to say good morning to any stranger they met on the way – and our staircase was always full of strangers, odd-looking people coming and going. See nothing, hear nothing and get behind your front door fast was the rule here. I was nervous about door-knocking with no idea at all who might be living here. I knew one squat used as a crack house had been raided and shut down just a couple of weeks before I moved in. I knew on the ground floor there were problems – an old alcoholic who often brought home a rabble of other drinkers to crash in his shambolic flat. I had also seen very young girls – brightly, lightly dressed – flit in and out of this old man's flat from early in the morning who looked as if they might be prostitutes, but it was only a guess. So I feared any stranger knocking on doors here might get a mouthful of abuse, but at least now I had a plausible excuse.

I met a nice-looking young black woman coming out of the flat opposite. I told her about the water and asked if they had the same problem. She smiled and shook her head. 'No, no water. But you'll have to ask my landlord about it. I don't know anything. He's not in but you could ask him later,' and she hurried down to the lift. A little later, as I went back into my flat, another young woman came out of the flat opposite and I introduced myself. She smiled and said her name was Mathilda. Did she live here, I asked. 'No, no, I live somewhere else. This is my grandfather's flat,' she said hurriedly, as if she didn't like to be asked. I had been too nosy. We discussed the water still pouring out of my front hall and she said none was leaking in their place. 'Talk to him when he comes back,' she said, but she was in a hurry to get to work.

When I knocked on one door there was loud music playing inside, the thump, thump of the base ricocheting off the walls. I knocked harder, banging the handle of the letter-box, but I was on my toes ready to duck and hurry off if necessary. I have spent many fruitless hours of my life canvassing estates like these, clinging tight to a clipboard, first as a Labour party member, later as an SDP candidate (failed), so I was well used to sharp rebuff. Suddenly the music stopped. Someone hissed angrily to a child to shut the fuck up, then silence. I knocked again and called out, 'I'm from upstairs. It's about the water coming in!' but there was no reply and I gave up. The same thing happened at a couple of other doors. It was a place full of secrets and people didn't open doors often.

Right beneath me I found a neatly dressed, highly respectable young black couple with two equally neat young children, in an immaculate flat that always had flowers on the table. They were sweeping out the water when I came down to talk to them, distraught at the destruction of their carpets and walls. It had happened before, the husband said, ruining a whole cupboard full of their clothes. As I chatted to his wife, she described their life in which they hardly saw one another except for part of the weekends. He worked nights and studied International Relations at university by day. She worked shifts to fit in with times he could be home to look after the children, a life of hard work and ambition to make ends meet and always the worry about bringing up their children here.

When I later tried the door opposite mine, from which the two young women had emerged, an oldish black man put his head out. I explained I was living in the flat across the hall and he broke into a beaming smile. 'Ah, so you are the one! I was wondering who moved in there!' I said I was Polly, he said he was Dominic, we shook hands and I told him about the waterfall. He stepped out into the passage to inspect the river flowing through my front hall and shook his head. He grumbled about the council, the state of the block, the state of the lift. 'I'm very glad to see you, because I have a problem,' he said. His telephone had gone dead and he wanted to report the fault. He gave me his number, I went back into my flat to call the engineer for him and then he invited me in for a cup of tea.

His flat was the mirror image of mine: two bedrooms, sitting-room, kitchen and bathroom. But he was living in one room, using it as a bed-sitting room, letting out the two other rooms to the two women I had already seen. Into his one remaining room he had crammed a double bed, a sofa, a TV and video on a stand, stacks of magazines and books, piles of things everywhere. On a cluttered coffee table was a plate with a sausage roll he was half-way through eating. He sat me down on the sofa and went to make the tea.

When he came back with a teapot and cups on a tray, I explained to him that I was here to write about the estate and the Clapham Park Project. (I had no need to lie to anyone on the estate, only to prospective employers and, with far more reluctance, to those I worked with.) Luckily Dominic liked the idea of being interviewed and launched enthusiastically into his views about the estate, its problems and the possible remedies. Like everyone I spoke to in the block, Dominic said security doors were the first absolute priority and I agreed wholeheartedly. A couple of mornings ago there had been a large pile of human excrement on the stairs just below us, a nasty surprise to step over on the way to work. 'It's because the

place just looks like a toilet!' Dominic said and laughed. It was
cleaned up during the day by the estate contractors. By the evening
some wit had scrawled on the wall above the spot, 'Shit happens!'

Dominic grumbled, 'Anyone and everyone comes in here, they
shoot up, they sell drugs, the prostitutes do their business inside the
doorway, kids in gangs jam things in the lifts so the doors break.' His
litany went on quite a while and he was right. Lying in bed at night
it was alarming to hear the downstairs front door banging about, the
sounds of shouts or scuffles or just running feet, knowing there was
nothing to stop anyone coming right up the stairs to your front door
and kicking it in. If they did, no one would run out to help.
Although I know the statistics – even here crime is much more
feared than real – that doesn't help at 2 a.m. An entry-phone would
have made a difference to the feel of the place, but it was not a part
of the planned refurbishment, too expensive for a block destined for
demolition. 'Mind you,' Dominic said, shaking his head, 'there have
been times when you would not want to be locked in here with
some of the people on the inside. The badness is sometimes on the
inside already. It is down there on the ground floor right now.'

A couple of nights ago there had been a lot of shouting outside.
'They were shouting at me,' Dominic said. Two men had knocked
on his door late on Sunday night. They claimed they were gas meter
readers but he wouldn't let them in. 'They kept knocking, saying
they had to see the meter but I don't have a meter. I said I was going
to call the police but they didn't go away until I said I had the phone
in my hand and I was calling them right now, and then they ran off
fast.' Did he call the police? 'No, I didn't dare. They stood outside
my window and shouted abuse at me. They said if I called the police
they would come back and get me, so I didn't.' The police have
been trying to encourage people to report every incident, even
anonymously – though it will mean crime on the estate will appear
to rise in the statistics as people report more of it. The police are
trying to map the worst trouble spots to deploy most effort in the
worst places. But Dominic said reporting it was just too dangerous.
Once people knew where you lived they could come after you any
time.

Dominic came over to Britain from Nigeria in 1970 as a student of finance and banking at the North London Polytechnic. When he graduated he got a job with a Nigerian bank in London, worked there for many years, and became a naturalised citizen. But then the bank went bust. 'It was the African method of banking!' he said with a laugh. 'People get loans but they don't pay them back, and then bang!' He was forty-five and couldn't find work in any other bank. He ended up as a security guard on £6 an hour until he got sick. His kidneys failed, damaging his heart and he is now too weak to run for a bus, leaving him looking much older than his sixty years. He lives on Incapacity Benefit of some £80 a week, less his rent and the £25 a week he spends on electricity. Because he is in all day, he needs to use far more than me to keep his freezing flat warm. Recently he was cheated by cowboys persuading him to switch electricity providers and the price of his weekly token shot up to £45 a week, but he has now switched back again. Gas and electricity touts working on commission selling lies about their prices preyed on tenants here: many others had also been duped.

People here often have secrets, good reasons for keeping themselves to themselves. For Dominic there was the way he obtained his tenancy. As a single man, he discovered, he couldn't get one so he found himself a girlfriend – a young student – and presented himself to Lambeth Housing as part of a couple, and got this flat. But she had now gone back to Nigeria. He said she might come back, but she was trying to get the necessary money to bribe the British High Commission for a visa, which he swore was the only way. One way or another, he was now 'very sadly, on my own'. Another secret: Dominic finally reveals that this is not really his name. He just felt safer at first telling me it was. Then he tells me his real name and I agree not to use it for fear of social security coming after him.

Eventually I dared to ask him about the women living in his flat. Tenants? Yes, he said, not a granddaughter at all but these things have to be talked about carefully. He is quite entitled to let out rooms and tell the housing office. But if he declares it, they will tell the benefit office who will dock his Incapacity Benefit by the amount he receives in rent. So the existence of these extra people, who they are and why, is just another of those common secrets in this place. Often people I met at first denied living there. There was good reason to say nothing, reveal nothing and never put yourself into a position where a neighbour might know and use something against you. This is blackmail knowledge, something small in the scale of human secrets, but big enough to be dangerous. Small fiddling on social security, secret tenants and often not the right people living in the flat at all, the rent paid in the name of someone long-gone several tenancies ago, secret payments, unknown exchanges, imaginary relationships and relatives – dealings well beyond the fathoming of the neighbourhood housing office.

I had been told that, not long ago, the housing office made a half-hearted attempt at a census, trying to find out who was and wasn't living where, checking up on the legality of tenancies. One man was told to be in at a certain time on a certain day with ID to prove who he was. He waited and no one came. Later he was asked to drop in to the housing office where all he had to do was sign in and no one asked for any proof of who he was. He could easily have been an illegal tenant so long as he knew the right name on the rent book, so long as someone kept paying the rent. With demand and rent rewards so high, the odds were strongly stacked against a hard-pressed housing office outwitting the powerful black market in rooms and flats. Letting spare rooms is in any case a good thing with London's extreme shortage of affordable housing.

But later this may come to matter a great deal to the Clapham Park Project. A time will come when tenants may be asked to vote on various options that will involve decanting them from old blocks into brand-new ones. It should be obvious that moving to beautiful new flats would be popular. But on the Aylesbury estate in Southwark, a New Deal that began earlier than this, the tenants ended up voting against any move to new flats because unofficial tenants were not included in the promise. The majority preferred to stay where they were, partly because so many were unofficial or were renting out their spare rooms unofficially and they would have no rights if there was a clear-out.

Thereafter Dominic became a friendly reassuring person whose door I could always knock on if need be. He had trusted me enough with his small secrets and I had been able to tell him everything he wanted to know about the progress of the Clapham Park Project. He had been to a public meeting or two, but was unsure what to believe. Essentially, until he saw an entry-phone on our front door and central heating fitted in our cold flats he was disinclined to believe anything was changing for the better, even though the repainting of our block, inside and out, was already clearly under-way. Long-term tenants have heard too many promises, seen new ideas come and disappear again, money offered only to run out. However, I was surprised when he suddenly burst into a riff of optimism about this government: 'I rate Tony Blair most highly,' he said. 'Almost as highly as I rated Harold Wilson. It was Margaret Thatcher that destroyed everything, and look, all round us here, this estate is part of her wreckage! Once we had caretakers on every block, but she took them away. She took everything away, cut everything.' He was shaking with anger at the thought of her as he took his Labour party membership card out of his wallet to wave at me with pride.

Between Dominic's door and mine there was another front door but I had never seen anyone come or go. One of Dominic's tenants said she thought maybe the bloke who lived there had gone away. I worked out that between Dominic's front door and mine there could only have been space for quite a small single-bedroomed flat. 'He's an OK chap,' Dominic said, 'very quiet,' which was his highest expectation of a neighbour.

Later when the tank-water came pouring in once again, I knocked on this door and, after a long pause, a shaven-headed man in his forties opened it with a frown. I stepped back instinc-tively. He had a pierced lip, pierced eyebrows, several ear piercings and a number of tattoos. He looked me up and down with a menacing kind of glare and at once I regretted knocking, but it was too late. I rushed out an incoherent explanation: I was from next door, awfully sorry to bother him and all that kind of thing, but I was checking if anyone else had a problem with water pouring down their walls at all . . . He looked at me steadily until I petered out. Then his face broke into a quite unexpected sunbeam of a smile. 'Well, it's so nice to meet you! I was wondering who was moving in, I was!' He was extremely camp, with a soft-pitched voice, a whoosh of friendliness, exuding an entirely unexpected gentleness. 'I'm Micky!' he said. 'I'm Polly!' I said, so relieved I was grinning like an idiot. We discussed the water feature in my flat, but no, his place was OK, except for the usual bucket catching water from the roof when it rained. He stepped back and showed me the steady drip in his kitchen, but it was nothing like mine. We chatted a bit about the block and I explained what I was doing here. He asked for my name again and I told him. 'Oh, you're the Polly Toynbee who used to write in the *Radio Times*! I used to love your columns! Really sad you're not doing them any more,' and we were off. There is, after all, nothing more pleasing to a journalist than to meet someone who has actually read something you have written (and does not appear to want to biff you on the nose for it either).

Next day Micky invited me in for a coffee – a delicious cup poured freshly from a cafetière. His small sitting-room was a radiant canary yellow and he had a collection of teddy bears grouped on the sofa. On the wall was that famous and most fashionable picture of a perfect naked man sitting hunched with his arms clasped round his knees in a dark nineteenth-century sort of landscape, intimate and romantic, though I dare say serious art critics think it naff. Anyway it is not only a gay icon but bedecks the walls of many women's offices too, including mine at one time.

How had Micky come to be living here, back in 1984? 'There were two of us then, a couple, me and Chris, only he buzzed off back to New Zealand, the little sod, so I'm all alone now.' They had moved in quickly after some squatters had been evicted and had left it bombed out. The council's deal was that if they moved in at once to stop it being squatted again, and renovated it themselves, it was theirs for life. It had been a great blessing. They had been living together on the Springfield, a vast sprawling old LCC estate on the Wandsworth Road, but their life there was hell. They were picked on and harassed by a group of kids, repeatedly burgled, had stones thrown at them and abuse shouted after them in a non-stop gay-baiting terror. Finally his partner went out one day and a few moments later there was a knock on the door. 'I only opened it without checking, didn't I? Fool! I just thought it was Chris, the dizzy queen, left his keys behind or something. But this guy pushed in the door, tied me up and took everything. I was tied up for four hours before anyone came.' After that, they fled the estate.

In Clapham Park, however, he feels relatively safe. 'I often come in late, maybe two in the morning, but I'm careful to come into the estate different ways, not always the same pathway, in case anyone's waiting. I like the privacy here, the way everyone keeps to their own flat and asks no questions. I've never had any trouble. If you get talking to people, they may be very friendly and not at all homophobic, but maybe they will tell their kids you're gay and their kids might tell other kids and before you know it, it could all start all over again. So I'm very careful who I talk to. I always say hello to anyone I see, but when they see the look of me they think I'm hard, a bit of a rough, don't they? I'm a total softy really, completely non-violent. Couldn't be violent.'

I asked about the people who had lived in my flat before me, though when he told me I wished I hadn't. 'Portuguese woman, very nice with two nice kids. But she made the mistake of making friends with another Portuguese family in the next block, see? This new woman friend seemed so nice and friendly, but she was just casing the joint so her son could come in and rob it. He burst in there twice at knife-point and took everything. The last time he locked her and the children in the wardrobe and they were all stuck in there for hours. I felt terrible because I was in here at the time and I heard nothing through the walls. Anyway, that did for her and she left a couple of days later. It's been empty for months until you came. The police did catch him and he asked for twenty-three other knife robberies to be taken into account. Look, if ever you want anything, just bang really loud on your hallway wall and I'll hear it in my sitting-room.'

As for himself, he had had a hard time in recent years. He was a residential social worker in Lambeth children's homes working with severely disabled children, but now all them had closed, some following scandal, most due to lack of funds and low standards. He loved the work, low-paid though it was. (The jobs as residential social workers I saw were advertised at around £12,000.) 'Some of the abuse stories that came out were horrendous, including a ring that involved foster-carers as well, though it never really came out in the open. It was a tragedy that Lambeth ended up with no children's homes.' He was diagnosed HIV-positive six years ago, about the time he lost his job and his world fell in. He said he had been busily trying to re-assess his priorities and live differently with death in mind when after four years another doctor discovered it was all a mistake. They must have mixed up the first blood tests, because he was completely clear. He got financial compensation from the hospital responsible for this trauma, not much and not enough to compensate for a nervous breakdown from which he is still recovering. He lives on Incapacity Benefit of £77.10 and pays rent, council tax and water rates amounting to £8 a week.

He thinks that at last he sees signs that the estate is getting better. He was delighted that the stairs and the outside of White House were now being renovated and said there are fewer addicts' syringes by the bins than there used to be. He too wants the old caretakers back who were cut in the 1980s. He mentions the water flowing from tanks in the roof into my flat: 'Those tanks are rotten. Not long ago we had a dead pigeon in one tank and everyone in the block got sick until they found it. Don't ever drink out of any tap except the kitchen cold, which is the mains.'

Knowing both my nearest neighbours, I now felt much better about the flat. Dominic and Micky might be out of sight behind their doors, but knowing who they were and knowing I could knock any time made all the difference. The more people I met, the more often I was reminded that there are no stereotypes of people who live here. Everyone has their own story, all different, all interesting. Nothing binds them together in some inevitable state of poverty. Some of them are not poor, if they are a couple with reasonable incomes and shared expenses. Those who are poor have a multitude of reasons that would not fit comfortably into any charts or statistics. The more people I meet, the more it seems to me some of the targets set for the Clapham Park New Deal are wrong-headed, if high-minded, and probably unachievable. But on the other hand, the more people I meet the more optimistic I am about the great majority of decent people who live here who could and should form as stable a group of residents as any upmarket street in Clapham. But the notion that everyone who lives in a place like this must be no-hope dysfunctional disasters from some underclass has lodged deep in the local social mythology. Most of the people here are just like everyone else – but without the money.

Water stopped pouring down my walls after a few days, but the flat smelled of mildewed carpet for weeks. Then, just as the walls started to dry out, it flooded again, soaking everything. The housing office later explained that when the tank had originally been shut off for repairs it had cut off some people's water. When these people complained, another emergency team from a different contractor climbed up in the roof and turned on the tank again, despite a large notice telling them not to. Even after the walls eventually dried out, the fungoid smell never quite evaporated.

No sooner had that problem been sorted out than the repairs on the exterior started in earnest. Water was blasted against the outside walls of the White House, spurting in through the wide gaps in the window frames, none of which shut properly. Cement, mud and water puddled on to the sills and the floor, darkening the windows with a thick murky spray. At times the noise of the drilling made the whole concrete edifice vibrate from end to end.

It was not for me to complain, since I was only there because the flat was unlettable until this work was finished. Tom Bremner was surprised that the other tenants didn't protest and demand their rents be stopped during this upheaval. He was unsure if it was a kind of despairing resignation, as if they had gone beyond expecting anything, or if their lack of complaint was appreciation that at last something was being done to improve the block. Things were getting better. Over a couple of weeks the entire internal staircase was water-blasted and steam-cleaned. The stink of decades vanished. For a long time I still held my breath walking into the block before remembering it was now unnecessary. The smell really had gone, soon replaced by the delicious odour of fresh new paint.

All the same, rubbish was still often strewn around, a scattering of used cotton buds, old chicken bones, little piles of ash where something had been burned, a baby's bottle, a shoe – all kinds of alarming and surreal objects came and went from day to day. People still urinated on the stairs. How long before it all returned to its former state and its old smell? This staircase was always full of crazy people. Sometimes someone in a woolly hat was just sitting on a stair, which gives you a fright when walking up and turning a corner to find them there. Sometimes people were running up and down with great leaping bounds, young druggy types, young prostitute types, odd little groups of shifty people who took off like a covey of birds when they heard someone coming up the stairs. Tom said this was the worst staircase in the worst block, by no means typical of most of the rest of the estate.

Only a day or two after the painting was completed, strange new graffiti began to appear. There were no tags, no obscenities, no names, just bizarre numerology on each landing. It started on the second floor beside the rubbish chute, a long list in felt tip with 'two' as its theme:

Two, duo, two, two the lily white boys, bilateral, twin, double, dos, as like as two pins, two for the price of one, two peas in a pod, two gentlemen of verona, two turtle doves, binary, bisexual, bi-annual, bi-ped, second, secondment, second best, second sight . . .

On and on it went from top to bottom of the wall, small obsessive writing, imaginative, well-spelled and drug-crazy. The next day exactly the same thing appeared on the third floor beside the rubbish chute: 'Tricyle, trois, tertiary, triangle, threepence, we three kings, the trinity, thrice, threesome, threepence . . .' Next night it missed my floor, the fourth, and moved straight on to the fifth: 'Pentangle, pentagon, fifth dimension, five-stones, fiver, five finger exercise, fifth column, five pointed star' Who had done it? Why? It must have taken hours to write. Graffiti suddenly appearing in your own home space is disconcerting, a personal invasion. Was this the same wit who had written 'Shit happens' so appositely, or perhaps the excreter himself?

One day a leaflet dropped on to my still-sodden front-hall carpet. The literature I got here was sparse and quite unlike the daily flow cascading through my letter-box on the smart side of Clapham. At home there are glossy magazines from upmarket estate agents almost every day. There is a lavish free magazine called *SW* that suggests everyone living in Clapham is rich. It is full of articles about restaurants and bijou shops set up by upper-class girls: cute little businesses selling pastiche heritage ware or garden statuary. Pizza leaflets shower the doormat daily, along with upmarket cleaning and ironing agencies, specialist carpenters who trained with Lord Linley and dinner party caterers. But here in the White House not even a pizza leaflet arrives. (I called a nearby pizza delivery service once and they said it was 'Out of our area'.) I did get a photocopied leaflet for a miracle healer who with God's help would cure everything, including lack of money, and I had a notice from the council telling me my rent was going up by £2 shortly, but nothing else. No one tried to sell anything to me here. So when this shiny leaflet from Berkley Alliance arrived I paid more than usual attention to it.

'Are You A Council Tenant? Have you ever considered giving up your tenancy? If so, you could receive between £6000–£26,000.' I had heard about estate-agent sharks on the prowl in Clapham Park. The project chairman, Oliver Higgins, and others on the board were worried that a large number of properties might be sold off. While the board was busy trying to decide whether land might be sold off to housing association developers to raise money for creating more social housing on the estate, too many flats might simply seep away through the right-to-buy, especially through these estate-agent scams. The Greater London Authority was talking of creating a staggering 3,000 more homes on Clapham Park (though later they scaled it back to 300), to meet the London-wide need for more affordable flats for key workers – teachers, nurses, police, social workers – to stem the flight created by soaring London property prices. Yet at the same time, large numbers of flats here might be lost to private speculators. Ever since the £56 million New Deal money for Clapham Park was announced, the estate agents had stepped up their blitz on buying into the estate. It was entirely legal, but an unwelcome gesture of faith in improvements to come.

So that evening when I came in from work, I called the free-phone number on the leaflet and a suavely fruity voice answered. I played dumb. 'I am considering giving up my tenancy, so how do I get this money you are offering?' I asked.

'Well, it would be silly just to hand your tenancy back to the council, when you could make some money out of it instead, wouldn't it?' said fruity voice. Yes, I agreed. He explained, 'You apply for the right to buy. We put up all the money and cover all costs and we buy the property. By law you would not be permitted to resell the property for another three years, so you assign us a twenty-year underlease – all totally legal and above board.' 'Sure?' 'Absolutely. You can tell them what you are doing and they can't stop you. We then rent out the property for those three years while your name is still on it at the land registry, and at the end of that time we sell it on.' He was entirely right, all this is absolutely legal.

He explained they already had quite a lot of council flats in the area and he named a few blocks where they have bought. 'Is this really desirable property?' I ask, thinking that one of the harder targets the New Deal has been set is to increase the value of property on the estate so it reaches the same value as the surrounding private property. Looking at White House now I think they have a long way to go to achieve it. 'Are property values here rising?' I ask him. 'To be honest the Clapham Park Estate has got a bit of a . . . well a bit of a reputation to live down, hasn't it? Since we started buying here two years ago, none of the properties has actually increased in value. But it is our belief that they will because they are planning a lot of improvements now. For example, they are clamping down on trouble spots on the estate, aren't they? We have so many people just queuing up to buy property here now, at these prices.'

So what is my flat worth? '£83,000 for two bedrooms, we reckon,' he said. 'However, the council is valuing it at only £78,000.' So is that the price I would pay if I wanted to buy it myself? 'Oh no, as a tenant if you have lived there for at least two years, you would be entitled to a 50 per cent discount. They would only charge you £39,000. You would get a very good deal, which is why we would want you to be the purchaser.' Oh! I exclaimed, still playing dumb. 'Yes, we're always amazed that council tenants just don't realise they are sitting on a gold mine. We can help you to realise some of that money.' So how much would I get out this deal if they purchased it in my name and I handed it over to them? '£7,000,' he said, which seemed a remarkably small amount of the profit they would make. How much would they rent it out for during the three years it had to stay in my name? 'Two bedrooms on Clapham Park? Oh, £180 a week, easy.' I explained that I was paying only £59 at the moment. 'Yes, council tenants often don't realise the real market value of their property.' I wondered how many vulnerable or deeply indebted tenants might be catastrophically seduced into this scheme, losing their home and their right to a council tenancy for ever in exchange for a paltry slice of the profit.

I said I would go away and think about it. Maybe this ought to be encouraging – estate agents licking their lips and gambling on the improvements they expected the New Deal to bring. But the more I thought about it, the worse it seemed. London is desperate for affordable housing for its semi-homeless, its badly housed and especially for its key workers. Yet there was no safeguard to stop a haemorrhage of housing on to the private market, never to be returned to the public sector. That target to increase the value of the property was an understandable one: it would be proof positive that the New Deal had worked and the open market had recognised that it was no longer an undesirable area. But if the better the estate became, the more flats it lost to the private sector, this would be self-defeating. At the end of the New Deal, instead of proving that a bad council estate can be turned into a good one with its existing tenants, it might end up ambiguous: it would show that improvements brought in private owners and the estate rose in standards because it had so many better-off home-owners. It might be said it had been achieved not by moving existing tenants up in the world but by bringing in better-off people who displaced them. It would just confirm prejudices that only heavily privately owned estates can be good places to live. It seemed to me that Clapham Park should be allowed special rules to protect its own investment: perhaps any tenant who bought from now on should have to sell their flat back to the estate if they wanted to move. As for Berkley Alliance, I discovered they would be making even greater profits than they admitted. They quoted the value of my flat at £83,000, but when I called Tom Bremner, he told me someone had just sold a flat in the White House – yes, in the White House itself – for £150,000. The Clapham property boom made even this location desirable – though it was still half the price of a small flat in the surrounding private terraced streets.

That evening was a particularly cold night, with the wind whistling loudly through the broken windows on the landings. I pondered on that sum. £150,000 for this flat? I was huddled up to the fire, feet in thick socks tucked up under me to keep them off the chill concrete floor. I calculated in my notebook how long it would take a minimum-wage worker to earn money like that: official estimates expect people to spend at least a quarter of their income on housing costs, in which case it would take seventy-two years, which shows how out of reach home-owning is on the open market.

And for this? After several weeks the place still felt desolate. Coming home from a long day's work to a meal of lentils, potatoes and a small piece of cheese with a cup of tea and no wine made it feel especially cheerless. I was watching *The Bill* on television and at one point the police raided a flat on an estate that looked just like Clapham Park's east side. Watching it from here, I realised these are the only images ever shown of council estates – crime, dysfunction and disaster. Ordinary people who live here and in the thousands of places like this do not figure on the national landscape at all. They are the forgotten, the invisible, only good for tales of mayhem in outlaw territory. These are the badlands of national imagination, not ordinary places where nearly a third of the population live ordinary law-abiding lives.

If I was here for life and not just for the weeks of Lent, how would it feel? In truth, I don't know, because this is not my life and I still cannot honestly imagine myself into it. Sometimes, standing at my fourth-floor misted-up window, I feel as far away as a foreign correspondent up in the hills of Kashmir or Afghanistan – yet I could run home in ten minutes from this other country.

To be sure, there was crime here, enough to blight the lives of the residents. Just one bad flat on my staircase terrorised all the other inhabitants, keeping people isolated from one another behind their own front doors. These estates are wrecked by a handful of people like Mr B or, more particularly, those who preyed upon him.

Mr B, the alcoholic in the basement, had been warned repeatedly by the housing department. He had been told to remove the undesirables from his flat, or else. They had already been cleared out once or twice, and, shortly before I moved in, the police had called to warn him but the rowdies were already drifting back. At first it was just a gang of fellow-drinkers but it was getting worse. Mr B was a vulnerable weak-headed chap who liked company, any company. He was used and abused by the prostitutes and the drug-dealers, but in a way they also befriended him. In exchange for using his flat for business they would give him money to stumble off down to the off-licence for enough drink to keep him out of it most of the time, which kept him happy. But things were getting out of hand. The people wandering about on the staircase were getting odder. The number of young girls flitting in and out was growing. I wanted to stop them and talk to them, but didn't dare. Some looked glazed and disorientated, others had a steel-hard gaze, as if ready to punch anyone who spoke to them. About this time the big boys moved in on Mr B, serious professional crack-dealers with their bouncers who fixed heavy barred fortifications to the inside of the door.

One night the police arrived in force in cars with sirens blaring and a swarm of armed officers wearing bullet-proof vests surrounded the back of the block to stop anyone escaping. People hung out of their windows to watch. Mr B's door was blasted down with a kind of pneumatic battering ram that reduced it to splinters. Evidence was collected, but at the time of writing, the case has yet to come to court. The housing office was confident they would at last win an eviction order. But it is not easy. The next day the council workers were round repairing Mr B's door, and he was back inside with more dire warnings to keep undesirables out, while the court case was still months away. But little by little the police were progressing through the estate closing down the crack-houses, making it too hot for the really dangerous individuals, and most had moved on. Little by little there are signs of things getting better, but as yet it is still hard to find tenants who will admit to noticing it.

Chapter 10

Cold-calling

Call centres and telesales sweatshops are the modern slave galleys of the labour market, with workers chained to their desks by their headsets. The TUC is running a campaign on their conditions; their research finds that call-centre workers earn around 40 per cent less than average earnings. There are over 400,000 call-centre employees – more than in coal, steel and car manufacturing put together. One in fifty employees now works in a call centre and the industry is growing fast. Not surprisingly, turnover of staff in this business is very high, somewhere between 30 per cent and 60 per cent. Just as Repetitive Strain Injury is the new disease of computer users, so 'acoustic shock' is the new industrial disease, caused by intensive telephone work, resulting in depression and inability to stand loud noises. After a few hours at this work, anyone will feel the depression. It felt to me like Repetitive Brain Injury.

Since it is now such a key industry, I thought I should sample it. Although I kept looking out for one, I never found any call-centre or telesales jobs advertised at the Job Centre. It is one of the categories of jobs that are mainly found in the pages of newspapers. In any case, most call centres are now located far from London in cheap areas with choice accents that inspire public trust, with polls showing that Scottish, Welsh and Yorkshire are the preferred accents, Birmingham the least trusted. The only job I found in the area was advertised in the *South London Press*: 'Full time telesales. Required by SE1 cleaning company. Excellent basic/bonus package. Experience preferred, although training will be given to enthusiastic beginner.' Beginner – yes; enthusiastic – not really, but I decided to try it.

The streets around Borough tube station are a hive of cleaning agencies, some specialising in contracts with the public sector, others working entirely in the private sector. I had already visited a couple of agencies there, all aptly near the site of the old Marshalsea debtors' prison. Plan Personnel in Borough High Street had offered me any cleaning or catering job in Guy's and St Thomas's hospitals after I had lined up with queues of other temporary workers, signing a commitment not to 'discuss what you know with journalists, politicians, pressure groups or anyone who may express an interest. You do not use what you learn for the purpose of writing any article, book or broadcasting on TV, radio or other media.' They had asked urgently if I could start that very day at St Thomas's. Never mind checking my references, they were desperately short of people, even someone like me who had never operated a big polisher before.

Behind the church near Borough tube station I found the offices of the company I was looking for. I shall call them 'Clean Direct', since there is no need to name and single them out among the many. They are only a medium-sized business competing fiercely in an increasingly cut-throat market for contracts to clean central London offices. As soon as I reached their relatively small front door, I realised this was not going to be one of those gigantic warehouse call centres with row upon row of teleworkers, forbidden from moving, timed in the toilet, listened into electronically and banned from diverting from their scripts. When I went in I was directed to the sales department upstairs, where I found a smallish room with just five telesales reps sitting at counters stretching around the walls. In the centre of the room was the raised desk of the supervisor who also hit the phone all day herself, while keeping an ear open on everyone else's progress.

Melissa, the supervisor, was a lively woman of about forty in bright flamboyant clothes who left her telephone to come out and interview me. She was warm and cosy, treating everyone as an equal colleague. She sat me down at a desk outside the telephone room and told me that there was no need for references, previous experience or any other paraphernalia here. All that mattered was whether you could sell on the phone. 'There is no knowing who can do it. You get kids who are brilliant, you get kids who are hopeless and older people who can charm the monkeys out of the trees. It's all down to you.'

This was the system. I would be paid £100 a week basic for a nine-to-five day, with a one-hour unpaid lunch break. One hundred pounds for a thirty-five-hour week was, I noted, considerably less than the minimum wage, working out at £2.85 an hour. So much for the 'Excellent basic' promised in the ad. Everything else depended on the bonuses and that depended on how well I could sell. 'Could you do it?' she asked. I said I thought I could.

So a few days later when I had finished my previous job, I arrived back at Melissa's telephone room at nine in the morning ready to sell, sell, sell. Could I at least sell my way into earning the minimum wage?

Melissa explained how the job was done. We were to phone businesses with central London postcodes, trying to persuade them to agree to make an appointment to see one of the company consultants who would give them a free quotation for all their cleaning needs. If we got that far, Melissa said the very first question always was to check that the company required at least two hours of cleaning, five days a week. If not, get off the phone fast because anything less is too small, a waste of time.

'All that matters to us in this office up here is getting those appointments booked for the consultants, whatever it takes. You get a bonus of £7.50 for every appointment you manage to make and put into the diary for one of our consultants. If it is ever a big one – I'm talking a large hospital or a store as big as Debenhams – then you would get a £15 bonus. But you only get paid the bonus once the consultant has been to the appointment.' There was a second bonus to aim for, she explained. Each week Melissa would set each individual a target for the number of appointments to make. If we hit our target we would get not just the £7.50 bonus for each appointment but a £75 super bonus on top. Because I was a beginner, my bonus for my first week would start at just two appointments a day, so if I reached ten in the week I'd get the £75.

I did a quick calculation and worked out that if I did indeed get my ten appointments, I would earn a handsome £320, or £9.14 an hour. But, she said, my bonus target would go up thereafter to whatever they thought I should be reaching out for. It was like the high jump: as soon as you get there, they raise the stick. Since, as yet, I had no idea how easy or difficult it would be to fix these appointments, I had no way of guessing what my pay might be. It could be anything between £100 and £320 this week.

She took me through the procedures, how to book apppointments in the diary and so on. I asked what we were to say if the companies wanted to know what cleaning prices we were offering? 'You just say whatever will get our consultant through that door,' Melissa said. 'The best thing to say is that it is approximately £4.50 an hour. But remember to be sure to say "approximately".' I thought that sounded extraordinary. How could this company operate at a profit when they must be paying their cleaners at least £4.10? 'That sounds very low,' I said cautiously. One of Melissa's many good qualities was her forthrightness and she said, 'When they ask what that will work out at, we find it's best to say that cleaning for two hours five days a week comes to about – always remember to say "about" – £65 a week.' But surely they will notice the discrepancy between the hourly and the weekly sums? 'Oh no, they never do. People aren't that good at working out sums fast on the phone. The real price we charge, by the time we have added on this and that, is over £7 an hour but we never say that over the phone, ever.' I must have looked doubtful because she leaned across the desk and gave my hand a friendly tap. 'Look,' she said, 'it is often necessary to tell little white ones, isn't it? Honesty gets you nowhere these days, it doesn't pay. Sad but true. It's just the way of the world. You have to say whatever it takes to get our consultant through that door, right?' Right.

I sat in on Melissa's calls for five minutes and then I was on my own. In front of me on the bench was a telephone, a blank notepad and a much-thumbed and marked business telephone directory that looked as if it might have been flung across the room a few times. My letter today was G. I had to call all the businesses with central London postcodes starting with the letter G. I was given a printed crib sheet to read from, but Melissa said we were free to use whatever words we liked. As I listened to the others, some stuck to the text, others ad-libbed.

I didn't like the text: 'Good morning. My name is X and I am calling from Clean Direct. May I speak to the person in charge of your cleaning arrangements?' Once through to the right person, repeat the introduction and continue with: 'Over the next couple of weeks I have a consultant in your area and I wondered if you would like a free quotation for your office cleaning. This is not to change any set-up you may have already, but so you may keep it on file should you need it.' I tried it a few times but the more I used it, the less I liked it. For a start, I hate the false intimacy of cold-callers who offer their Christian name in the first breath. Who cares what you are called? It only adds to the aggravation, so I dropped that. Then I hated the last line more every time I used it. 'This is not to change any set-up you may have already . . .' Of course it was and what fool would believe otherwise? Though after a few calls, it turned out that some sentiment of the sort did work quite well. No, not well, because nothing worked well, but it did allow an extra fraction of a second's pause for thought or sheer incredulity before the phone was slammed down.

'No THANK you!' 'Not today.' 'We are suited, thanks.' 'No, you can't talk to anyone.' 'You lot called only a couple of weeks ago. I can't believe you're calling us again after we explained last time that we are very happy with our present cleaning company.' 'Oh God, not another one!' 'Certainly not. How dare you! What a nerve! You should know we fired you a month ago! Your company was a bloody disgrace!' 'What are you talking about? We're a client of yours already! What kind of company doesn't know its own bloody clients, eh?' 'Fuck the fuck off, with your fucking phone calls!' 'If any more cleaning companies call this fucking line I'll fucking come round and clean the fucking lot of you up, so take us off your fucking computer, right!' It was more surprising that most people were very polite. 'Frightfully sorry, but we've got an awfully good cleaner we're really fond of. But so kind of you to call.' 'I'm sure we'd like to receive your literature, but our office manager is a little tied up just at the moment.' 'I will make a note of what you say, and get back in touch if we ever need a cleaning service.' 'I'm afraid we're a bit busy in the next couple of weeks, but thanks all the same.'

There is an intimacy and immediacy about talking to someone on the telephone. That is why cold-calling makes people so indignant at the impertinent intrusion on deep privacy, uninvited straight into the vulnerable earhole. It doesn't matter that I don't know the voice and the voice doesn't know me, the rules of human engagement, however depersonalised, still apply. I had to make my pitch as a person to a person, trying to create an instant relationship by gleaning whatever I could from the tone of their first Hello. Shall I be posh, bossy and confident? Or matey and breezy? Or timid and try to command pity? Whatever the strategy, rule one is to talk so fast they can hardly get a word in. Then listen hard for any hint as to the character on the other end and adapt to their tone. Sometimes a rapid-fire command, 'Put me through to your office manager, would you?' did the trick if someone sounded hesitant. Sometimes a more intimate wheedling worked better at prolonging the conversation: 'Our consultant is dropping by tomorrow in the W1 area and he'd love to pop in for a quick chat.' Sometimes the effort of acting all day was too much and I just read out the script in a bored monotone, like Lee next door to me, a young boy who was hopeless at the job.

I have never known the hands of a clock tick by so slowly, slower than double geography at school, slower than time passed in any other job I did. I ached with boredom as I tapped out number after number, repeating the same phrases over and over again, with ever-sinking spirits. Every repeated phrase spoken by the other reps in the room became familiar and deadly too. I am not pedantic about grammar but for some reason I could have strangled the woman who made the same two grammatical errors over and over again all day: 'Could I speak to WHO would organise your cleaning arrangements?' and ' . . . to keep the quotation on file should the matter DO arise in the future.' The dreadful power of repetition going on incessantly all round the room magnified even tiny irritations as the day wore on.

But it was the swaggering salesman next to me I really could not abide. Gary was a handsome, elegantly dressed, honey-coloured young black man in his early twenties who considered himself the king of the room, no contest. Poor Lee cowered before his contempt. Gary claimed he sometimes DJ'd at the Ministry of Sound, and he let us know he was the company's hottest seller by far. He drifted in late morning, that was his deal, and it was fine with the boss so long as he kept the appointments flowing. He had his own special high chair and a telephone that no one was ever allowed to touch.

Once he got on that telephone he canoodled and giggled, sympathised and made excruciatingly lame jokes. He used funny voices, deploying an artillery of fake bonhommie and office chat argot. 'Ooh, on holiday is he? Lucky man!' 'Did you say his name was Don? Is that like Don Corleone then, ha ha!' 'Manager gone out, has he? Bet he's skiving!' 'Look, this is just a courtesy call, but I did think you would like to know that we do have our very best consultant in your actual street tomorrow . . .' How he oozed and bamboozled, and how I hated his smarm. But it worked. Or at least it kind of worked. Of course like the rest of us he had the phone slammed down on him most of the time, an earful of insults or weary No Thank Yous. That is the name of the game, repeated refusal, after refusal, after refusal. But he did get three appointments fixed in the four hours he was on the phone, so he was king.

Lee got no appointments all day and said he was thinking of giving up. In the lunch-break I encouraged him to go off and find something better than this dire work. He nodded but said glumly, 'All I can say is this is better than the door-to-door selling I was doing before. At least you let your fingers do the walking here.' He liked the idea that he was a salesman, a step up from more obviously manual jobs, even if he was the world's worst salesman, timid and defeated.

As for me, I clocked up 163 calls in my seven working hours that day, and I got just one appointment. It sounded a pretty dubious one at that. An innocent and dim-sounding young lad on the line at the General Osteopathic Council agreed to make an appointment for a consultant to call on his office manager who was out. I had a strong impression that when the manager returned he would probably bawl the boy out and cancel the appointment immediately. But even if it held and I got my £7.50, I would only have earned £3.96 an hour that day. To get my bonus I would now have to get three appointments next day. But I didn't stay. I couldn't stay. It was unbearable, claustrophobic, mind-crushing and soul-wearyingly pointless. Every other job I did had a proper purpose, something useful that had to be done by someone. This was so much emotional effort for so marginal a cause. Who cares whether one rip-off cleaning company manages to hijack a contract off some other equally seedy outfit? All these contractors defraud their workers grievously, usually charging double what they pay their cleaners. In this job I was an 'overhead' living, albeit on thin pickings, off the labour of the office cleaners whose services I was trying so hard to sell.

Competition is the motor of capitalism, but here competition did no productive good to anyone. It helped drive down the cleaners' wages perhaps, though all the companies seemed to pay virtually the same.

That very week Gordon Brown was extolling the virtues of small business, promising them special tax breaks. I wondered if he had ever spent any time in an average small business and understood that small is sometimes not very beautiful. It is often small for good reason, because it doesn't deserve to grow. Small companies can be the worst employers, their chambers of commerce and their Institute of Directors the most mean-minded and selfish sector of employers. However much the anti-globalisers may rant against the iniquities of global companies, at least they have a brand name to uphold and minimum standards to maintain. Bad small businesses in the gloaming of the economy can be the worst there is, yet they are often overglorified, exempted taxes and excused working-condition regulations that should be enforced with equal vigour to protect their workers. If treating their workers well and paying the same taxes as everyone else sends them to the wall, that may often be a good thing. Other better, more sustainable companies will absorb their trade and improve things for their customers as well as their workers. When the minimum wage was first mooted by Labour, it was the small employers who objected vigorously, while many large employers made exactly this point to the Low Pay Commissioners who fix the minimum wage: small outfits that only struggle and survive by underpaying workers and offering a second-rate service are not worth protecting.

I wondered how Melissa could have stood the mind-numbing boredom of cold-calling for Clean Direct for eight long years. She gave the usual mother's reasons. She started part-time, fitting it in with her children. She knew and liked the boss and felt at home. 'I've been here so long now I don't dare go for interviews. I can't use computers, what could I do?' She was bright and likeable, efficient and a good manager so there were plenty of things she could do with a bit of extra training. 'I know I could, I know I should, but maybe other employers wouldn't be so flexible about my children? I just don't know enough about what other jobs are like and it makes me nervous to think of moving.' Here it was again, a mother's natural caution and anxiety about taking any risks. Anyhow, when I called next day to leave a message for Melissa to say that I wouldn't be returning, she was the only ex-employer who called me right back, keen I should get the money I was due. (I had to squeeze my pay out of most others.) She said with friendly warmth that she absolutely understood why so many people couldn't hack it and left almost at once. She just had to do it, and that was that.

The pay I actually received from Clean Direct was utterly baffling. The pay per day seemed to be £28.58 or £4.08 per hour which was more than the £100 a week basic I had been told. Even more mysterious, another £5.96 arrived later, presumably repre-senting the £7.50 commission I should have had for completing one successful appointment. But I have no idea as no payslip arrived to explain. That is why when you ask many low-paid people exactly what they get per hour, they are often surprisingly im-precise. Complex systems of bonuses they do not understand, or in this case commissions, alongside the different lengths of the months and payslips that do not explain how pay is calculated make it difficult to make sense of.

Just out of interest, I applied for a job as a cleaner with this company a while later. They were offering £4.50 an hour, better than many, but then they were charging their customers over £7. After I had done the job trying to sell the labour of office cleaners, I thought I should try doing the work myself. It was a great deal preferable – and marginally better paid – than cold-calling all day. Not far from Clean Direct was another much larger cleaning contractor, City and Kent, who trawled for cleaners for the NHS in the *South London Press*, so I tried them, too. I preferred to work for the NHS than cross the river to clean West End offices.

Chapter 11

Early-morning Cleaning

In the dark at the night-bus stop there was already a row of tired people slouching on the bench. Some of them had their eyes shut, leaning their heads back against the glass of the shelter, deep breaths billowing out into the cold air. Most of them were women but there were a couple of men waiting there, too. It was four-twenty in the morning and everyone there was on their way to work. When the bus trundled up we climbed on board sleepily and it ran along its dark route picking up more drowsy passengers as it went. Outside Stockwell tube station there was a street sweeper already at work in his fluorescent jacket, silently shovelling up rubbish. Out here was a night world I had rarely seen, cars and motor bikes on the move. At this time of the morning there is a mini-rush hour – not late-night clubbers returning home groggily or late-night lovers sneaking home to bed but a new day beginning for people who did not look as if they welcomed it much.

I had answered one of the many local newspaper ads for early-morning cleaners and I felt at this strange hour as if I had suddenly sleep-walked into another time zone. No doubt if I did this often I would get used to it and my body clock would re-arrange itself around this new idea of night and day, but on my first morning it felt like falling into a ghost world.

In a dark, blowy side street just off Borough High Street were the offices of the City and Kent cleaning company. It was on the outer edge of the compound of Guy's Hospital. A man opened the door eventually when I pressed the bell, said not much, more of a grunt, and led the way down a dark corridor to the back of the building and then through a series of locked doors, across a darkened courtyard and suddenly, mysteriously, we were inside Guy's, walking up the steps to a building I knew, the Sackler building. This all felt dreamlike, silent, weaving through narrow entrance-ways and security doors into the bright lights of reception, where about a dozen women were sitting on a bench or leaning against the walls, waiting quietly. The woman I sat next to on the bench was heavily pregnant and dozing. Behind the desk two night guards were gazing at security cameras, not moving much. Two African women began talking together quietly in their own language, others had their eyes shut for a last nap.

Five minutes later Heather, the supervisor, arrived, bustling in wearing her company royal-blue fleece and her company polo shirt, emblazoned with the City and Kent logo. Everyone got up and she started assigning various jobs but most knew where they were going already. 'You the new girl?' she asked. 'Come with me and I'll show you. You're filling in for a girl on holiday.' She gave me a company royal-blue tabard overall and I followed her along winding corridors, through more security doors, across courtyards so I lost all sense of direction. We arrived in another clinic and stepped into a reception area where a freckled security guard was reading yesterday's *Times*. He jumped to his feet and tried to look busy as the supervisor stopped to discuss some recent break-ins here, the reason for his presence, though this little fellow didn't look as if he would deter anyone.

Heather took me upstairs through more fire doors, while I suffered the usual extreme anxieties about the first day in a new job. I worried the job might be difficult, might involve complicated polishing machinery or tasks I might not know how to do. When she explained I was to work here alone for the next three hours, I realised there would be no other cleaner to ask. As she opened the door to the corridor that marked the start of my patch, she explained that this was the drug-research unit. People come here to act as guinea pigs for new drugs. Once drugs have been administered, experimentees have to sit about all day being monitored and tested for reactions. 'Do you know, they are paid £120 a day!' she said. 'I wouldn't do that, not for any money, never. None of us would. What kind of people would do that?' She kept returning to the lowness of their guinea-pig trade as she bustled about tutting and tssking her disapproval. 'They make such a mess. Who do they think is clearing up after them?' People who were so lazy and work-shy that they chose to sacrifice their bodies when they could perfectly well be cleaning for a living instead was to her a gross affront to decency. Though if she was right about their fee, in one week doing nothing they were earning £600, which would take nearly a month of cleaning for forty hours a day.

The drug-testing unit was light and modern, newly furnished, with several sitting-rooms, some with televisions, some with books and games, a computer room, a smoking-room, a billiard room and finally a changing-room full of lockers. There were two dining-rooms, one at each end of a central kitchen where the meals were cooked, with a servery and a tea and coffee station littered with used plastic cups. 'Just look how the staff always leave their dining-room so clean, but the patients, well, you can see what sort they are from the state of their dining-room! They leave their mess everywhere!' How she despised these unseen people we never met as the lowest of riffraff. She showed me the cleaning cupboard stacked with supplies and handed me a big bucket filled with Pledge canisters, detergent sprays and cloths. For once there was no scrimping on key utensils. I was greatly relieved at the sight of the vacuum cleaner, a manageable small Henry, one of those round semi-industrial ones with a smiley face painted on it, strong yet easy to handle. There was no daunting polisher or heavy backpack vacuum cleaner like the ones I had spied cleaners using in some workplaces.

We paced the length of my corridor, looking into each room I was to clean as I tried to get my bearings and remember all her instructions. Polish the chrome table legs in the staff dining-room. Empty the bins. Take out the rubbish in big bin bags. Wipe down the glass plates on the doors. Watch out for coffee drips on the walls. 'These patients get coffee everywhere!' Vacuum all floors. Then she left, telling me she would be back in three hours' time at eight o'clock to escort me out again with her security pass. When she had gone I walked the route once more to make sure I had this right. It was quite simple once I had worked it out, just one long winding corridor to be cleaned, with all the rooms leading off it.

I started at the far end in the staff dining-room, vacuuming the floor, cleaning the tables and chairs, wiping down the edges and ledges, the window sills and skirting boards. Then I vacuumed the first stretch of the long corridor, pulling along the Henry with the smiley face like a small robot following me wherever I went. It was easy cleaning, all new carpets and paintwork, not much furniture or clutter. I was wide-awake now, and this was satisfying cleaning, quite enjoyable once you got into the swing of it. Bright modern furniture and carpets were easy to make smart and there is a pleasure in creating order, cleanness and neatness when you are paid for it. It was also a relief not to be watched but to get on with it in my own way at my own speed.

I finished more than an hour early. I thought at first I had made a mistake so I retraced my steps carefully several times in case I had left anything out. I could have done it much faster, but on the first day it takes longer to find where everything belongs. I went back over it all again with squirts of Pledge. I scrubbed away at old marks on the walls. I cleaned underneath the lids of the waste bins in the dining-rooms and the bottoms of the bins. I polished the legs of the billiard table. I cleaned the windows, though that was not part of the job. I opened every cupboard and door I could find in case there were other rooms I had missed, but at the end of two hours I had done everything I could think of, some of it several times over. I had nothing to read and anyway I didn't want to be caught slacking so I wandered about with the Pledge and a cloth pretending to be busy in case a supervisor came by.

A man turned up to clean the kitchen, which was categorised as kitchen porter work and not part of my duties. He said a friendly hello and I leaned across the hatch watching him polish the already pretty clean modern cooker. It didn't look as if he had overly much to do either.

'Have I missed anything out?' I asked. He came out and paced the corridor with me, checking the rooms.

'No, you've done it all fine,' he said. 'I used to do your job sometimes. I got it down to half an hour.' He smiled. 'These are nice easy jobs,' and he went back to a slow wipe-down of the small kitchen's surfaces. 'Good jobs for students,' he said over his shoulder. 'Plenty of studying time in these mornings.'

It was getting light outside by now and I leaned out of the dining-room window looking at the pink dawn coming up over the large council estate opposite. That is where most of the cleaners lived, the kitchen porter said. I wondered why my job had been assigned three hours when one hour would have done it and an hour and a half would have been generous. The more I thought about it, the easier it was to imagine how it had come about. Most of these hospital services have been contracted out for years now. I imagine the contractors would tell the hospital managers how many hours each job was worth and charge accordingly. The cleaner might only get the minimum wage, but the contractor would charge double, so every extra hour was more profit to them.

No doubt in-house services were often inefficient in the 1970s, but now a new generation of hospital managers has grown up with no real hands-on experience of day-to-day management of cleaning work, relying increasingly on the contractors' estimates. The unions report that, increasingly, the same group of contractors for the NHS and local government between them run what are effectively semi-cartels. The NHS or a local council may change contractor from time to time, but effectively these companies divide up the work between them at similar rates. They are not intent on creating ferocious competition to drive down their rates. I could see how, now that the hospital's NHS managers were no longer directly responsible for hiring and supervising the cleaners, they had lost the knowledge of judging exactly how long a job should take. Their managerial effectiveness had been deskilled and they no longer understood the details of cleaning work.

Another effect of hiving off these services to separate companies to do different parts of the work meant there was no way managers could easily re-design jobs to make sure they were done with the greatest possible efficiency. Why was I not given the kitchen to clean as well, for example? The medical parts of the hospital, the wards and operating theatres, were done by at least one other company. There was a ward at the end of my corridor where the guinea pigs were given their drugs, but that was medical and so it belonged to another contractor, though I could easily have cleaned that too. But City and Kent only had the contract for the office spaces not for any medical spaces. So I just did what I was ordered to do by the company, and a nice job it was too.

The hospital portering work I had done at the Chelsea and Westminster Hospital suffered from the same problem. No one was going to think creatively of ways the porters might relieve the nurses or the clinics of some of their work and offer a better and friendlier service to the patients, at least in moving them in and out of beds, trolleys and wheelchairs. No one was going to bother to up-skill porters, because the nurses were hired by the hospital while the porters and cleaners belonged to Carillion, the contractor, and that demarcation was rigidly laid down by contract.

How many times have Tony Blair and other ministers demanded 'flexibility' from public-service workers, extolling the virtue of breaking down old demarcations and urging people to explore imaginative reforms that would make people work more co-operatively across old disciplines? Yet the contracting-out process encourages exactly the opposite. It creates far stricter demarcations as private company managers instruct their employees to do precisely what they have been contracted to do, and nothing else. Tom Bremner said he was driven to distraction by it. When he took on the post of Housing Manager for the Clapham Park Estate in 2001, he found that there were between fifteen and thirty different contractors at work there, all with different tasks, criss-crossing each others' paths, visiting and revisiting the same problem properties with just their small area of responsibility instead of looking at the jobs holistically. It infuriated tenants when time and again the 'It's not my job, Guv' approach meant the man who came to fix one thing wouldn't mend some other small defect while he was there because he was not contracted to do it.

Just before eight o'clock Heather arrived promptly to lead me back out, after making a brief check round the rooms to see that everything was done well enough. Maybe not all the jobs were as easy as this, because she said to me as we walked out, 'We're in bad trouble today. They are saying the guy we sent to empty the fryer over the weekend hadn't done the job right. They said the thing all boiled up and frothed when they tried to use it on Monday morning. They are complaining we don't use trained cleaners any more.' Certainly emptying and cleaning the fryer was one of the nastiest jobs that had to be done in the primary school kitchen where I had worked. But who had the right to expect skilled workers at these pay-rates? Maybe the hospital managers did not even know what a small proportion of the money they paid contractors for each hour's cleaning went to the people who actually did the job?

So this was the easiest job I did. Apart from getting up at a cruel hour of the morning, it was simple and pleasant. It did leave me with a kind of jet lag the rest of the day, but I was only doing it as a reporter, not for a lifetime. Most of the other cleaners were going on to other jobs and Heather assumed I was too, telling me that if I had trouble reaching my next job on time, I could always choose to start earlier in the morning if I wanted. I met a few people in Clapham Park who did not two but three jobs a day, morning and evening office-cleaning as well as a full-time day shift elsewhere. If they were on the minimum wage, that means they might be working a twelve-hour day Monday to Friday with four journeys in between for just £246.00.

City and Kent paid me £4.10 an hour, which was puzzling since any cleaner here could walk up the road to where Clean Direct were employing cleaners at 40p an hour more. Then I realised that mothers and other poor workers could get to Guy's Hospital on foot in the early morning from many nearby estates. At Clean Direct they would have to travel in to do the cleaning in central London offices which would take them much longer, adding possibly an unpaid hour and a half to their working day. It would only be worth their while to pay for the journey there and back if they already had some other central London job so they were anyway buying their £8.50 a week bus pass. Yet again, the market for mothers' labour, which is most of the market in low-paying jobs, works on very different principles from the ones economists design. They do not float free to follow the ebb and flow of economic tides.

Chapter 12

Cakes

It was a hard place to find. It was hidden away in a network of streets in a dismal part of Bermondsey, curiously old-fashioned, a location that might be chosen for a film set in the 1940s or 1950s, mean streets, multi-occupied, forlorn. The factory itself felt like a throwback to that era, as did the people who worked there and the cakes it baked.

The ad on the Job Centre computer said: 'Packer, £4.10 per hour. Applicant must be able to recognise different types of cakes sold in a baker's shop. Duties will include packing and counting cakes into boxes and crates. Some paperwork and other such tasks. MUST KNOW ABOUT DIFFERENT TYPES OF CAKES.' I quite liked the sound of it, packing cakes sounded leisurely and easy. When I called the number I was given by the employment service a brusque middle-class woman's voice asked, 'Do you know cakes?'

'Yes,' I said. 'I worked in a cake factory,' without mentioning that it was thirty years ago.

'Would you know an Eccles cake?'

'Yes.'

'Well, what is it then?'

'Round, made of pastry with currants inside.'

'OK then, come and see me at six tonight.'

The bakery was set in the service area at the back of a big council industrial block but it didn't seem to have a door or any sign. Only a high brick chimney suggested baking might be going on inside, and the lorries crammed together outside loading crates. By squeezing between the trucks I found a narrow open doorway. It was difficult to push my way in with so many crates stacked high at the entrance and I wondered if this was the main door, but it was. Inside it was dark and cavernous with frosted high windows only offering a frowsty light. People were scurrying about and it was hard to attract anyone's attention. Eventually a man in a grubby apron and old T-shirt stopped close by and I asked for the boss. 'Up there!' he said and hurried away again. Finding the stairway was a problem, but after trying several doors, dodging people shunting crates back and forth, I eventually found a dark staircase round a corner and went up. A harassed-looking woman in her fifties with a sharp face and piercing eyes came out of a box-like untidy office into a passageway stacked with cardboard boxes.

'I've come about the job,' I said.

'You'll have to see my daughter. I haven't time now,' she said and I recognised the voice on the telephone. She clattered past me down the stairs and out of sight, and I perched on some boxes and waited until a woman in her twenties in an apron and cap came up to see me. She explained she was the owner's daughter and took me into the poky office space, taking out a piece of paper and a pen. She asked for my name and address and what experience I had. I told her about working in the Lyons cake factory in Earl's Court and luckily she did not seem to know it had closed down some twenty years ago.

'You know cakes? We have about a hundred varieties here, so you need to be able to pick them out to make up the orders.'

'I can do that,' I said. She asked the Eccles question again and when I gave the right answer she nodded.

'When can you start?'

'Any time.'

'But the thing is, we're not sure there is a job right now. It all depends on if we get this big new order at the weekend. If we do, then we will need someone extra. Call us Friday and we'll tell you.' This was the first job where no one asked for a passport or work permit, National Insurance number or reference.

On the way out I paused at the bottom of the stairs to look around. The pace of work looked fast and scrambled, involving climbing over and under things, shuttling forward and back round haphazard crates of cakes piled everywhere. They were the most chaotic working conditions I had seen so far.

I called on the Friday and got the owner on the phone. 'Sorry, we've given the job to someone else. It's someone who's been working in a bakery, so she knows cakes.' Another wasted trip. 'Of course, she might not turn up. Lots don't turn up on the day, so we'll keep your number just in case.'

It was never nice to be turned down. Even if a job at £4.10 is no one's idea of desirable, it was surprisingly bruising to fail. I had forgotten that it doesn't matter how low the job, rejection is always an affront which is another reason why people don't job-swap upwards as much as they should and could. It is not pleasant to subject yourself to scrutiny and risk failure. What was wrong with me? At the start of this project, I had assumed I would be turned down everywhere and getting jobs would be hard. What would they make of me? Out of prison, drug rehab or mental hospital? My voice, my language, my overconfident demeanour would arouse suspicions, I thought, and my age might rule me out. But until now I was treated just like anyone else desperate enough to want one of these jobs, just another pair of hands who could push a broom or scrub a pan as well or badly as anyone else. I had got used to being hired for any low-paid job I was interviewed for without changing anything much about myself, except perhaps that I was more genuinely nervous and sheepish than usual. In any case, I put the cake failure out of my mind in pursuit of other jobs.

It was Sunday and I was not thinking about work. I was walking on Clapham Common with my family, and we stopped by the pond to sail my two-year-old grandson's boat across the windy water, watching it heel and capsize. I began kicking a football about for him and he was squealing with laughter when my mobile phone rang.

A gruff foreign voice said, 'Can you come in to work today?' I had no idea who or where. Recently I had applied for a spate of jobs and had not heard back from many: if you don't get to the *South London Press* early enough, the jobs are often gone, but you leave your name all the same. 'What's the job?' I asked. The voice sounded put-out, as if there could only be one job in the universe. 'Bakery, of course,' he said. 'We need you right now, big rush on. How soon can you get down here?'

'Where, exactly?' I had applied for two bakery jobs. He gave the address.

'Paula said you know the place, you been here before, yes?' I wanted to say no and enjoy the day but I was curious about this factory. So with deep reluctance, I said yes I'd be there in three-quarters of an hour. 'Just ask for Manuel,' the voice said. It was one of the odder wrenching moments in my shuttle between my real life and that other world.

Evidently the other woman who had got the job instead of me had not been able to face it after all, or else she had wisely found something better. The big new cake order had come through and suddenly the factory was short-staffed.

Squeezing through into the same scuffed entrance-way, past yet higher stacks of crates, I saw the head baker transferring cakes near the doorway. 'I'm Manuel. Go and leave your stuff upstairs and get right down here,' he said. Upstairs sitting on packing cases was a group of women in assorted T-shirts and old aprons, smoking and chatting while several young children were fidgeting about. The women looked blankly at me but didn't say anything. 'Where do I leave my stuff?' I asked. 'Oh, just dump it anywhere,' a thin young woman said. I added my rucksack and coat to a heap on top of some cardboard boxes and went downstairs. I had on a white polo shirt and my black work trousers, and at the bottom of the stairs a large woman gave me an apron. She was the supervisor of the day, tall with curly hair and a bright red face. 'I'm Joanne, and I'm exhausted!' she said, and then smiled and introduced me to various other workers hurrying past. 'I've been up since three this morning. Been selling cakes all morning at Nine Elms, and now this! I can't go on much longer!' Despite that, she was kindly and put me with Gina, a young girl of about seventeen, to teach me what to do.

Gina had been lounging about joking with some of the lads. 'I don't work here any more,' she said. 'I've just dropped by to see some mates, but I don't mind showing you.' She took a long computer printout from a pile on a sticky table, pulled out a Biro and explained that I had to get a big crate and go and fetch cakes on the list, fill the crate, and watch out for anyone else pinching them out of my crate while my back was turned. She scrawled 'Western

Bakeries' on a spare piece of bakery paper and pronged it on to the crate so the van drivers would know where my crates had to be delivered once the order was filled. She pointed vaguely around the nooks and corners, explaining where different types of cakes were to be found – pastries at the far end, doughnuts this end, and everything else 'just wherever you can find it'.

It is hard to do justice to the disorder and pandemonium in that place that day. Restaurant kitchens often look to the outsider like chaos, with the shouting and clashing and weaving in and out of many bodies in a small place between cookers, sinks and fridges, but after a while a very precise method in the apparent madness begins to take shape. Any half-decent kitchen operates a strict system which might be carried out on the run amid a hail of curses and yells but is efficient none the less. But not here, not on that Sunday. Everything was almost as haphazard as it seemed at first.

'It's a pity you weren't here first thing,' Joanne said. 'Then you would have seen where all the different cakes are kept.' The problem was that by this stage in the proceedings most of them had become mixed up in a chaos of half-filled and muddled crates, scattered all over the place. The narrow alleys were crammed with much jostling between people stepping over and between the crates, carrying other crates here and there.

There were indeed scores of different kinds of cakes, and their descriptions on the list often bore no resemblance to the actual cake. First let me describe them: they were not the kinds of cakes to be seen in any ordinary supermarket, let alone an upmarket coffee bar or restaurant. They were enormous, heavy, doughy things – the weight of a full crate felt like carrying a load of lead. They were the biggest individual cakes I have ever seen – twice the normal size and five times the weight, gigantic doughnut rings with thick hard icing on top, vast cream puffs stuffed with white artificial cream and a squiggle of lurid red jam. Biggest of all was something called a king, a huge loaf-sized oblong éclair, full of white cream with inch-thick anaemic chocolate icing on top. It was impossible to imagine one person eating the whole thing. These were the kind of cakes you sometimes see in old-fashioned works canteens, the kind of cakes only very hungry men would eat after doing hard physical labour, the worst of old English baking I hadn't seen in decades and had thought driven to extinction by the superiority of Mr Kipling and other branded varieties. I could see why they might sell early in the morning to the fruit and veg porters at Nine Elms market.

As the job ad had warned, the problem was identifying them all. How was I to know that something called 'cheesecake' was a large white pastry square covered all over with coconut shreds – or were they icing shavings? I had to keep asking what things were and it wasn't easy as the twenty or so other workers hurried about filling up their own orders. Ten custard tarts, easy, except they were large and wobbly so that carrying a whole bundle of them was precarious. Most of the cakes we carried in handfuls or armfuls to and fro between crates, so I would fetch eight vanilla Devon slices in my hands, trying not to squash them and trying not to be jostled by other people. Sometimes there were not enough of a particular item to be found anywhere, creating an incomplete order. Forty-five custard doughnuts? Only thirty-three to be found. Ten cream slices? Only eight. What is the difference in name between a chocolate-covered doughnut with chocolate sprinkles, and one without? When all the fruit Danishes look the same, how do you know apple from apricot or from one called just 'fruit' on the printout? And you did indeed have to watch out that no one pinched anything from your already half-completed order while you were over the other side of the room piling up pink iced buns; or worse still that you didn't pinch anyone else's by mistake, not realising a stray crate was someone's half-filled order.

The thin-faced young woman who had been smoking upstairs when I arrived was now angrily shunting crate stacks up and down, cursing, 'I'm getting the fuck out of this fucking hell-hole, this shit-hole, I'm not fucking staying!' to herself as she went. It was only after a while I stopped to realise I had not washed my hands. I had seen nowhere to wash them and I was shown no sink downstairs. I saw no one else washing either. The floor by now was quite dirty and cakes did sometimes fall on it. Cherries often toppled off and had to be retrieved. I don't suppose anyone could be poisoned by cakes that fell on the floor, since there was no meat involved, but the grubby, crunchy sugar, torn papers and general muck underfoot grew by the hour. Yet the cakes had to look good. Any cracking of the sugar, sometimes caused by a top crate crushing a layer under-neath, had Manuel prowling round weeding them out. Today's big new order, he kept telling everyone, had to be perfect – or at least it had to look perfect.

What really made the place impossible was the children. I wasn't sure whose they were, but there were now three or four of them aged between five and seven. They tore up and down between the racks, whizzing about on a broken office chair they had found. They prodded the cakes and tumbled about fighting in the middle of the narrow aisles. Sometimes someone shouted at them but not with much force, which suggested they might belong to someone in authority because the impulse to bellow at them or shut them in a cupboard was strong in the rush, yet people resisted it. At one point the children were perched on top of the doughnuts shredding a telephone book all over the place.

In the end I had to go to Manuel and tell him my second order could not be completed because there were not enough cakes to be found. He and Joanne shouted about the useless computer, the inexplicable shortages that always happened on Sundays, never enough. They went off into the vast walk-in freezer and brought out frozen doughnuts and buns, rock-hard bread pudding slices that even unfrozen were the most unrelenting of all the cakes. Manuel plonked the frozen doughnuts on to the custard spike and filled them up, handing them over to me as he went so I could roll these frozen rocks in a box of icing sugar and add them to my order.

Some orders were worse than others, especially those requiring cakes in ones and twos which meant tearing back and forth for a few of everything, two cherry slices, two custard Danish, four cream puffs, two vanilla kings . . . Best were big orders – forty-five chocolate rings – where you could just bring along a whole crate at a time.

The last orders were for 'wrapped' cakes. I was put next to Maria to operate one hot-wrapping machine while she used the other. She went at about three times my speed, whizzing each cake under the cellophane, pulling the cake and wrapper over the metal plate, slamming down the hot lid that melted and sealed the paper's edges.

At first it seemed quite easy, but that was when we were wrapping round flat cherry Bakewells. Apart from often losing the cherry and having to fish it off the floor, there were few difficulties as the tarts fitted the paper. It was the big tall cakes and the large buns that were difficult to seal. Any cake wrappers left even a little open were spotted at once by Manuel and he slung them back at us. Worst of all was the wrapping of custard tarts and the long open cream-filled doughnuts. They were almost impossible to wrap without squashing the custard and the cream, but they had to look good. I don't know if some shops and canteens wanted wrapped cakes because they thought them more hygienic: if so, they were in a fool's paradise – wrapping just meant yet another set of hands had touched them. But perhaps wrapping helped them last longer out of the air.

Maria and I worked fast, but if I tried to keep up with her I got into trouble, twisting the cellophane roll, crushing the cakes or squashing the cream. She seemed so professional I thought she must have been there a long time. 'No,' she said, 'only three weeks.' She was in her mid-twenties and came from Madeira. She had recently been chambermaiding in hotels in Bournemouth. 'But then I come to London, what a crazy thing to do! Bournemouth is a nice place, London is terrible!' She rolled her eyes and looked around the room, the detritus on the floor, the darkness and the stacks of cakes still to wrap.

I asked her about pay. Since she was clearly such a fast and good worker, intelligent and diligent, I wondered if they paid her a bit more, now she had proved her worth. 'I get £3.95 an hour,' she said. I thought I had misheard with all the clattering and banging around us, but she repeated it. She was getting even less than me and I was on the minimum wage. 'But how can you be getting less than the minimum wage? It's against the law.' She shrugged and rolled her eyes again. 'What can I do about it?' Manuel was suddenly standing behind us again, watching, so we speeded up. When he had gone I asked her if she knew there was a minimum wage and she said, 'Yes, but what difference does it make?' She looked guarded and I was in danger of getting too nosy so I worked on in silence, wrap, slam, wrap, slam, the rhythm of picking up a cake, pushing it under the paper and slamming down the hot welder.

If she was from Madeira she was within the EU and not an illegal worker who might be working without a permit and thus obliged to take whatever wage she was offered. I had not come across employers even in these low-paid jobs who would take on anyone without a permit, certainly no agencies, which are the main dealers in cheap labour, and certainly nothing advertised at the Job Centre. Why should an employer break the minimum-wage law just to a save a rotten 15p an hour? I had no actual proof from her payslip.

Later when I thought about Maria I did contemplate calling the penny-pinching mother-and-daughter owners of this bakery, pretending to be an Inland Revenue inspector, threatening to descend on them for failing to pay the minimum wage. But they might just have sacked Maria and any others like her on the spot to ensure there was no one around to tell the story if inspectors came.

The cake-wrapping was not finished until eight-thirty that evening. Most of the other workers had already left. They all departed with big bags of spoiled and broken cakes and Tom, an amiable old man, stopped on his way home to urge me to remember to take a good-sized bag too when I left. 'It's a perk!' he said, though I didn't fancy the look of them at all. Maria and I carried on working, slam, wrap, slam, wrap, until they were all done with Manuel still at our back, returning bundles of them if he found so much as an unsealed crack in a wrapper. It was a curious perfectionism over the appearance of these cakes, with so little concern about how often they were touched by human hands. Then it was over, with the last crate finally filled and finished. We were the last ones left and we were both exhausted by the end of the shift, struggling up the stairs to collect our stuff and wash off the sugar, cream, custard, jam and general gloop at a small sink in the toilet that Maria showed me. There was still sugar in my hair and fingernails as we left the building. It was silent outside in the cold dark cul-de-sac now that the lorries had left with all their deliveries. With a brief wave Maria hurried off into the night in one direction, I in another, as Manuel was locking up the doors after us.

I was not going back the next day as I already had another job arranged for Monday morning. But I felt that more days of cake chaos were unlikely to reveal significantly more about the work, though I might have found out more about the workers. Most of them were white English of all ages; there were virtually no black faces, which is rare in rock-bottom jobs in South London. There were roughly equal numbers of women and men, old and young, and some foreign accents, some Eastern European I guessed.

Why were they all there? Many were transient, but this was another job that was good for mothers and for people wanting to combine several jobs because there were various shifts that fitted school hours or other commitments. Why had some of them stayed for several years? Here too was that special camaraderie I had seen in the school kitchen, a bonding born of trying to do a difficult job in bad conditions. There was plenty of laughing and joshing between those who had worked there together a while, grumbling and joking in turn, perversely proud of their stamina in surviving it all. There were other better jobs to be had in the area, so this was another example of the non-existent labour market that economists believe in, another reason why the minimum wage needs to be much higher to protect those with few choices. There is no perfect labour market that will itself push up wages in a healthy competition for these workers. People do jobs and stay in jobs for a multitude of personal reasons, logistic and geographical – if, for example, they can get there on foot and avoid fares. Pay and conditions are not the most important factors in many people's job choices.

When I worked in the cake factory in West Kensington in 1970 I was paid £14.25 for a forty-hour week. It didn't seem much and the women I worked with were poor. True, it was a big Lyons factory rather than a small business, and large companies often pay better. It was an era of full employment and strong unions, before the 1980s downsizing managerial culture that judged a manager's prowess by the sweat he could squeeze out of every penny spent on wages. But even then there was no slack and the pace of work on the assembly line was grindingly hard. It meant hours a day of relentless concentration, forced to work fast and repetitively at precisely the speed the machines ran, no slower, no faster, spreading cream on to the layers of angel cake slices. It was harsh work for low pay and no prospects.

According to the Institute for Fiscal Studies, that £14.25 would translate now into £239.45 (Tom Clark of the IFS says every £1 in 1970 should now pay £16.80 in wages.) If I had worked a forty-hour week in this bakery at the minimum wage, I would only have been paid £164. So in 2002 I was now being paid far less in real terms than in 1970 when there was no minimum wage – £75.45 less. This is something I did not expect when I started out on this book, yet whenever I could make the comparison, I was now always on lower wages despite the great increase in national wealth since then. It was the most shocking discovery.

In fact, it turned out worse. When I called back at the bakery to collect my wages a couple of days later, I was turned away by the owner's daughter with some excuse that her mother had the money and she wasn't there. I was persistent and turned up again, but again I was sent off with nothing. On the third visit it must have been the black look in my eye, because with marked reluctance the daughter sent me up to her mother upstairs who slowly reached for her handbag and counted out my money from her purse – no paperwork, no receipt to sign. When I looked at what she had given me it came to only £4 an hour. I thought I should complain but from the forbidding look in her eye, I feared she might say I had been worth no more than that, useless at the job, lucky to get anything at all, or some such. I hadn't the stomach for a fight so I took the money and gave her back her apron, nicely washed.

Chapter 13

Care Home

I was always drawn towards the more welcoming, less forbidding job ads because it was never my intention to seek out the worst jobs with the worst employers, but just the average, everyday at around the minimum wage.

> Care Assistant. Required to work within a private residential centre to assist qualified nursing staff. Experience desirable, qualifications an advantage, but caring and understanding more important than either. Must have good English to understand instructions and be co-operative to work in a friendly team environment.

The only drawback was the usual one: just £4.85 an hour for shifts that included evenings and weekends.

Hazeldene turned out to be a genteel nursing home with the air of a respectable if somewhat depressing modern provincial hotel set down on the border between Lambeth and Wandsworth. Its receptionists were good at the Have A Nice Day smile and the care assistants all wore smart hospital uniforms subtly suggesting hosts of fully qualified nurses. However, even if this was a posh home, like all the others it didn't pay posh wages or a London weighting allowance.

As with everywhere else, applying for a job could not be done by post or phone. Cheap labour's time is priceless, meaning unpaid. Never mind the time of day or breaking into working hours, you have to leg it here and there to get a job. I had to take two buses down there and two back again to collect the application forms, another double bus ride down there again the next day to return the forms with all the required documents, and then come back a week later for an interview. The interviews were only on Tuesdays in the early afternoons, breaking into the working day, hard for anyone already in a job: the boot is always on the employer's foot.

There was something overawing about the atmosphere at Hazeldene. Their genteel air made them even better than other employers at making applicants for jobs feel nervous, apologetic, uncertain, in fear of rejection and grateful for their time in considering you. The lower paid the job, the more employers make you feel it is you who is being done the favour. They keep you on tenterhooks, conveying a general expectation that they are more likely to reject than accept you – until suddenly, before you know it, you are working for them. Then you realise that, never mind the airs and graces of employers, virtually anyone not visibly mad or bad who will take these wages can get any of these jobs. Brooms, mops and wheelchairs will be thrust into your hands with a lofty *de haut en bas* that cleverly disguises employers' eagerness.

My interview was with Sister Prunella, the Head of Nursing, who was a stately black middle-aged woman wearing the company office uniform of patterned shirt and matching pleated skirt, like an air-hostess. She had the stern air of an old-fashioned matron, a way of looking you up and down with a slight hint of disfavour. Scuffed shoes? Broken fingernails? She explained that the company now has forty-six nursing homes, with more opening all the time, including a brand-new one that was being built next door to this for care-assisted independent living.

I knew that many small independent nursing homes were going to the wall because the state pays too little for each patient, especially in the south-east, but I knew also that the big companies in this sector are booming. This was founded in the early 1980s at the start of the great Thatcher boost to private nursing homes. The Conservative government caused local authorities to close most of their homes by offering DSS payments for patients who went into private homes, but no funds to councils for those in local authority homes. Here at Hazeldene, said Sister Prunella, there were 140 patients on four floors, mainly in their late eighties and nineties. Some were privately paid-for, some were NHS-funded, 'But we make no distinction whatsoever in how people are treated.'

She was far more diligent in checking my application form than anyone else. I was impressed (and alarmed). Her interviewing technique involved going back over the same questions, looking for any slight discrepancy, a clever manoeuvre because it is easy to lie once but harder to remember your lie afterwards. For example, I could not now remember exactly how long I had claimed to work for my mother – two years or three? Sister Prunella tripped me up, I stumbled and she eyed me severely. Nor could I remember exactly what job I had claimed that I did for my partner. Cleaning? Housekeeping? I got by, just, I thought. Like all the other job-interviewers, she was scrupulous about taking my passport. She also took my police check and said she would write to both my references. She was the only employer who actually bothered to write to my referees and wait until she had received back good references before I was offered the job. (No employer is proof against mendacious references from private referees.)

'We aim to be not good, not better, but the best!' was a mantra she kept repeating with greater emphasis each time. I was genuinely impressed. She talked most about treating the patients with kindness and above all with respect. 'I don't want any of that "John, darling, just pop into bed!" talk. Some of these people were professionals or doctors and they deserve our best respect. You must find out how they like to be addressed first.' She spoke warmly of the residents, some physically weak, some mentally weak, some, she claimed, just living there for company because they were lonely. I would, she said, be part of a team caring for a group of patients whom I would get to know, so I would learn what each wanted and how they liked to be treated. She returned often to an ethos of kindness, politeness and respect: 'Not good, not better, but the best!'

This was the most effective instruction I encountered, emphasis-ing the things that matter. Carillion's staff at the Chelsea and Westminster Hospital certainly got none of this, it was just 'Here's your wheelchair and off you go', without a word about kindness to patients. The difference sprang mainly from the fact that Sister

Prunella was hiring me directly rather than through an agency. Her own standard of work would be judged by the quality and behaviour of her own staff. Carillion, on the other hand, were using distant agencies and anyway were not themselves directly responsible for the hospital's reputation, which remained, precariously, in the hands of the NHS managers who no longer hired or managed their own people. The closer to the actual employer, the stronger the sense of belonging, for both sides. Sister Prunella was a force to be reckoned with: she made it seem a great honour to be summoned back for a second interview the next week.

So I made a fourth visit to Hazeldene, sixteen buses in all and now a whole morning in the middle of the week without any warning that this second interview would in fact take several hours. As I arrived the crisp young receptionist at the desk, decked out in the universal company air-stewardess kit, looked briskly at me as I asked where to go for my interview. Tossing her golden pony-tail, she pointed rather imperiously down the corridor to a residents' lounge.

There I found myself with seven other women and one man, when to my surprise the receptionist herself followed me through the door and joined us. I had got her quite wrong. She turned out not to be imperious but rather nervous as this was her first day in her new job and she too had been sent in for induction and a viewing of the company videos. This was a good example of the powerful effect of uniforms: they give the passing public a spurious trust in the competence, qualification and experience of even the most transient of workforces.

Now we came under instruction from Jody, the Nursing Manager. What we expected to be more interviews turned out to be an induction session, without anyone formally offering the job, laying down the terms and conditions or giving us a written contract to take home. Jody was about my age, a jolly-hockey-sticks kind of nurse who had trained in 1965 at Bart's Hospital, full of bounce. She took us through the fire drill and showed us a company fire-safety video. Our instructions were startling: if the fire bell goes, forget heroism, abandon the patients and get the hell out was the basic message. 'Suppose you are all residents,' she said looking at us grouped in the residents' chairs around the television in the lounge. 'Suppose that television set blew up and caught fire. You should just leave the room, shut the door, set off the fire alarm, shout Fire! out in the corridor and leave them. Yes, I know it sounds terrible, but they are behind a fire door and if you open it the flames and the fumes will spread and kill a lot more people than them. Just get out.' I am sure this is all standard fire-brigade doctrine. The tenor of much of our induction seemed to be about protecting the company from being sued either by patients or by staff. 'If you do not obey these instructions, you could be legally liable, as well as the company.' The video taught of dangerous toasters too full of crumbs, irons, Carmen rollers, televisions and above all cigarettes. 'OK team?' Jody would ask, after each point. We were already a company team.

We were taught how to lift patients – never by the arms but by grasping them round the waist and shoulder, always with bent knees. Mainly we were being warned not to lift them at all. EU law says men cannot lift more than twenty-five kilos – a sack of potatoes – and women no more that sixteen kilos (eight bags of sugar). If we lifted any weight more than that, the company would not be to blame for any damage we did to our backs. If a patient was dropped, the company was not to blame but we would be for lifting too heavy a weight. So we were introduced to the electric Sarita hoist and the Trixie Lift hoist by which patients were to be heaved out of chairs or off the floor and on to beds or commodes. The Trixie took a long time to settle a patient into. It was a complicated sling device that left the patients swinging helplessly in the air, undignified but safe and painless for both carer and patient. This was all serious and essential information, for Jody described how she had destroyed her back during her nurse training, lifting patients without help in the days before hoists or instruction.

Listening to this good advice and looking back, it seemed all the more perverse that Carillion's Chelsea and Westminster porters were given no such instruction. It only took a couple of hours to learn and after that porters could have been far more useful around the hospital, lifting patients the right way instead of leaving it all to the nurses because they were 'trained' for it, wasting time waiting for the nurses to come and do it instead of doing it ourselves. But saving nursing time would be of no interest to Carillion as they only employ the porters, not the nurses, the workforces inefficiently divided between different employers. As for electric hoists, I never saw one at the Chelsea and Westminster and suspect the nurses were still left to lift far more than the EU rules permit.

The Hazeldene training on respecting patients' rights was good, too. Never restrain a patient: the company can be sued for false imprisonment. So those who keep falling out of bed at night can never be tied in, but must sleep on mattresses on the floor. People can never be left alone even for a moment belted into a wheelchair. 'We asked a social worker if we could just belt in one difficult patient briefly to give her meals, to stop her pacing up and down all day and night, but her social worker said no, it would be against the law. These are free people, as free as you or I. You can no more force someone here to do something against their will than you can some stranger in the street.' (Which is all very well in theory until confronted in real life by a patient insisting on climbing inside a broom cupboard, convinced it is her bedroom: a certain amount of force turned out to be necessary to stop another one choosing to sit in among the buckets and bags of soiled pads, whatever her rights.)

Jody gave examples of the dangers of institutionalisation. 'If a patient decides she doesn't want to go to the dining-room one day, no problem, you bring her lunch to her room. Then if she does it again the next and the next day, you do not, repeat NOT, assume that from now on Mrs So-and-so always has her lunch alone. That is institutionalising her. You take the time to find out why. You ask her and you get her to tell you. Maybe she'll say she hates the way someone eats who she sits next to on her table. No problem, move her table in the dining-room. Maybe she'll say she's had a bowel movement and she's afraid she smells. Well, sort out her problem. Meal times here are very, very important to the residents, the most social times of the day, really looked forward to.' All this sounded like good care. Sister Jody was as thorough and as enthusiastic as Sister Prunella, both of them keenly proprietorial about their residents – 'Not good, not better, but the best.'

When I arrived to start work the next week, the staff changing-room was packed with care assistants hurriedly putting on their uniforms for the shift. There were not enough lockers to go round and there was a waiting list for them, so the rest of us piled our bags under Sister's desk for safety. Sister Prunella issued me with a second-hand light-blue nurse's jacket with epaulettes and the company logo on the pocket, together with a pair of navy blue trousers. I liked it very much. Like a magic spell, it made me feel like a nurse as soon as I put it on, crisp and capable. A whole new uniform would be ordered for me, for which £10 would be deducted from my wages. She said she was giving me an easier start on the partly private second floor, where she handed me over to the floor sister on duty that day, Sister Davina, who sat me down and explained, 'On this floor many people are paying a lot of money, so we have to go the extra mile. When they call on the bell, we answer however often they call. Whatever they want, they can have.'

It was shift change-over time and Sister Davina read out the case notes of each resident to the gathering of all the care assistants on this new shift. I was the only white face on the floor, all the others being West Indian or African, with a few Indian nurses who had been recruited from India by the company a few months ago to serve out their time at Hazeldene as 'adaptation nurses'. After these indentures they would eventually become fully qualified nurses in Britain, free to work anywhere. (There has recently been a scandal about the many nurses employed in this way by some care homes, and often paid less than ordinary nurses, one in three having paid large sums to the employers or agencies who brought them over. But I had no reason to suppose it was happening here.)

For my first day I was assigned to Dorcas, the senior care assistant, who had worked there for six years. Dorcas was one of those dynamos on whom employers so often rely without ever acknowledging the value of what they have. 'Don't you worry!' she said, sensing my anxiety. 'It's a lot to learn but you will pick it up, the same way we all did!' and she threw a welcoming arm round me. 'We are all nice people here, that's what keeps us going, isn't it?' The others laughed, breathing in her infectious camaraderie. Majestic, warm, wise, meticulous about details, fussy about every kind of cleanliness and gentle with the residents, Dorcas was approaching her fiftieth birthday within the week, with a husband, seven children and eleven grandchildren to help her celebrate. She was given to breaking into hymns from time to time. She hugged everyone and everyone hugged her. She was the star of the second floor, invaluable and beloved of the residents whom she took me round to meet, going from room to room to introduce me to each of them.

Even after six years at Hazeldene and many more years' experience in other nursing homes before that, Dorcas was still paid only a little more than me, something over £5 an hour. Like most of the others, Dorcas did at least a 48-hour week, because, she said, it was the only way she could pay her bills. Her thirty-year-old daughter used to work as a care assistant here on the floor above, but she had given it up for higher pay as a bus conductor, a job with a fraction of the responsibility, worry and sheer hard work.

As Dorcas took me to say hello to each of the thirty-five residents on our floor, the full dreadfulness of what lay ahead hit me. They were very frail indeed, most of them demented to varying and often deceptive degrees. Virtually all were incontinent, which is usually the last straw preventing people surviving in their own homes. The routine, Dorcas explained, was bathing and dressing them to get them up, which took most of the morning. Then there was lunch and feeding and, before you knew it, it was time to do it all over again to get them back to bed. That was our day's work and the residents' whole lives.

You get used to changing wet and soiled pads reasonably easily. The first time you think you might not, but surrounded by all these care assistants who do it scores of times a day without a thought, you just get on with it because it must be done. Someone has to do it and that someone is us. The real fear is the danger of knocking people over, letting them fall, hurting them or doing the wrong thing. But after changing people a few times, wiping and washing bottoms and elderly genitals, the shock of it wears off. That is not the true horror of this job. What never wears off is the shock of the old. Dealing all the time with the most pathetic old people – most of them in pain from various sores on their legs, in misery and despair, many wishing to die – strikes you through the heart. I left the place after each shift hardly able to speak with the wretchedness of it all. In their little dying rooms, no amount of ruched valances, potted plants on the window sills, photos of smiling fit great-grandchildren could ever overcome the awfulness of their condition: they had come here never to return to the outside world. This was it, all there was left of life, nowhere to go. Their varied lives had shrunk down to the narrow confines of the dull and sometimes painful routines of eating, being washed, dressed and undressed. Yes, there were cookery, flower-arranging, exercise classes and other activities on offer but most were too far gone for that. It was not the fault of the nursing home – this was superior to most – but watching over these people's fragile remnants of life made the job hard to bear. No prison is so lacking in hope. This is death row.

My first evening I took a tray in to Minnie who was sitting hunched in her chair, plucking at her knitted waistcoat. I was bringing her a small plate of elegantly cut sandwiches without crusts, a dish of tapioca with a dollop of jam and a cup of tea.

'Take it away!' she said. 'Take it away!' I urged her to try a little. 'You see,' she said very clearly, 'I am hoping not to be here tomorrow.'

Was she leaving, going somewhere? From the furniture in her room – they were allowed to bring in anything of their own that would fit into their rooms. Her chest of drawers and a small dresser looked as if she was here for good. 'I feel,' she said, looking up at me, 'I feel that one ought not to go on a full stomach. It doesn't seem right, does it?'

I tried a smile and said, 'You'll feel better if you eat something. It'll give you strength.'

'I just want to die tonight. I think I will.'

I wondered if she knew it would be tonight, as in those old tales of premonition or even sheer volition. She pushed away the sandwiches but eventually agreed to try a little tapioca.

'So you think I should eat a last meal, like a condemned man?' she asked me with a dry laugh. 'Well, I'll try.'

The trouble with moments of lucidity was that they tended to be like this, moments of all-too-rational despair. Dementia was often preferable. Many were described as 'depressed', as if it were a medical condition, when it was only a reasonable response to their plight.

Later that evening a young care assistant, vivacious Vicky, and I came back to wash and undress Minnie for bed. We got her hobbling and shuffling across the room to her bathroom on her wheeled Zimmer frame. She had an odd habit of referring to her stroke-paralysed left leg as Jane. 'Come on Jane,' she would mutter to it under her breath. 'Come ON Jane!' urging it along. Vicky explained that Jane was the name of an old much-loved house-keeper Minnie once had. For some reason now in her mind the Jane of old had transmogrified into her bad left leg. 'Jane!' she would rebuke it in irritation when it failed to obey her. We manoeuvred Minnie on to the toilet, managed to wash her backside and started to get her going back towards her chair when she began to wobble badly and fall backwards.

'Stand up, stand up!' Vicky called out to her.

'I'm not doing it on purpose! It's Jane!' Minnie said.

'Quick!' Vicky said, flinging her arms round Minnie, hauling her upwards. 'Quick, get her legs or she'll fall!' Together we managed to lift her uncomfortably on to her bed. This went against all the rules of our induction but there seemed to be no alternative at the time. I said nothing but Vicky said, 'Look, we are not supposed to do that ever, but we do. I know I shouldn't be showing you the wrong ways, but that's how it is.' What should we have done? 'We should have let her fall slowly on to the bathroom floor, holding on to her as she went. Then we should go out and get the hoist, put the sling around her and hoist her up and on to the bed. But it would be worse for her. Falling is frightening for them. It would take a long time to do it that way and the hoist is not nice for them either. And anyway we have a lot more patients to get into bed tonight. It was the quick way.'

While we were undressing Minnie, Vicky said, 'You see, we get no sick pay here. If we pull our backs or arms so we can't work, and we do it from lifting patients, they pay us nothing at all. It is our fault. But sometimes you have to and that's that. Of course the managers know we have to do it sometimes but it's not their responsibility.' Minnie's undignified and probably slightly painful method of getting to bed that night was at least better than a fall, a long wait and an elaborate hoist off the floor. In the next few days, if Sister wasn't looking, we lifted and hauled quite a few patients in unorthodox ways because it had to be done. But if there were any accidents, it would all be our fault, not the company's.

Coming in next morning, the first shift took a tour of all the bedrooms to check everyone was still breathing: never trust the previous shift, look at them for yourself, we were told. When we came to Minnie's room I held my breath. I thought (and hoped) she might have died quietly in her sleep as she had wished but she was as alive as ever. She was just gazing up at the ceiling. No doubt whichever night she does die – this year, next year, whenever – someone will say, 'The amazing thing is, she knew she was going that night!' She hoped she was going every night but her God was not merciful.

In another room Dora was curled up in a foetal position all day and night, her eyes always closed, her television always on in the vain hope it still gave her some contact with the outside world. Daft afternoon game shows and inanely chirpy presenters may have drifted somewhere into her consciousness, but if so there was no response. She had been in this state for at least three years, according to Vicky, but some of the carers remembered her from before that when she was not so bad. We rolled her over one way, changed her soiled pad, washed her all over, rolled her back the other way, changed her nightdress and left her still curled up and propped up on pillows. The only response she ever made to anything was when eating. She ate a lot, as much as you could shovel into her. Was eating her last remaining pleasure or was this just a reflex response to a spoon on her lips? There was no way of knowing, but however sorry you felt for her it was impossible not to ponder on this waste of everyone's time and energy, pouring food into her at one end and cleaning it up at the other day after day for a life that had long outlived any chance of happiness. You could only hope she had no consciousness left. But those things were never said between us because once you started to think that way it could lead to callousness and I never saw any of that. If at times people were treated less than perfectly, it was always through lack of staff and time, never through unkindness.

In Dora's room when it came to washing and cleaning her, the pot of bedsore cream had run out. Care assistants were always pinching it from other rooms as there was never enough to go round. On my first shift I had been puzzled when a kind assistant shoved a bundle of disposable rubber gloves and disposable wipes at me, warning me not to let go of them but to keep as many as I could fit into my pockets. There was always a shortage of wipes, cream, soap and gloves in most rooms. Also in the mornings clean sheets and towels often ran out. Yet these were the key tools of our trade, indispensable for all the wiping and washing of bodies and bottoms all day. Once Sister Davina caught a care assistant handing out a lot of gloves and wipes she had found in a store cupboard. Sister immediately demanded to have all boxes of these supplies brought to her. 'I have to keep control over them from now on!' she said sharply. 'We are issued with enough for the week every week, but if you people hoard them then there are not enough when we need them. You people go off duty leaving your little supplies in your lockers and secret places and we can't be having that!' She took command of the few remaining boxes in the store cupboard and kept them in her office. Could she order more? I asked. 'We are issued with enough,' she said firmly and then added that it was difficult to get more because she would have to give special reasons to the admin offices downstairs. Petty meanness over essential equipment was something I encountered frequently in most of these jobs. Cheap labour does not deserve much spending on its tools.

Only a short while afterwards on the same day, Sister Davina and I were giving a bed bath to Edna, an almost totally paralysed woman with excruciatingly painful sores on her heels. She had been a nurse during the war but although she sounded superficially sensible, when I talked to her while feeding her lunch spoonful by spoonful, it was clear she remembered nothing very much. She was one of the many who just sat in their chair all day doing nothing. When it came to giving her a bed bath under Sister's supervision everything was done the right way as a demonstration of perfection. There was certainly no heaving people about with Sister watching. I fetched the hoist to lift Edna from her chair into the bed in the correct fashion, which took much time and indignity, then we wrapped her in towels, rolling her this way and that to wash her all over. I noted that Sister herself had no wipes or gloves and kept asking to share mine from my pockets, using wipe after wipe until I had none left. But she didn't offer to replenish my supply afterwards.

Most of the residents were touchingly endearing. There is something about dementia that is affecting – it is not just pity but a fascination with a condition that throws up memories, thoughts and feelings in random ways. There is the lack of inhibition, there are sudden surreal exclamations and snatches of long-ago conversations. Sometimes, among the grander residents, orders were given to unseen servants. 'George! George! Fetch me a packet, fetch me a packet!' one woman shouted repeatedly one morning. Childlike, yet sometimes sharply acute, they often surprised you. The care assistants were genuinely fond of most of them and I could see why.

Alice was a sad case. Dainty and thin, she wore her pearls most days with smart clothes, but she was profoundly depressed. She lay fully clothed on top of her bed all day unless you got her up, when sometimes she would wander up and down the corridors in a daze. 'So sweet,' Vicky said, stroking her hands when she walked up to us, looking about with a vacant smile. Vicky said she had lost her mind with grief after her much-loved husband died. She had never recovered from the shock. She had no children, though other relatives visited her. 'Mrs Knightsbridge', Vicky called her, and she looked and sounded exactly like a lady shopping in Harrods. Her hair was done each week by the hairdresser and you could have taken her anywhere without anyone realising there was anything the matter with her. But all that was left were phrases and wishes. 'Oh, would you be most awfully kind . . . most awfully kind,' she would say but forget what she wanted. When you tried to get her up to go for lunch she would say, 'Oh no, thank you so much. I don't think I will today . . .' and you would have to swing her legs off the bed and urge her to her feet to lead her to the dining-room. On the first day I asked her which was her seat and she led me to the wrong table, a serious *faux pas*. I sat her down on the mostly more sensible table and everyone there looked quite affronted but they couldn't quite articulate what was wrong. She fidgeted and looked distressed until another care assistant hurried up to point out my mistake. It was very difficult to get her to move again; thrown into a muddle, she demanded to take all the cutlery with her to her own table. Later, walking her back into her room, making polite conversation, I complemented her on an embroidered footstool she had propping open the door. 'Did you embroider it yourself?' I asked. 'Of course not, you silly woman!' she snapped, suddenly not so sweet. 'Why on earth would I do it myself!'

When it came to dressing and undressing her, I had to go down to the Sister's office to fetch the keys to Alice's cupboard. Her wardrobe was kept locked to stop her opening it and throwing everything on to the floor. Dressing her was a pleasure since, unlike some of the others, she had a plentiful supply of nice clothes to choose from, and she looked so smart when she was done. But she hated to be bathed. 'Oh no, I really don't think I'll take a bath today. Awfully kind, but not today, thank you so much,' she would say emphatically. I could see why no one liked baths. In the bathroom, once she was naked, I would sit her on the chair attached to a hoist and winch her up, swing her over the bath and winch her down into the warm water full of bubble bath, wash her all over and winch her out again. However kindly we did it, it was not much fun and certainly not dignified. She had no memories left, or none she could communicate beyond the phrases she had used all her life, all politeness and refinement until she would shock you by blurting out, 'That's bollocks, all bollocks!' for no particular reason.

The mostly more sensible table in the dining-room didn't in fact make very much sense, although they looked like a cosy group of ladies chatting together in a tea shop. As I listened in, what looked convincingly like rational conversation was generally not, though there would be times when they all alighted together on the same subject. But usually the comments they made to one another were random, which made it difficult for them to catch one another's train of thought, though they tried. It was plain each thought the others dotty and they smiled indulgently at one another's foibles. Things went best when one of them held forth with a long story and the others listened, then added some unconnected story of their own. But on some tables they never spoke.

Mrs Knightsbridge was seated opposite Marina, a woman in a wheelchair whose mouth hung open all day, victim of a paralysing stroke. She could feed herself – just – with a large bib and much splattering of food down her front and across the table, but Mrs Knightsbridge didn't seem to notice. Marina had a bigger room than the others with some fine paintings, including one huge eighteenth-century landscape that filled a wall and looked as if it had come from a big country house. Marina could not speak at all, but she frequently shouted out great 'Aaaaaah's, in a rhythmic modulated rise and fall that was distressing to hear going on and on for hours. I couldn't tell how much mind she had left. Sometimes in the morning she would sit reading *The Times* or the *Mail* for hours, turning the pages awkwardly but looking intently at them. Was she reading? Was her mind intact, trapped inside? The day I arrived there had been a loud shouter, a Lady Someone-or-other, who bellowed odd things like 'Your stomach is flatter, your stomach is flatter!', the same phrase all day long. She was due to be removed upstairs, a floor I never saw but assumed was a good deal worse than mine.

The residents' possessions were a dangerous problem. A couple of days earlier a very valuable necklace went missing. The woman's room was searched, everything was checked – the back of all seat cushions, under the mattress – but it was not found. We were told it was insured for £12,500 and there was a panic. But it turned up the next day. The resident smiled and took it out of a tiny reticule she had been clutching. It was decided that it should be returned to her relatives: her diamond rings had already been given back and the family had been encouraged to bring some valueless glass jewellery instead. 'You are responsible for all, I mean ALL their possessions. If anything goes missing, it is down to you,' Sister said firmly at the next hand-over meeting.

One old woman had died a few days before I arrived. Dorcas and I were sent to clear out her room and Michelle the cleaner came along to help. The relatives had said they didn't want any of her things returned, but here was a wardrobe full of grand clothes. 'It should all go to charity,' Dorcas said. 'But I've seen what they do here. They throw it all in the bin downstairs. I've seen such good things go in there.' She was holding up a sequinned jacket and a silk embroidered blouse. 'She was such a lovely lady, she was so sweet,' Dorcas said. 'She gave no trouble to anyone and always had a nice word for us. It was a shock when she went so suddenly like that, not expected. I miss her.' Michelle was superstitious and she shuddered. 'I don't know how you can touch a dead person's things!' she said. Cleaners were mainly women who couldn't face the caring work or the long hours involved. 'Nonsense, this should all go to charity if the family doesn't want it,' Dorcas was saying, when Sister put her head round the door. 'You are not to take anything!' Sister said, rudely I thought, because Dorcas would never dream of taking anything that was not hers and Michelle wouldn't even touch it. 'It should go to a charity shop. I know they throw it out downstairs,' Dorcas said. Sister replied tartly, 'That's none of our business, Dorcas. We obey the rules, that's all. The rules say we put it in bags and send it down for administration to do with it whatever they think fit. But I'm warning you, take nothing!' and she gave me a stern look as if I might pilfer. We packed it all away and sent it down.

Relatives were a frequent source of trouble, Dorcas and Vicky said. 'Maybe it is because they feel guilty. If they come here and give us a hard time it eases their conscience and they pretend they are doing something good for their relative.' Some relatives were pathetically grateful and nice to us, but others were demanding monsters, always complaining about small things, finding fault with trivia, keeping us on our toes, especially about possessions. I remember one marching into a room when we were trying to get a fallen patient off the floor, and demanding a vase, 'Right now, or these flowers will wilt!'

There were only two male residents on this ward. Alfred was completely paralysed from Parkinson's disease and just sat in his chair, dribbling on to a large bib. He too had *The Times* every day, and probably could read it and make sense of it, but he couldn't really speak. When Sister wasn't there, we heaved him into his wheelchair and on to the toilet several times a day and often he sat there too long, despite having a bell in his hand to pull. Once the toilet seat left a round red indentation on his skinny buttocks. He looked about sixty but I could glean little about his life, except for his hippie jacket over a chair, made of woven bright-coloured ethnic stripes, and an embroidered purse on a string round his neck. The other man was a new arrival, a Major, who stayed in his room and watched television all day. All he really wanted were frequent cups of cocoa.

Only one or two residents were bad-tempered. Dolly had her own electric wheelchair, but its battery had broken down temporarily and it was a very heavy machine to push. She was sometimes full of complaints and would bark out in a sharp South London accent, 'I don't get what I want! I want what I want!' Other times she would cheer up and tell a string of dirty jokes that seemed to have lodged in her otherwise vague mind. She was allowed a tot of whisky at lunch and dinner, but she was no longer allowed to keep the bottle in her room as she had been drinking so much she fell out of her chair. Now she had to be wheeled to the Sister's office at mealtimes to have it measured out to her from a medicine cabinet. One or two others had a glass of wine at meals from their own bottles kept in the dining-room cupboard for them. 'They can have whatever they want,' the Sister kept saying. 'This is their home.' But the wine didn't seem to add noticeable sunshine to the empty remains of these old ladies' days.

I was embarrassed when one or two relatives would automatically turn to me as the only white face with an unpleasantly conspiratorial air, implying we white folk had to stick together. Although I was by far the most junior and useless person on the floor, they just assumed I must be a figure of authority because of the colour of my skin. I would give them a frosty answer and refer them at once to Dorcas or Sister. The residents seemed to adore their carers, asking where they were each day, especially any day Dorcas was off duty. In this part of London, in many of the jobs I did, race was a marker for low pay. Wherever there are a lot of black faces, there the pay will be lowest, the work the hardest and the jobs the least desirable. I have not referred overmuch to race because that was just a feature of where I had chosen to base myself. In other parts of the country these jobs are all done by white women, wherever mothers need work and will take anything that they can fit around their lives.

The work here was hard, physically and emotionally, but at least it was never dull. There was Margaret, a tiny shrunken old lady with beaky, hawk-like features who walked up and down the corridors all day. Everyone would smile at her and pat her hand as she passed and she always smiled back. She seemed to make reasonable sense, but you could never tell. I was dressing her one morning, chatting away to her about what she wanted to wear, discussing her wardrobe and where her clothes had come from. She didn't get things quite right, claiming she had worn this or that on her wedding day, but it didn't matter. She chose a blue dress but once I got it on her with a bit of a struggle (she was not good at working out where arms should go), I found it had no buttons left. She was a compulsive button-puller. So I put a salmon-pink jumper on over the top to hide the button deficit, brushed her hair, and she smiled at herself in the mirror. I sat her in her chair where she took happily to shredding Kleenexes, which was her favourite occupation, while I made her bed and straightened the room. I was turning to walk out with a wave goodbye to her when Sister came in. 'Have you checked the bin?' she asked. I hadn't because the cleaners did bin-emptying a bit later. 'Ah,' she said. 'With Margaret, always check the bin.' I did and it was full of urine and Kleenex. 'She does that every night,' Sister said as I emptied it and washed it out. 'Why don't we take away the bin if she gets confused at night, and maybe she'll find the toilet?' I asked. Sister said, 'Because her relatives don't like to come in here and find no bin. Everything in the room has to be just so. It's the rules.'

Relatives may often have been a nuisance to the care assistants, but the staff were more distressed by those residents who had no visitors or only very rare ones. In all closed institutions the constant watchfulness of outside eyes makes all the difference to standards. Nothing was allowed to slip, everything that happened here was on display, open to sharp eyes and noses. If some relatives grumbled and complained, it was not really about standards, it was about the general misery of the place. There was not much we could do about that, except be unnaturally cheerful and friendly, which most care assistants were persistently all day long, but beaming gets tiring too. I found the gloom oppressive however chirpy we were, due to the wretched condition of people who had outlived their bodies and their minds, for which we had no cure.

However well-managed this home was, some things would never go smoothly with residents such as these. One morning one of the room bells rang and I went off to answer it. Paula, a very large woman, was sitting in her chair. She seemed entirely rational, had a room full of books, mainly histories of the monarchy. She had an intellectual way of talking with a most convincing air. 'I know I must be a frightful nuisance, but I wonder if you could be awfully kind and just help me a bit?' She was struggling to get her large bulk out of her chair on to legs that plainly would not support her. I told her to stay sitting down while I did it for her. 'You see those books over there? They need straightening.' The books on the window sill were leaning very slightly to one side. 'I absolutely must have them straight!' Then she wanted various ornaments repositioned by a few inches this way and that. 'I am most awfully, dreadfully fussy, I know,' she said. She was but I did it for her just as she requested with a smile, although we had pressing needs of other residents to see to at that busy hour. 'I have all these people coming today I think.' (Sadly, she was one of those with no visitors.) 'I'm not sure. I was thinking about, thinking about . . .' but her thoughts petered out and she forgot what she was saying. With her, it was often difficult to gauge what was sensible and what was not.

I was just leaving her room when she said, 'I want, I want, you know, to go there.' Where? 'Oh, over there, over there!' She was pointing at the window. Vicky was passing by, looked in and asked bluntly, 'Do you want your commode, Paula?' Paula nodded yes. I didn't know if it was the remnants of embarrassment or just aphasia that had made her unable to find the right words. So we brought in the commode and between us managed to manoeuvre her on to it, a difficult job given her large size. No doubt it should have been done with a hoist, but we did it ourselves. 'Ring the bell when you've finished,' Vicky said, putting the bell–string in her hand, and we went off to the Sister's office for a hand-over meeting.

The meeting went on a while, going through each patient's notes, describing what was happening or mostly not happening with each of them. As the time ticked by I worried about Paula sitting there on her commode, but her bell did not ring and I assumed Vicky knew better than me. Suddenly there was a big commotion out in the corridor. Paula had fallen off her commode, again. We hurried back to her room and there she was, her great baggy body sprawled on the floor, skirt above her head, the commode tipped up and a large pile of excrement and urine on the floor, stinking. Sister hurried in to supervise us and check that no harm was done. Paula seemed to be in one piece and in no particular pain. Her legs moved, her hips weren't broken, nor any other bones, and she just groaned a bit. 'Why didn't you ring the bell?' Sister asked her, but got no comprehensible reply. Getting her large frame off the floor with the Trixie hoist took a long time, putting the wide sling round and under her by rolling her one way, then the other, attaching the sling to the hoist brackets at four points, strapping her in and slowly pressing the lift button so that she gradually swung upwards, dangling like a monstrous baby brought by the stork. We pushed and pulled and swung her over the bed, lowering her gently back down.

As there were no cleaners on duty in the afternoons we cleaned up the floor as best we could, but the smell remained overpowering until next morning when the cleaners came back on duty and shampooed it. Keeping smells at bay was a major part of our routine, obeying the rule that nothing must offend the visitors, and it worked. The stench of urine in geriatric wards or less well–run homes is a trademark of such places, but not here. Everything dirty or smelly we sealed in plastic bags immediately; everything was washed and wiped and a visitor might not guess almost all these residents were incontinent.

Sister explained to me later that some people considered Paula to be an attention-seeker who would fall on purpose to make people come running. 'But I don't think like that, and you must not either,' she said sternly. 'These people are very confused and what they do is not to be considered in the same way as with normal people. They cannot help themselves,' which was a kindly attitude. But the good intentions were not always matched by practice. Although I never heard any care assistants get angry with residents, insensitive treatment was sometimes inevitable with so much to be done by too few of us. People were often left too long on toilets or commodes. They often had to wait too long to be got out of bed in the mornings in rotation, or to be given breakfast. Hurrying past some rooms, you sometimes had to harden your heart to people who called out to be done next when you were half-way through doing someone else. We were worked very hard, with no slack in the system. More staff would have allowed us more time and better care.

'Going the extra mile', 'Not good, not better, but the best!' just was not possible on many occasions. Most residents were remarkably patient and uncomplaining, but there was no way they could all be got into or out of bed, into and out of chairs and commodes, or have their food brought to them precisely when they wanted it. It must often have been insufferable for people whose lives had been reduced to basic things not to have small wants and needs dealt with quickly. Minor frustrations grew quickly to desperation among those who could not do the simplest things for themselves.

I don't know how the staffing ratio at Hazeldene compared with the average: this national information does not exist, according to Laing and Buisson, the care sector analysts. But Dorcas thought there were too few care assistants for so many residents and I trusted her experienced judgment. There were thirty-five residents on this floor and each shift had one care assistant assigned to a group of between six or seven residents, with one trained nurse (Sister) in overall charge. That felt like a very heavy load since so many of the residents were entirely helpless. Dorcas had worked in a small independent home in Tooting before moving to Hazeldene. She said in that home there had been three care assistants on duty every shift caring for just eleven patients with a Sister in charge as well – a ratio of more than 1:3 whereas it was 1:6 here.

All I know is the first shift that I was given six patients to myself was deeply alarming. I hurried yet I didn't want to hurry, since washing and dressing and chatting required time and patience to do it well with gentleness. Six people to get up, washed and dressed; six precisely correct breakfasts to be assembled – porridge or cornflakes, with or without sugar, prunes or All-Bran, eggs or bacon, toast with or without marmalade – all took time. For example, I spent a lot of time going in and out of Margaret's room, persuading her that her toast was for eating: 'This thing here is so strange,' she kept saying, tuning it upside down and pushing it about the increasingly sticky paper doily on her tray. 'I need to take time to decide what it is, don't you see? I can't quite understand it.' Sometimes she could be very articulate about what she could make no sense of. 'Is it something for my hands?' she kept saying as I tried to explain that it was toast and toast is for eating.

Time ticked by and my last resident was still not out of bed by 11 a.m. – and nor, I noted were some others, so it wasn't just my inexperience. Making up the beds, straightening the rooms, putting away their clothes, scurrying along to the sluice room two corridors away to dispose of soiled bags and dirty washing while trying to maintain an air of relaxed friendliness was not easy. Baths took a long time, hoisting and lowering people into the water, fearful of letting anyone slip, drying and powdering and rubbing their buttocks with cream, waiting while someone stopped for a long time half-way through putting on a dress, frozen as if suddenly struck by some far more important thought.

Nothing goes to rule. Just as you get one person finally settled and you start on someone else, the bell goes. Sister and everyone else could see when one of your residents was ringing, and you had to drop everything and hurry to answer it so that you could get the alarm switched off fast. It might be something easy – fetch me a drink – or it might be someone having an accident on the way to the toilet, which took a long time. You could never take the risk of ignoring those bells. No doubt if I'd stayed longer I would have got better at it. But I rarely saw the others have a minute's rest, except for the miserly fifteen-minute break we were given in every six-hour shift. I actually fell asleep in the staff room on a quarter-hour break one morning and had to be shaken awake by the others. Occasionally in the afternoons there was a little time just to sit and talk to residents, keeping them company in their rooms, but not often. The first day I had my own group to care for, one or two care assistants were off sick. One of ours was sent away to cover on another floor and her work was spread between everyone else. Management did not appear to budget for spare pairs of hands, nor was there any extra pay for care assistants working twice as hard to cover for others.

Laing and Buisson say local authorities are now paying about £100 a week too little for each patient they put into residential care. Many owners are abandoning the small nursing-home business before the government brings in rigorous new quality standards, requiring expensive new fire escapes and bigger rooms (the government has since relaxed standards because of this). At the same time the property price boom in the south-east reduces the incentive for care-home owners to work so hard turning a marginal profit when they can sell the place handsomely to developers and retire. The big companies have moved in everywhere as economies of scale make better profits, so they expand while the independents go to the wall. The government at the time of writing has yet to provide a staff/resident ratio guide, which is difficult to fix as it all depends on how feeble the residents are. As residents' dependency status keeps changing, usually for the worse, it makes it tricky to set hard-and-fast regulations. But Dorcas had told me she thought the work here was too hard and the staff far too few for such fragile patients.

According to Laing and Buisson, this company made some £3 million this year out of its 3,200 beds nationwide. That means, says William Laing, they make around £1,000 a bed per year clear profit after all capital and running costs. Those profits depend on keeping wages at rock-bottom. This, he said, is a growing company that does well out of building nursing homes in affluent areas and charging high prices to those who can pay, while also taking block contracts from the NHS, which pays more than local authorities to place its patients, because by definition NHS patients need more intensive care and the price for each can be negotiated individually. It is all a question of what it is worth a hospital to pay to unblock one of its acute beds by decanting a patient into a nursing home.

Dorcas complained vigorously about the low pay. She had to work forty-eight hours, including long twelve-hour shifts at the weekends, and it still was not a survivable wage. For reasons neither she nor I could understand, she got no overtime rate, no time-and-a-half or double-time for these terrible extra weekend hours. But at least here she could always work as many hours as she wanted when she needed to earn more, which is one reason some employers get away with low pay. Many jobs have no chance of extra hours, and many are now advertised for thirty hours or below with shifts to suit employers' heavy-pressure times. This was taken to extremes in places like the Clement Atlee school kitchen, with its unpaid half-hour in the middle of a three-hour shift. Kinderquest's 'temporary' status was doing the same thing. I asked Dorcas if she had ever thought about joining a union, since unionised workplaces get better rates of pay. She nodded enthusiastically and said they had often thought about it. Once or twice people had suggested it and had tried to get something going, 'But it didn't happen. I don't know why. Of course there should be a union in here and the pay might improve. But the people who tried to organise it a few times, I don't know what happened to them. They don't work here any more. Maybe they walked away, I don't know.'

It is expecting a lot of people who already work so hard to take on the task of trying to organise union recognition in their workplace. It feels scary and dangerous, it is unknown territory, and in a 48-hour week with bad shift times and children, how was someone like Dorcas supposed to do it? I didn't suggest she should, though she nodded her head and said, 'Someone ought to. That would be a good thing.' It made me feel guilty. I should have stayed here a while, helped to organise a union ballot, tried to make things better. But staying any longer than strictly necessary for reporting purposes was more than I could bear. Dorcas said she often thought of leaving, but the trouble was that many jobs that paid more per hour, like her daughter's bus conducting, didn't offer enough hours' work to match her present total wage. Anyway, as I had already found, it is not so easy to change job without suffering several weeks without pay, leaving debts and rent arrears which someone like Dorcas would never countenance without fear.

I quit before the weekend, when I had been rotaed to work two twelve-hour shifts, all day on both Saturday and Sunday in that claustrophopic place. Those three long windowless corridors where we worked, hardly seeing the light, were darkly oppressive. It was emotionally draining work, hurrying from drama to drama, from one suffering and demanding person to another, torn between pity, anxiety and irritation. It had its rewards when a resident smiled and expressed pleasure or gratitude, when you had time to do something extra, to listen to them and talk a while. These were pleasures I saw all the carers take in their work from time to time, coming out of a room with an air of satisfaction after making someone more cheerful: they talked about the residents with affection and involvement. But I doubt this is work many would choose if they had a real choice, not at this low pay and low status. Nurses often have to do this same caring work and the same dirty work, but they are better paid, (even if still not well-paid enough). They are professionals with ladders upwards if they want to take them and good qualifications to their name. They have general respect, even admiration, coming top of public esteem in opinion polls. Care assistants have none of that: health ancillaries feature nowhere in the national consciousness. Since I am lucky and I have the choice, I walked away from here with a sigh of relief.

I left Margaret, Minnie, Paula, Mrs Knightsbridge and all the rest, but they haunted me for weeks, daytime ghosts. It was more demanding work than the school kitchen, since the scrubbing of inanimate pots and pans was nothing compared to the washing of fragile old people with raw sores on their legs, who winced at the pain. The strain of engaging emotionally with all that misery was exhausting. The kindness and hard work of the care assistants here was worth far more than they were paid. But this is unseen, unmentionable labour, hidden away in these human oubliettes we would rather not think about. Considering directors' pay rises and weighing up the value of their work compared with the work of these women here, what is the scale of worth that puts care assistants at the bottom of every heap? Where do these values come from?

It is because caring is women's work. That attitude is embedded still in the values society apportions to the jobs people do. It is why there will never be equal pay until women's work is regarded with equal respect. There were no male care assistants here, only one or two male 'adaptation' nurses from abroad who were on their way upwards. Women's work is still treated as if it should be given almost free, a natural function. Any woman can do it because we are born to it, trained to it from infancy. Cleaning bottoms and being kind doesn't require qualification, only being a woman. At the heart of the low-pay problem lies the continuing low valuation of what are regarded as women's skills – caring, cleaning, cooking, teaching and nursing. Things your mother did for you she did freely out of love, and there is an unspoken expectation that all women at work should be society's mothers, virtually for free. The low value put on their labour springs from a deeply ingrained belief that they do these jobs because they love them. The gap between women's and men's pay will never be bridged until the value put on women's and men's work is re-balanced. Why does a mechanic cleaning sparking plugs rank higher than a care assistant cleaning old people? Companies like this rely on that gap to make their profits.

The standard week here was forty-two hours. That earned just £203.70. Of all the jobs I did, none made me so outraged at the pay. How could such good work be worth so shamefully little? Whenever anyone accuses me of naivety in imagining that these things can be changed, if anyone lectures me on the immutable laws of the market, I just ask them how they can justify paying £203.70 a week for work such as this?

Chapter 14

It Doesn't Have to Be This Way

Mr Jones, I shall call him. He is the chief executive in one of the larger care-home companies: it is a secretive sector and it is the policy of this company never to give on-the-record interviews. He is anyway better left anonymous as an archetype who could be speaking from any era down the ages. In Dickensian days he could have been in the flue-cleansing business, speaking of the economic disaster that would follow if chimney-sweeping were over-regulated and little boys were banned from fulfilling their economic destiny. As it happens he suited this part in appearance too: plumpish with small eyes and a bright pink silk tie.

We start off politely enough discussing the problems in the care-home industry. The government pays too little per patient, probably about £100–150 per resident per week too little in the south, driving some companies out of business. His own, he says, is among the most efficient and takes more private patients, which is why the Chairman's message in the company's annual report records 'profitability at a record high'. The introduction of the minimum wage, reports the Chairman, has had little impact on the company. (Which must be evidence the minimum wage was set too low, if even a low-pay, labour-intensive industry like this had no problem.)

Around two-thirds of Mr Jones's clients are government-funded residents. He wants the government not only to pay more for their care but also to force local authorities to close their remaining care homes and place their patients in the private sector. State-run homes are, he says, inefficient, badly run and their real costs are double private homes. I asked him why the few remaining local authority homes cost so much more to run.

'It's the usual, their staff are feather-bedded.'

'In what ways?'

'Oh, you know, the same as ever. They are very overstaffed by our standards and so feather-bedded.'

'How exactly?'

'All those pensions, holidays, sick pay, overtime pay and so forth.'

Those were all the things that were reduced to a bare minimum or non-existent for the staff at Hazeldene, as with agency staff and contracting companies everywhere. He is quite right that this is where the margins of profit and efficiency have been made in the private sector. I asked him what he pays ordinary care assistants.

'Around the £5 an hour mark,' he said (though I discovered the 'around' meant it was 25p less).

'£5 is not a wage they can live on, especially in London,' I said. Mr Jones gave me a beady look. 'They are working very hard,' I continued. 'Most care assistants work forty-eight hours and even then they still can't make ends meet. Your business's success depends entirely on how well they do their job and how well they treat your clients, yet they can't afford to live on their pay.'

He sat up rather emphatically in his chair. 'We pay top-of-the-market rates and wages are our biggest cost,' he said. I bit my tongue and said nothing. 'Look, we all work hard, don't we?' he said, leaning back in his chair. 'You and I, we use our heads. You and I work very hard and we sometimes have to work until late at night, don't we?'

'But we don't work as hard as care assistants, nothing like.'

'Look, what exactly are you getting at?'

'OK, I'm not pinning this on you in particular or on your company. But care assistants aren't being paid enough to live on, not a living wage. We as a society, private or government-funded, are just not paying the going economic rate for having old people looked after. It should cost more. It should cost enough to pay carers a living wage, shouldn't it? Not just in this industry but wherever people are being paid less than they can survive on. If you and I eat in a restaurant where the kitchen staff can't live on what we pay for the meal, we're getting it too cheap. We are not paying the market price.'

'But the market price is whatever you can produce and sell something for.'

'No. It is a distorted market if it depends on sub-survivable wages. It is a below-market, fraudulent price, not the true price. The result is the government has to give out tax credits to subsidise low wages. The government subsidises every restaurant meal when they top up the pay for washing up our plates. Do you think that is acceptable? Why should the tax-payer subsidise the services you and I purchase? Why subsidise a restaurant meal? But above all, how do you and I justify earning large salaries while these hard-working people struggle?'

Mr Jones pulls himself up to his full importance and leans across the desk to deliver the quintessential well-off man's reply. 'Look, this is the way I see it. I believe this is a free country. I believe in this modern age that everyone has their opportunity. Everyone who really wants to reach their goal is free to do it. If making money is your thing, you can go for it and make it. If it's education you want, you can get educated. Otherwise, if you try to even everything out what do we get? We get soaring wages, soaring inflation and then soaring taxes to pay for it and then what? Communism? Is that it? Doesn't work.'

So he shall remain plain Mr Jones who is a middle-of-the-road chief executive of a middle-ranking company, nothing exceptional, with a very ordinary director's view of society to match his very ordinary director's salary. Checking his company's annual report, he earns £162,000 a year, plus his 387,100 shares in the company which, according to the report, will have yielded him another £85,162 in dividends. Although that gave him an income of £247,162 last year, it still puts Mr Jones at the low end of the scale for company directors. He probably does not regard himself as especially rich, certainly not as any kind of fat cat, since he compares himself with those in his own occupation, forgetting that he is still among the 0.5 per cent richest earners in the land. Instead of counting his blessings, Mr Jones will be looking up enviously at the median (not the top) earnings of directors of the

FTSE 100, FTSE mid-250 and FTSE small-companies indexes, which he will find is nearly twice his salary at £416,000 and rising fast. The median, including small companies! It is rising meteorically, astronomically above the pay increases of their staff. Since 1994 directors' pay in these companies has risen by 107 per cent while the average salary of their collective employees rose by just 31 per cent. In other words, directors have had pay rises that outstrip their employees by a ratio of 3:1.[1] The gap is not just widening, it is stretching out of sight. So Mr Jones at £247,162 per annum does not think he is a rich man.

It is curious how in the bars of the Institute of Directors, their own pay increases are not discussed in the same horrified tones as the threat of raising the minimum wage. There is not much said about how all these directors' pay is inflationary and jeopardises economic stability, yet they will protest that putting up the minimum wage by so much as 50p would cripple the country. They will speak of the danger that increasing the minimum wage will cost not just as a dead-weight sum but as a knock-on effect right up the scale as other workers want their differentials restored. (So far there is little evidence of this.) Yet they never question whether their own stupendous increases might have the same inflationary knock-on effect encouraging their staff to demand to have their differentials restored upwards with boardroom pay. 'Ah, but that is the politics of envy!' they might say with magisterial distaste, as if envy were a more deadly sin than their own greed. However, neither envy nor greed is as socially corrosive as lack of empathy, lack of sympathy with others, a pathological and deliberate refusal to put yourself in someone else's shoes and ask that essential question: would your society still look morally justified and fair if you were no longer looking down on it from the heights of ease, but up at it from the sluice room of a care home?

However, putting callousness aside, Mr Jones's view of society and how it works is the one to be answered. 'Everyone has their opportunity,' he says, and that is his comfortable justification for gross social inequality. It could be at least a tenable position to believe that if we all start out equal together then the race to the trough is to the swiftest: those with their snouts in it earned it fair and square. The modern myth that class is dead and education and advancement are open to all is not particularly modern. It is a delusion Orwell records among the well-off, and many reactionary voices pretended to believe it a century before him. Every generation regards itself as uniquely modern and in modernity is the idea that old structures are falling and progress is breaking down old barriers. It was never as true as the historical Mr Joneses used to pretend, but at least there was slow progress then. Mr Jones now has to face the fact that the story of gradually improving equality and opportunity for all is over. Social history ground to a halt in the 1980s. Nor is there much sign that it will be kick-started again, despite mighty efforts by the Labour government which so far is running hard to stand still, running uphill with tax-credit subsidies against a market that last year gave the top 10 per cent of earners a rise of 7.3 per cent while the bottom 10 per cent had a rise of just 4.5 per cent. In the US – always more extreme in everything – Will Hutton has recorded how the decades of conservative intellectual ascendancy have now created a society whose higher echelons are far more impenetrable than ever by the poor, far more rigid and immobile than Europe, an end to the American dream.[2] There is now a solid platform of middle-class wealth from which it is virtually impossible for its children to fall, or for those below to climb up on to. The danger is that Britain, which still has one foot in the European social and tax model, and one foot in the American, is now like the US battening down the hatches on the bottom 30 per cent, locking them in.

The delusion of a new, modern, classless equality remains. It is deep in the television and advertising culture which assumes we are all consumers now. To be sure, people will say, there is the problem of the hopeless, feckless, dysfunctional poor but that is a particular social issue to be dealt with as Labour does. Are there no programmes, schemes, regeneration of estates like Clapham Park, parenting classes to break the generational cycle, carrots and sticks of every variety? Otherwise, no, class is dead now that one in three go to university and the doors are open to all. The classless delusion began in earnest with my own generation, the spirit of Woodstock and the Isle of Wight inviting all of us there to pretend we were the same and always would be. Hip is always classless and now the royal princes rave to rap from the ghetto, but so what? I have avoided discussing class in this book because it obscures instead of illuminates the question of growing inequality. Mention class and in no time the British will start to discuss accents, tastes and how class-free the media has become now that a Yorkshire or Welsh accent is a broadcasting asset. There is no doubt that demotic is cool while my own South Kensington origins lack any regional hip zip. But modern egalitarian style only helps cloak how difficult it remains for those in the bottom 30 per cent to rise up, or for their children to escape the poverty they are reared in.

But for Mr Jones and anyone else doing nicely, modern egalitarianism is a necessary myth. It makes it easier to sleep at night, as there is no other way to justify the way we live. Every human being has to find a justification for their own life and behaviour, an explanation that satisfies their own self-image as a reasonably good person: without that we all wither and die. Criminals create for themselves a story that saves their *amour propre*. Privilege also needs its self-justification, however self-deceiving, and it is found in the opportunity story.

The left wastes time arguing about whether equality of opportunity is enough of a goal, or whether we should go for equality of outcome, which frightens the right with its soviet implications of centrally controlled wages and prices, or abolishing private wealth. The old left's accusation against Tony Blair and New Labour is that they are heading for the meritocracy model: only make sure the doors are open to all, then it doesn't matter if the superior skills/birth/luck of some earn them far more than the pay of the unskilled/low-born/unlucky. In *The Rise of the Meritocracy* Michael Young raised the horrible spectre of a new inequality ordained and justified by ability, in which those at the bottom would be even worse off. Better by far to be cast in an inferior role by the loaded dice of parentage than by personal failure.

But this is all an artificial angels-on-pins debate because it is entirely impossible to devise a society in which every baby enters the starting gate equal, with only its own talents and determination to speed it on its way, if the winners are still allowed to earn 200 times the pay of the losers. Of course they will pass their power and money on to their children who will then not start out equal in the next generation. In other words, the goal of a fairer society is indivisible: it must confront both opportunity and outcome. But in seeking the acquiescence of Mr Jones and the conservative-minded everywhere, it will always be easier for governments to proclaim they are striving towards fairer opportunity for children because not even Mr Jones can argue with that. New Labour was right to stress 'opportunity for all', and right to frame its egalitarianism as 'abolishing child poverty'. The question now is whether they have the nerve to make it happen, because it means a great deal more redistribution than anything they have contemplated yet.

What of Mr Jones's economics? He and his world suggest that any significant attempt to share out earnings more fairly will bring the entire economy crashing down and the poor would lose out alongside the rich. Look at how Communism failed, he says triumphantly, as if there were not a wide range of options and destinations between the market red in tooth and claw and red revolution. But it is an assumption many make. They assume that the necessary trade-off between capitalism which works and Communism which doesn't is that we have to tolerate great inequality. Since the Thatcherite There-Is-No-Alternative 1980s this has become a sad-but-true factoid so widely believed that New Labour still dare not challenge it head-on, so it needs careful examination.

The most important overriding fact is that other countries manage to be both more equal and more successful economically than Britain – almost all the rest of Europe does, especially Norway, Finland, Sweden, Denmark and the Netherlands. When the Western economies are laid out in terms of economic success and social justice, there is not much correlation. The crucial fact which Professor Tony Atkinson has proved with econometric precision is that lack of connection.[3] Nations make their own destinies voluntarily. They can decide how fair or unfair they will be. How they share the proceeds of their economy has little effect on the success of that economy, though Atkinson's evidence suggests that the more fairly they share it, the better they will do, with a cohesive society and a better-educated workforce.

The next Mr Jones assertion is that if pay at the bottom rose, inflation would take off again. Reading the newspaper on the bus on the way back from working in Hazeldene one evening, I saw that new official wage statistics had just been published. Commentators were praising the government on the surprising 'wage stability' in the economy, despite a tight labour market. There was no 'inflationary' push in wages because pay at the bottom was not rising, nor was there a ripple-up effect from the minimum wage. Economists were surprised, but then economists often are. Fashions in economics come and go. Under Mrs Thatcher everyone watched the monthly monetary supply figures, hearts in mouths. Under Harold Wilson it was the balance of payments figures. Now those orthodoxies have passed. However, it remains an orthodoxy that rises in wages must be inflationary so they must be held down – at the bottom if not at the top. Memories of the runaway inflation of the 1970s are burned deep in the national political psyche, when Harold Wilson warned the country, 'One man's pay rise is another man's job loss.'

That experience has left the powerful impression that putting more money into people's pockets would be worthless as it would just push up prices with too much cash chasing the same number of goods: no one would be any better off (though in fact the inflationary late 1970s delivered the greatest equality ever). In other words, an iron economic law makes it impossible to live in any other way than we do now. This ignores a multitude of differences between otherwise similar countries, and profound differences between the economic climate of the 1970s and now. It was a time of global inflation, kick-started by the 1973 oil crisis, whereas now world inflation is at a record low. Those were also high-tax days but now, with Britain the lowest taxed in Europe, any hint of inflation can be squeezed out of the economy easily enough by raising taxes. In the end, no real progress towards justice for the poor can be made without taking from higher earners to give to the lower earners, which would redress any inflationary tendency. Money in the pockets of the poor is healthier for the economy than money in the pockets of the rich: it is spent on local products and it rolls through the economy several times more, multiplying its good effect as it goes. Money in the hands of the rich flies abroad instantly on extra foreign holidays and foreign goods.

One way or another more money has to be put into the pockets of the low-paid. Either higher earners must pay more for their services directly by paying the full market rate in restaurants, for their domestic work and care, or they must be taxed more so the low earners are subsidised by higher tax credits, or a bit of both. But none of these approaches is inflationary, none upsets the fiscal balance overall. Incidentally, the impact of what high earners are paid has a remarkable effect on the annual figures. Look at annual pay tables and you can see the big bounces in the pay figures which are accounted for only by the bonuses the City pays its boys in red braces, yet apparently these are not considered a danger to the smooth running of the economy. Nor does the fact that top pay has now vanished off the graph and disappeared out of sight. If you look at the table on page 214, which shows the weekly earnings of all full-timers, it indicates how income is distributed.[4] Yet this only gives a rough impression of the pay of the top earners. If the graph actually included the highest earners on the same scale, it would stretch from wherever you are sitting to somewhere down the corridor.

If the minimum wage were to rise to the European Union-agreed 'Decency Threshold', the figure the Low Pay Unit uses as its benchmark, it should now be fixed at £7.32 an hour or £292.80 a week: that sum represents two-thirds of male median earnings, a reasonable benchmark. That is also where the equivalent lowest earnings were, relatively, in 1970, so there is a long way to catch up. If the minimum wage were to be set at half of male median earnings, as New Labour first proposed, then it should now be fixed at £5.38.

The East London Communities Organisation (TELCO) is starting a Living Wage movement in London, trying to get large employers in the East End to agree to pay their workers enough to live on. They have fixed on £6.30 an hour, following research by the Family Budget Unit which found that this was the minimum a woman and two children could live on at a 'low cost but acceptable' standard. This seems to me an achievable and quite modest target.

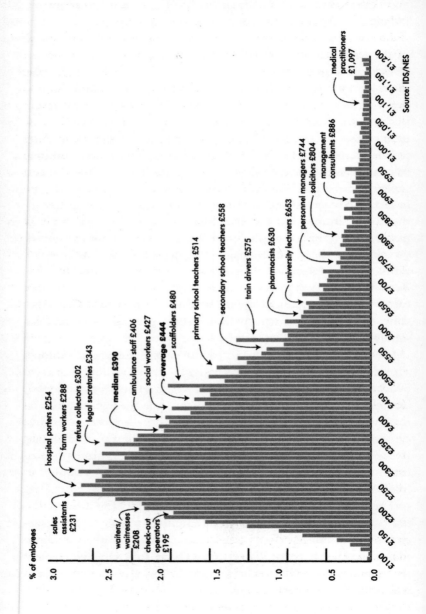

% of employees

sales assistants £231
hospital porters £254
farm workers £288
refuse collectors £302
legal secretaries £343
waiters/waitresses £208
check-out operators £195
median £390
ambulance staff £406
social workers £427
average £444
scaffolders £480
primary school teachers £514
secondary school teachers £558
train drivers £575
pharmacists £630
university lecturers £653
personnel managers £744
solicitors £804
management consultants £886
medical practitioners £1,097

Source: IDS/NES

Working forty hours, it would provide £252 a week for three people, which is hardly generous. But it is a reasonable starting point because Rome was not built in a day and Sweden, Norway and Finland took many years since the war to develop a consensual path towards greater social justice. No one is seriously proposing a sudden devastating increase in one step. What is required is a national determination to keep moving upwards towards an agreed goal of giving every worker a living wage. Whatever the exact sum, the minimum wage needs to rise year on year in a declared strategy, allowing time for adjustment. After a one-day strike in July 2002, directly employed local authority workers won a promise of £5.33 minimum pay by 2004. But that does not cover the majority of the low-paid public workers who are contracted out in private companies.

How much can it rise before it starts to cause widespread loss of jobs? Ask most economists and they will tell you in all honesty they do not know. I asked many and Professor Mark Stewart of Warwick University Business School, who did research for the Low Pay Commission on the effect of the minimum wage, says, 'No one sensible claims to know.' Much research on this was done around the time of its introduction, trying to predict but working in the dark. Consider how diverse the sectors are where pay is low – from McDonald's burger-flippers to the village hairdresser, from a student bartender in a Manchester pub to care assistants and school cleaners in Westminster. All agree there must be a point at which jobs are lost but few claim to know where, when, how many or in which sectors. The behaviour of consumers constantly outfoxes the forecasters. Just when people should be staying home cowering from an expected recession, they go out shopping, drinking, holidaying and spending right through it. If, say, the Ritz is forced to raise the wages of its dishwashers, economists do not know exactly what fraction of the price of the meal in that opulent restaurant would be affected. Bar staff are among the lowest paid, but the proportion of the price of a pint that is attributable to an increase in staff wages will vary wildly in different types of pubs and bars around the country, and a pint of beer is just one commodity among millions to be assessed to make this calculation. Then consider how this calculation will shift according to the state of the economy at any one time.

However, one man thinks he knows precisely how many jobs will be lost for every penny extra on the minimum wage. He is Professor Patrick Minford, Mrs Thatcher's guru, who has always advocated a pure unfettered market approach to wages and labour laws. He used to preach that Britain should take the Asian Tiger route to riches, undercutting all competitors by paying the lowest wages. But that was before the Asian Tiger economies lost some of their snarl. Professor Minford has an economic model, he says, which demonstrates precisely how many jobs would be lost as the minimum wage rises. His model proclaims that if the minimum wage were to rise by 8 per cent (which is only 33p), it would cause the loss of half a million jobs. If it went up by 24 per cent (only 98p), then 1.4 million jobs would be lost and at the same time national GDP would fall by an alarming 7 per cent. His model predicts yet worse doom: if the minimum wage rose by that same 33p, although only 5 per cent of workers would benefit, the knock-on effect would create an overall 4 per cent increase in the total national wage bill.

The only trouble with his model is that it proved to be monumentally wrong about the introduction of the minimum wage at its original supremely cautious £3.60. Professor Minford predicted that it would lose a quarter of a million jobs. Research from a number of bodies, including the Low Pay Commission itself, suggests the minimum wage lost no jobs – or what was officially described as 'insignificantly different from zero'. Any losses were unmeasurable since a million more jobs were created after its imposition. Even Professor Minford now says, 'Yes, we would resile from the position we took then. But our model still holds good.' But how did the model get it so wrong? 'We can explain that. We think that many jobs were not lost because there was a great deal more evasion of the minimum wage by employers than has been reported and many more did not actually pay it.' But there has been little evidence that this was widespread, with the Low Pay Commission and Inland Revenue scrutinising it assiduously. 'Well, the other explanation is that employers cut back on other conditions such as holiday pay, sick pay and pensions. That is how they absorbed the cost without causing job losses,' Minford explains.

It is worth noting in his model that he estimated that the minimum wage should have caused a fall of 1.2 per cent in GDP – and this too failed to materialise. However, one part of his model does work because it describes exactly what did happen, measurably in Treasury records for all to see. He calculates the extra income flowing into the Treasury from the extra tax and National Insurance brought in by higher wages as a result of the minimum wage was £1.4 billion, even after allowing for the extra the state had to pay out in public-sector wages. In other words, for so long as there is not significant job loss (which costs the exchequer £1.4 billion in social security and lost taxes for every quarter of a million lost jobs), then raising the minimum wage is pure gain to the state – and extra money can be spent on poverty-reducing programmes which in turn employ more people.

Professor Minford was not the only one who was wrong about the dangers of introducing a minimum wage. A good example of how the art of economics bends with the political fashion is the Department of Trade and Industry's 1995 report on the likely effect of a minimum wage at the sort of rates Labour was then proposing. It made headline news in all the Conservative press and it gave Labour a fright. The DTI opined that Labour's plan would lose a staggering 1.7 million jobs. (This came from supposedly politically neutral civil service economists, which only goes to show that the Conservatives suborned Whitehall long before New Labour.)

Because economists cannot predict where the minimum wage might bite dangerously into jobs, there is good reason to keep increasing it boldly until it does begin to do harm. 'Suck it and see,' said one LSE economist. 'That is the only way to tell.' Most of these jobs are in the service sector, so they cannot disappear abroad to Thailand or India. Manicures, sandwiches, cocktails, dishwashing, bed-baths and bin-emptying can never be done anywhere else but here. Nor can many jobs in these sectors be shed. From my own experience and from any number of labour-force reports, there is not much slack, no 'feather-bedding', as Mr Jones would say. Ever since the savage downsizing 1980s with its contracting culture and outsourcing within the private as well as the public sector, the myriad battalions of management consultants have pinched and squeezed the last drop of sweat out of virtually every workplace. The story of the Clement Atlee school kitchen is replicated everywhere.

Nor is it only taking place down in the depths of the kitchens: this pinch and squeeze has happened right through the workforce. Study after study is showing a sharp increase in hours worked, causing rising stress and a matching sharp decrease in work satisfaction in the last decade, reaching right from professional and managerial down to low-paid jobs. I can rarely remember a time when such a welter of diverse reports landed on my desk almost weekly on the same subject, pointing unequivocally to the same conclusion about growing work intensity. Most recently, the government-funded ESRC's Future of Work Programme finds people everywhere working harder and longer, with only half as many (a mere 16 per cent) happy with the hours they work as were satisfied in 1992.[5] Nearly half work more than their basic forty-hour week, with 81 per cent working long hours not because they enjoy it but because they need the money. The TUC reports 4 million people – one in six workers – working over forty-eight hours, which is more people than when the EU 48-hour rule was brought in, with the UK having the longest hours in Europe. The Work Foundation (previously known as the Industrial Society) records 'job satisfaction has plummeted over the last decade'.[6] The so-called 'high performance management techniques' introduced over the same period have made the entire workforce profoundly unhappy, yet have delivered no measurable increase in productivity.

So it is highly unlikely that many more jobs can be squeezed out of Britain's service sector even if the minimum wage were significantly increased. Small badly run companies – often the very worst employers – might be thrown out of business but their work and their employees will simply be picked up by bigger, better companies instead. (These might include the bakery I worked in, or the cleaning company for which I did the telephone cold-calling.) Big companies always did whisper behind their hands that they welcomed the minimum wage as it would drive out the worst firms in catering, cleaning and care. In fact the rate was set so low that even that did not happen.

However, all economists agree that there must be a point somewhere along the scale where too high a minimum wage would start to throw people out of work and on to the dole. Workers would be priced out of some jobs if consumers began to cut back their spending on optional leisure, beauty or eating-out. In the remaining manufacturing jobs there is always a danger of factories moving abroad in search of lower wages. Look how home-grown inventor-entrepreneur Dyson has just taken his bag-less vacuum-cleaner factory to low-wage Malaysia.

But once the minimum wage seems to have hit its safety ceiling, there is another imaginative route the government can take. It can create what is, in effect, a two-tier minimum wage. Look across the Atlantic and an unexpected un-American change is beginning to take hold. It all started in Baltimore in 1994 when a group of community organisations and churches called BUILD persuaded the city council to pass a bylaw requiring all companies that have contracts with the city, or receive subsidies and tax breaks, to pay their workers a living wage – a wage well above the minimum. The national US minimum wage is only $5.15 an hour and has lost 30 per cent of its real value since 1968: to keep pace it should now be $7.37. The Living Wage laws have currently fixed the price at $8 an hour (£5.51), a sum chosen because at $18,100 a year it is enough to lift a family of four above the federal poverty line. The campaign has taken off across the US with remarkable success and has now been passed into law in eighty-one cities and counties (most are Democrat-controlled), including Boston, New Orleans, Santa Fe, Santa Monica and New York City. Suffolk County has become the first Republican authority to adopt Living Wage laws. Maryland is about to become the first entire state to adopt the Living Wage.

Time magazine, hardly an organ of the left, recently examined the research evidence on the effect the Living Wage was having. Had it thrown people out of work in a society that regards sub-zero pay as the key to economic success in recent years? *Time* looked at the work of Professor David Neumark, an economist of Michigan State University who started out as a sceptic of all Living Wage-type laws. But when he researched what the effect had been on the economy of thirty-six cities, to his surprise he concluded that there were only slight job losses and these were more than offset by the decrease in poverty among working families. Neumark found that higher wages meant many businesses had productivity gains due to lower staff turnover and greater staff loyalty, which in turn helped offset the extra wage costs.

Some US cities held referendums first and the debate centred on what duty businesses owed to the communities they drew their profits from. At this point, as so often, comparisons between American and British social policy cease to be useful. The great difference for the US working poor, as Barbara Ehrenreich describes so powerfully in *Nickel and Dimed*, is that they not only have a lower minimum wage but no welfare state, and virtually no dole for the unemployed. Crucially they get no housing benefit subsidy towards their rent and no free healthcare. That makes the question of the social obligations owed by companies far more pressing, since the lack of a welfare state is why companies and individuals pay such low taxes. In Victorian Britain the great industrial philanthropists saw it as their duty to take care of their workers in the days before the state developed those functions. The best of them built their workers model towns, Sir Titus Salt's Saltaire in Bradford, Cadbury's Bourneville or Lord Leverhulme's Port Sunlight. Now, however, it no longer is or should be the duty of British industrialists to provide mini-welfare states for their workers. But it is their duty to pay them a living wage, without which these companies' goods and services are subsidised by other tax-payers in topping up their workers' pay.

On a recent visit to Saltaire I read in its history that while these great philanthropists would provide better conditions for their workers, the one thing they would never do was raise the pay. The philanthropists' workers' pay was no better than that of local bad employers, a cartel of mill owners combining to ensure wages were held down. Something of the kind still seems to operate now, keeping wages lower than they should be in a market with such fierce competition for workers, especially in the south-east. Unions report that employers are increasingly offering other incentives, flexi-time hours or even cash bonuses, but they will not raise the basic wage.

In Britain a living wage for all state employees and for all those working in contracted-out companies would be easier to implement than in the US. With the relatively generous tax credits that Labour has introduced, the more people were paid directly in wages, the less they would cost in these subsidies, and the more tax and National Insurance they would pay. One great advantage of the Living Wage is that the state pays and controls all the extra money paid out in this higher tier of wages: it would have to increase the price paid to contractors to cover higher wage costs. The Living Wage cities in the US discovered that although sometimes as few as 1 per cent of the local workforce was actually covered directly by the Living Wage law, it did help to pull up the lowest wages in the area by setting a benchmark other employers found themselves obliged to move towards if they wanted to keep their key workers. But that is not the same as forcing it upon every struggling corner shop or local hairdresser.

The Treasury prefers the WFTC top-up approach to raising wages. They say that raising wages does not target poor working families as precisely as tax credits do. All kinds of people – students doing holiday work, single people – would see their pay rise too. One riposte to that is, so what? The labourer is worthy of his hire. Students now need to earn to survive and so does everyone else. The other riposte is to point out that tax credits are not in fact well-targeted as they miss a lot of poor families who fail to apply for them. TELCO's research found many more poor families failing to claim WFTC than actually receiving it.[7] Since 70 per cent of the low-paid are women, raising the wages for all of them would hit a high proportion of the target families.

But the simple answer and the best answer is that in justice no one should work for forty hours a week and still not earn a living wage. No doubt tax credits would always have to remain as a part of the armoury against poverty, but most of those who work should expect to be paid a wage they are proud to take home to their families.

When I ask ministers or Treasury economists what is the long-term answer to a poverty-stricken workforce being paid too little to live on, one reply is always 'education and training'. If only these

people would up-skill themselves, then they could move up the
ladder. These economists tend to describe the jobs I did as 'entry-
level', which is a curious phrase. It implies this is where the young
set out on their upward journey through life, a humble first step on
a ladder to success. Alas, 'entry-level' is a euphemism: where people
enter the labour market on the bottom rung, there they usually
stay.[8]

Of course good training is badly missing from low-wage workplaces, the necessary escape route upwards for the many able people
who are cemented to the floor. But if employers were forced to pay
their staff more they would value them enough to offer them
training to enhance their skills. Education and training can never be
the primary solution to low pay for the one glaringly obvious reason
that is gently skated over by policy-makers. The thin ice is this:
come what may, training or no training, millions of people will
always be required to sweep and clean and cook and care. However
many NVQs they have in their back pockets, the basic hard grind
still has to be done, day in, day out and night-time too. Dorcas will
still be there, hoisting her six old people out of bed and into their
baths every morning. Maggie and Wilma and Winston will all be
hard at work, too. The only question is, why do they not earn a
living wage for the essential work they do?

Chapter 15

Then and Now

Standing in the long, bleak road on a cold windy morning outside Templeborough in Rotherham, I can see the bare ruined sheds of the steel industry stretching far into the distance. I stop a middle-aged man walking his dog and ask about the fate of Steelo's, as Steel, Peech and Tozer used to be known. He sighs and says yes, this was where it had been and he had worked there until it closed. 'Times have changed,' he says, shaking his head, and ambles on after his dog.

In 1970, researching my book, I spent time living with an old steel-worker, Reg Atkinson, and his wife, Mary. He had lost his hand in Steelo's when he went to work there at the age of thirteen. As a paint boy he had crawled under a carriage which rolled over and crushed all his fingers. He was guaranteed a job for life and was later given a Steelo's retirement cottage as compensation. At least the industry lasted for his own working lifetime. He had taken me round the mighty works, crossing the catwalk over the melting shop, then the biggest in the world, where six gigantic furnaces exploded with a noise beyond imagining when electrodes the thickness of pillars of the Parthenon were lowered in. At times sheets of flame roared twenty feet out of the furnaces. When the molten metal lava flowed out into troughs, the whole shop glowed bright and the chimneys roared like fury. It was a heroic sight but for the men it was a dangerous spectacle. Yet despite the danger and the sweltering hard work, it was, they said, partly glorious too.

Why? Because the wages were high for a manual worker, £35 a week standard (nearly £588 a week now) with many earning more.

That was well above the national average for all occupations and professions and that pay gave them the status of worker-kings. It made the jobs desirable despite the hard conditions that showed on every melting-shop man's face, pitted with black marks from the spitting metal branded deep into their skin. In these 'heroic' industrial jobs of the old days, it was money and industrial power that conferred pride: money and power are what counts, as every rich man knows. A similar job I saw back then was a tyre factory, stinking hellish heat and a gut-churning stench, but that was not 'heroic' because the pay was the among the lowest, so the work was done by new immigrants rather than worker-kings. Yet the conditions in the steel-works were in some ways worse: the work was more perilous, with far higher accident and mortality rates. If it had been high-paid work, the tyre factory would have engendered the same sense of pride as the steel-works. Pay is everything. If care assistants were highly paid, they would be proud queens instead of the downtrodden. There are plenty of satisfactions in manual work, as I found myself. If well-managed and decently timed and equipped, manual work is not of itself unpleasant. There is meaning in cleaning. It is only the low pay and thus the contemptible status that make these necessary jobs demeaning.

Steelo's finally closed in 1993. Inside a part of the old sheds is now Magna, a science visitor centre for children. Among its many attractions is a visit along the same catwalk I crossed with a simulation of the sounds and sights of the old melting shop. It is powerfully affecting and the commentary inevitably elegiac in recounting a proud history gone the way of the hand-weavers, cotton mills, shipyards and every other shifting phase of economic history, each glorious in its heyday, each cruelly painful in its passing.

When I was staying there in 1970, I went down a Rotherham coal mine, Manvers colliery, one of the twelve pits in and around the town then, now gone. The conditions were horrific and dangerous, the journey at pit bottom starting with a long ride on an underground locomotive and a half-mile walk stooping low in an increasingly hot, dark tunnel often ankle-deep in water. To reach the seam itself required worming along 200 yards of tunnel never higher than two and a half foot. At the coal face men spent their entre shift operating lethal coal cutters in a tiny confined space while crouched between hydraulic pit props a foot or two apart. When they stopped for a rest they could only sit with their heads tucked between their knees. Not surprisingly some 700 miners a year nationally were killed or crippled. But already by then the pits and the steel-mills were starting to close; in Rotherham unemployment was rising fast, the glory days were coming to an end and everyone knew it and talked of it.

The suffering of the old mining, steel and ship-building regions continues. A generation or maybe two was lost, towns and villages have lost their purpose, and there is scant reason for other industries to come to many of the farflung spots that once were the hub of the economy and the empire. Drugs are rife, youth once absorbed into their fathers' workplaces are left listless and lost. It was bad to send your son down a pit, but worse to see him go nowhere.

None the less, this industrial earthquake, tragic though it was for those regions, was only a small part of the social history of the last forty years. Millions more people have gained than lost in the social revolution that was taking place as I wrote. It has been a story of progress for all but the bottom 30 per cent, who were left behind. Back in 1970 there was still a mass working class, a solid blue-collar majority, a few well-paid but mostly not. There was little, in my view, to celebrate about this: the romantics who yearn for yesterday's cloth-cap masses, ferrets, pigeons and 'honest toil' are mainly regretting the use that could be made of this well-organised force to fuel political machines within the unions and the Labour party. Most people's lives have improved immeasurably since then. They may have lost a sense of close working-class community that was built on mutual deprivation, but it was a loss people eagerly swapped for better jobs and better standards of living if they got the chance.

By 1970 things were already changing fast. Home-ownership was on the rise. The children of blue-collar workers were getting better chances through comprehensive education and the new plate-glass universities. I was a sixth-former at one the very first comprehensives in London in the 1960s and its spirit in the early days was all about modernity, mobility and opportunity. The children of the comprehensive were escaping from their parents' blue-collar work into white-collar, better-paid and better-status jobs in the growing service sector. Although Labour's education policies had helped it happen, the party was instinctively ambivalent about these shifting social sands in its very heartland. At one point Harold Wilson's government tried to arrest the inevitable and support blue-collar manufacturing against the burgeoning services with a Selective Employment Tax, designed to increase taxation of the services in a vain attempt to bolster manufacturing exports. The rising service industries were feared to be like the bad old days of domestic service- low-paid humble work lacking the masculine nobility of the old heavy industries. But the net result has been embourgoisement, with two-thirds of the people now solid home-owners. That is probably the best definition these days of middle-class: a new mass with a stake in wealth and something substantial to hand down to their children unimaginable to previous generations. Opportunities for the majority of children have widened, their horizons broad, the universities filled with students whose grand-parents never dreamed it possible. That was genuine progress on a mighty scale, never to be underestimated.

This book is about the one-third of people who have been left out of this social evolution, for many of whom things feel worse since then. Unemployment is low, now roughly the same as 1970: now as then it is largely restricted to those who for geographic or personal reasons cannot find work. Most of the poor are now in work and working as I have described, ferociously hard, often at two or more jobs. They are workers as surely as miners and steel-workers, but they no longer have a strong national voice. Where once they were part of a relatively united and powerful class with a confident image of itself and its muscle, now they are stranded. Even if the poorer workers were always on the underside of that class and largely ignored by the strong trade unions, by hanging on to the idea of a united working class, gripping its coat-tails, they too could feel represented by its class politics. The strength of the majority was to some extent on their side, too.

That is no longer the case. The mass has moved up and away,

atomised, de-politicised, de-unionised, sprawling between myriad occupations that sociologists and census-takers now find increasingly hard to categorise in class terms. Is it income or is it clean hands? Is it property or is it education that defines class categories now? Mrs Thatcher's declaration that there was 'No such thing as society' described what was happening anyway, with or without a strong push in that direction by her. It took Labour time, but it too had to grow away from its cloth-cap image as the voice of a mass working class that was rapidly dissolving. When Labour eventually emerged from its chrysalis eighteen years later it was as a fully fledged middle-class butterfly: New Labour for new social times.

New middle-class Labour retained a social conscience, but in promoting policies to redistribute wealth towards the poor it now had no mass constituency to appeal to, nothing but the voters' better natures. Nervously testing its wet new wings, New Labour hardly dared put faith in that. In the old days the strong workers and their unions were willing – just – to pull along the poor with them, to some extent. But now there was not even that nominal power behind poverty, only a weak appeal to voters' sense of fairness. Labour seems to doubt that voters have consciences to be touched and so far they have not had the courage to test them. The admirable aspiration to abolish child poverty has not yet been matched by a willingness to admit what it must cost everyone else: nothing is for free. Labour has not yet dared tell the majority of voters that to achieve it they will have to hold back their own ever-rising growth in living standards to allow those at the back to catch up. It need not mean a real cut, it only needs to skim off and slow future income-growth for the well-off. Used to the idea that rapid social progress eventually sweeps all but the most feckless poor upwards, people need to be warned that it has stopped happening. It ground to a halt at the end of the 1970s when all the measures of equality started to move in the wrong direction and the children of the left-behind now no longer have the same ladders of escape. Poverty pay, bad schools and social-housing silos trap them below, and without radical government action they will never become the new home-owners of tomorrow.

Looking back at the jobs I did in 1970 and making comparisons

with pay now, I have been shocked to find that many pay-rates in
the bottom jobs are much the same or mainly lower in real terms
than thirty years ago, tangible proof of how the low-paid have been
left behind. Back then I worked at one of the many Lucas factories
in Birmingham, a gigantic old redbrick building in Great King
Street, blackened with Midlands grime, but it stands empty now.
Lucas was one the mighty elements of the British car industry,
supplying parts to most motor manufacturers, but it has long since
been broken up and sold off in bits, much of it sold on again and
again. I was a switch cable operator, cutting lengths of wire and
fitting them into small bulb holders. I was on piece-work, sitting at a
bench all day slamming down the foot pedal on the hot cutter, not a
bad job, sociable, plenty of conversation while you worked,
reasonable working conditions, a strong union and a weekly wage
for a day shift of £13.85. What should that now be worth, to keep
up in relative terms? The Institute for Fiscal Studies calculates that
those earnings now should be £242.70 to level-peg. To make the
comparison, the nearest equivalent job is on an assembly line at the
former Lucas factory in Perry Bar, now renamed TRW Auto-
motive, manufacturing electronic ignitions. Workers here are paid
£250 for a standard weekly shift, so they have gained a real increase
of £7.30 a week, a minuscule advance in thirty-two years, because
during that time average incomes have more than doubled. In real
terms they have had a real increase of 3 per cent in over thirty years,
compared with the average increase of 100 per cent. But averages
are meaningless to the bottom strata of workers when inequality has
grown so rampantly.

The more I thought about it, the more I realised that I should not
have been surprised to find pay in these jobs had made so little
progress. If you take the broad figures for the growing or shrinking
levels of equality, this is exactly what it means down at the bottom.
The top shoots up and away into a stratosphere out of sight of
everyone else, and the majority jumps upwards too, but pay-rates at
the bottom (and therefore benefits that are more or less pegged to
them) fall right back or barely change. National average growth
means nothing to them.

But averages include people who have gained. I went back to

Port Sunlight to visit the Unilever factory. In 1970 I worked in the vast old redbrick Number 3 building, the Scourers Department, making fancy plastic bathroom packs of Vim, and sometimes Dot, a now-defunct lavatory cleaner that burned your tights if you spilled it. I stood at a conveyor belt where the powder poured down a chute into plastic canisters and a packing machine slammed the lids on. I had to pick out the ones with faulty lids: at the next stage down the line they were turned on their sides so if you missed one, it spilled on to the belt and the floor. The packing machine broke down regularly, and I would have to heave great armfuls of canisters off the belt as they kept spewing forth. Apart from the thick sneezing dust and detergent in the air, it was not bad work and at the time the pay was average factory pay, £13.50 a week or £227.30 as the present-day equivalent.

But everything is different now. Where once 7,000 people worked, now there are only 1,000 producing far greater volumes of soap products. The packing machine in Number 3 building now turns out millions of Persil Aloe Vera tablets with a tiny number of machine-minders. We worked as a great unskilled mass of women packers, in a strict hierarchy. There was the supervisor above us in a blue overall, there were foremen above her in white overalls, and then the managers who wore suits and were rarely seen on the floor. All that hierarchy has been swept away. The workers are grouped in small teams of four or five, with a team leader, and they have to hit their targets each week. If they miss them, they work longer hours for no extra pay to catch up. They are all responsible for how hard they work, at what rate they work, and for how much they produce. Annual bonuses for hitting targets are part of their pay and their 37 ½ -hour week is annualised, so they may work twelve hours in peak times and have time off in slack periods. They now work shifts so the machines keep flowing through the night and they get one week in four off, not as part of their holidays. Demarcations between packing workers and engineers are breaking down as the packers (still hired as unskilled) learn to fix minor faults on their machines: in the old days if a packer touched an engineer's job the engineers would have marched out on strike. This slimmed-down, self-supervising, multiskilled workforce is entirely unlike the one back in 1970, when we did the minimum amount of work we could get away with, spent as long as we could smoking in the lavatory on an elaborate system of 'spelling' one another. We didn't care at all about output as any shortfall was good news because it meant more overtime. A lot has changed. When I met the Works Manager and the Head of Human Resources, both men were, to my surprise, dressed exactly the same as everyone else, in polo shirts emblazoned with the company logo and, like every other worker, their own name embroidered on the front. The overalls and suits that denoted jealously guarded status in the 1970s have long gone in favour of the new demotic, all-in-this-together style of running the place.

How was all this change negotiated? By paying the workers far more money. In 1970 I was paid the equivalent of £11,340.00. But now these workers are paid an average of £25,000 a year: more than double. So a small select group of workers have moved up to a higher level, with middle-class incomes and infinitely better working conditions (Internet cafe in the canteen, gleaming new computers in the union-run learning centre), more responsibility, more autonomy in their teams and they sound happy. There is zero turnover and if ever the company advertises a job they get more than a thousand applications.

There has been one other change, though. In 1970 I was one of thousands of women who worked the packing lines. When the great culture change happened, the company went over to rotating shifts but women couldn't by law work nights, so almost all of them left. (That law was repealed in 1986.) A large, poorly paid female workforce has been exchanged for a small, high-value, well-rewarded male one. It was not intended by the company, it is just the way the soap flakes crumbled. Low pay is women's work, high pay is men's.

When I went back to study some of the employment statistics for 1970, I leafed through the monthly government *Employment Gazette* for that year. It was the year the ambitious Prices and Incomes board collapsed, an anti-inflation policy designed to keep down pay claims by holding down prices, but both pay and prices burst out at the seams. I looked at how equal or unequal pay was then. To my surprise, I found that the bottom 10 per cent of manual workers then earned 67.3 per cent of median earnings. The minimum wage still has not even reached up to the 50 per cent of male median earnings which Labour originally proposed (which would now be delivering £5.38 an hour, or £215.20 a week). To return to 1970 levels for the lowest-paid 10 per cent, that 67.3 per cent of median earnings (currently £390 a week) would now deliver a minimum wage of £6.55 per hour or £262 a week – a living wage, unlike the pathetic £164 of the current minimum wage. That is the true measure of how far social justice has slid backwards since then.

I was stunned by something else I had completely forgotten and I admit that I am shocked that it featured relatively little in my book. It was something I mentioned sourly now and then yet I seem to have accepted it as an immutable fact of life. The *Employment Gazette* for April, summing up the end of the financial year for 1970, notes: 'The earnings of full-time men are again roughly twice the earnings of women, not only in the middle but also near the top and bottom of the distributions.' Month by month the *Gazette* reports the wages of every type of job in every sector, and in every category it gives a listing for women and a listing for men doing exactly the same job, with the women paid half as much. It was true in the factories where I worked: there was a women's rate and a men's rate for identical jobs.

The unions insisted on it as well as the employers. Virtually all unions were profoundly suspicious of women working at all. They wanted women to be paid less and yet because they were paid less, special agreements had to be drawn up to make sure management did not try to sneak cheaper women workers into men's jobs. At the start of 1970 the written house agreement between Vauxhall and the unions said this: 'a) Women will not be engaged if suitable men are available. b) Existing male employees will not be replaced by women. c) Women will only be employed on jobs broadly specified and agreed.' The work 'agreed' would of course be women's work which no self-respecting man would do – the catering and cleaning (and here in the motor industry it was also car-seat machining). Otherwise women would be kept out of higher-earning jobs that might compete with the men. Women were regarded as weak

union members who would accept low pay because it was assumed
that they were always earning a second wage in the family, although
by then already many were single parents and primary earners. If
anyone is inclined now to get misty-eyed about the grand old days
of strong trade unionism, there were some good reasons why they
were often unloved, especially by women.

Later in that year came Barbara Castle's magnificent battle for an
Equal Pay Act. Roy Jenkins, Chancellor at the time, was opposed.
He had trouble enough in the economy without a potentially
inflationary increase in all women's wages and it was not an easy
time to push for something so radical. Industrialists were indignant,
protesting that they could not afford to pay women more. It would
mean doubling their pay at a time when pay was anyway rising fast.
Virtually all the unions were opposed, too, some openly, others in
surreptitious ways, knowing their position was morally untenable.
The unions at the time, it should be remembered to their shame,
were also strongly opposed to a statutory minimum wage which
Barbara Castle had tried to introduce. They feared it would under-
mine trade-union power, as workers might not bother with union
membership if their pay was already secured by an effective national
minimum.

It is hard to recapture how extreme was the radicalism of the
government's knife-edge decision to push the Equal Pay Act
through late one night. As with every historic social advance in
history, the forces of conservatism are quick to forget now how
strong was their outcry against it. But opposition to it was formid-
able. The voices of the women in favour were a pathetically weak
political force – the *Guardian* and the *Observer* (for whom I then
worked) supported it; the *Daily Mirror* was equivocal, and that was
about it. There were a few feminists, but they were hardly a loud
voice in the land. Mainly it was done by Barbara Castle's sheer
determination against all the odds. She was allowed to win something noble since she had just been savagely betrayed by her
colleagues – notably Jim Callaghan – in her valiant attempt to
reform trade-union law which might have saved the Labour party
its wilderness years had she won. With the Equal Pay Act she
transformed the thinking, the language and the reality of women's

lives so radically that we can no longer imagine a time when industrialists and trade unionists agreed publicly to pay women half men's wages for the same day's work sitting at the same work benches.

The Equal Pay Act did not, alas, transform women's earnings overnight. If it had I might not be writing this book now, for women's low pay is still the true heart of the problem. It has been a slow and steady fight to ease women's pay upwards and stamp out the tricks that let managers continue to hold down their pay. Many companies simply segregated their workers so low-paid women worked in jobs where there were no men to compare their pay with. Low-paid women always were and still are in largely segregated work doing women's traditional three C's – catering, cleaning and caring: the men who take these jobs have to accept female status. The result is that well over 70 per cent of the low-paid are still the women, their work still officially and systematically devalued because it is women's work. The bad treatment of women remains the key reason for working poverty in Britain. Change has been snail's-pace slow. A good example of how slow was the impact of the Equal Pay Act can be found in the Vauxhall agreement that had to be drawn up later in 1970 to take account of an Act neither managers nor unions wanted. It was now called an 'Understanding' and not a firm 'Agreement', which would have been illegal. The Company 'Understood' that: 'No woman will be recruited into employment if suitable men are available and no existing male employee will be required to accept a lower classification as a result of the recruitment of women.' So it is not as if the culture or the reality changed enough to cause any kind of economic shock. As with Labour's ultra-cautious introduction of a very low minimum wage, there was none.

None the less, passing the Equal Pay Act at an extremely difficult economic time was a remarkably bold gesture. It was an act of great daring done not because there was any heavyweight political pressure for it but because it was right. Compare that with this government's exaggerated fear of any bark from business. Would they dare to bring the minimum wage up to what the bottom 10 per cent were paid in 1970? Business would howl its protest. The

CBI and the Institute of Directors would proclaim economic catastrophe; it would send a cold sweat down the government's collective spinelessness. Yet it could be done. If the minimum wage were now set at the equivalent of what the bottom 10 per cent were earning on average in the 1970s (i.e. 67.3 per cent of median earnings), that £262 a week would lift millions out of poverty. No Labour government has ever been in such a phenomenally strong position to do the right thing. It has the power, it has no opposition, its first bold tax-raising budget was a resounding popular success, it has the longest-sustained strong economy since the war and it would have social justice on its side.

The working poor are a popular cause as they are unequivocally the 'deserving'. Their only social problem is the undervaluing of their labour. Until I read through the *Employment Gazette* for 1970, I had forgotten that it was also the year when Sir Keith Joseph first announced that he would introduce the Family Income Supplement. That was the prototype for Gordon Brown's tax credits: a top-up to guarantee every working family with children would always be a little better off taking a job than living on social security.

The Institute of Fiscal Studies calculates that in 1971, when FIS was introduced, a family with two children, working a 35-hour week and earning the modern equivalent of £147 would have received the equivalent of an extra £74.81 in FIS, making a total income of £221.81 in 2002 values. How does that compare with Gordon Brown's Working Families' Tax Credits? An identical family with an identical income would now gain an extra £100.27. That means they are £25.54 better off in real terms than they were some thirty years ago: an improvement, but not much during a time when national income doubled.

Brown's WFTC is designed to be his chief method of lifting children out of poverty. It is a fiendishly complex system to calculate, but click on to the Inland Revenue website and it gives an automatic WFTC calculator. I fed in not the lowest possible wage but the one I have used all through this book, my original £4.35 a hour for a forty-hour week at the Chelsea and Westminster. The website instructs applicants to feed in their pay after National Insurance and tax deductions, which for me was £150. I added in my one teenage child and up came the sum of £70.83 WFTC. Add that to my £150 post-tax wages and that brings me up to £220.83. That sum would cover the costs of my son, delivering me £5.52 an hour. But life on this with a teenager would still lack most of the same things, such as holidays, presents or meals out. Once he leaves school, I would lose the money.

Sir Keith Joseph's income subsidy was founded on a very Tory idea. Now followed by Labour, the idea is to let the labour market take more or less its own course, allowing employers to pay sub-survivable wages to workers with the state coming in as back-stop with a top-up subsidy. This artificial work-incentive is necessary in order to protect social security budgets, unless, as in America, the state is willing to cut social security to starvation levels. It may be necessary to keep WFTC in the armoury against poverty for some cases, but in the long run fair pay is the only answer.

As a thought-experiment, imagine what would happen if the government were to withdraw all WFTC. Suddenly low-paid work for families would pay less than current social security rates, and all low-paid workers would give up their jobs and go on to benefits. What would employers do, in what they misdescribe as an already 'tight' labour market? (Tight only because of their tight-fisted refusal to pay more and entice more people in to work for them.) Without WFTC employers would have to put up wages until they made it worth people's while to go back to work. Employers would have no choice but to pay a living wage, instead of letting the tax-payer take the strain. Of course it couldn't be done, but the experiment proves the point. There is no honest labour market, only one already greatly distorted by Sir Keith Joseph's original subsidy to low-paying employers.

Since 1970 the unions have gone through their own eighteen-year chrysalis stage and they have emerged better equipped to represent the poorest workers who need them now more than ever. But their past failure to win public sympathy and the resultant retaliation that was meted out to them by Margaret Thatcher has left them weak, with only 65 per cent of the many fewer public workers now belonging to unions, and only 19 per cent of the privately employed. The poorest workers who need a union most are still the least likely to have one in their workplace. In 1970 the miners and steel-workers managed to command such high pay even though there was no shortage of men who would eagerly have taken their jobs, because of sheer industrial muscle through trade-union power. Care workers, in the main, do not belong to unions. There is no tradition of it and women's lives are so hard-pressed that only the occasional heroine manages to set up union recognition in a women's workplace. At least since Labour came to power, workers have for the first time the legal right to union recognition once enough of them vote for it, but making it happen asks a lot of a weak, poor and time-starved female workforce. Their erratic shifts also make organising meetings almost impossible.

But imagine if they did. The muscle of the care workers would be greater than that of the miners. Their power has the same potential as the police or the prison officers, for if the care workers all walked out of their nursing homes one fine morning, no other battalions of people could be found to do their work: death and mayhem would ensue in days. That is only a fantasy because, like nurses, care workers would be loth to do it. Trade unions are different now, too, in many ways more effective and a great deal more sympathetic than in their old confrontational mode. Unison (NUPE in the old days) is now the largest union with 1.3 million members. It represents people who work in public services and in private companies providing services to the public and it should be representing most of the people I worked with. In recent years it has finally moulded itself to represent the women who always were some 70 per cent of its members, with women at last featuring in its hierarchy and priorities. Unison and other unions now devote energy not just to pay but to other things their members urgently need. They are making deals with employers to provide free workplace-training programmes to make sure their members get the literacy, numeracy and English language skills to help them move upwards. They are now far better at listening to what their members actually want; for women this often means flexi-time. Workplaces with union recognition are on average 10 per cent better paid than those without, but there may be a chicken-and-egg problem here, with better-paid workers more likely to be union members.

Membership is starting to rise again, slightly, but unions are trapped in a spiral in which they can only spend a small fraction of their income on recruiting. It is hard for them to divert too many resources from the needs of their existing members who expect their money to be spent on services for them, not on putative future members. Setting up union recognition in new workplaces, especially among those with no union experience, is a long, hard and expensive process. At their present rate of progress, with such a small membership base among the low-paid, the trade unions alone are not likely to be the force that can make a real difference to most of the working poor, though the more members they have the stronger their political voice in calling for a universal living wage.

The unavoidable fact is that the story of union representation of the low-paid has been one of broad failure over the years. They have never succeeded in getting their members' work revalued and repositioned in the general scale of rewards, even though back in 1970 almost all public-service workers were union members. That suggests that unions may altogether have had less historic power than is imagined, even in their heyday. The strongest unions were in coal, steel, cars, ship-building, the docks and print. What was the nature of those workers' power? When they came out on strike large sums of money were lost, so employers tended to give in and pay higher wages rather than see balance sheets suffer. The trouble with the low-paid in the public service is that if they strike no one loses any money, they just damage hospital, school or care-home users while employers make savings on their pay. Service workers' power has never been cashable in the same way as the producers of high-value goods. They have no profits to share in, only a demand upon tax-payers to pay them more. The point of this comparison is to show that while unions do some good to their members, in the last century they effected relatively little social change.

Only government can make a real impact on markets, only government can force real redistribution of income and revalue the national system of rewards. If the politicians started to tell the voters the shocking fact that the low-paid are getting less than they did thirty years ago, it could begin the necessary national debate on a fair living wage.

I left my flat with no regrets at all. I cleaned it up as well as I could but the flood had left its indelible marks as had the repairs to the block that sent wet cement through loose window-frames. But although still unfinished, the White House felt much better now the stairwells had been painted and the original smell banished. All the same, no one would choose to live there if they had anywhere else to go, not while it was still an uneasy open house to any stray weirdo passing by. Not while Mr B was still in his basement flat welcoming in the crack-dealers and their clients, his boozing friends and local prostitutes. But there was no doubt things were improving and the housing office was sure they would secure Mr B's eviction when the case eventually came to court. If I have given too dark a picture of Clapham Park, I keep reminding myself it is because I was deliberately put into the worst block, the only one available. Other staircases in other buildings were nothing like this.

I sent all the furniture back to the Shaftesbury Society with another £100 donation for their efforts: the lift was out of order again that day and so they had to carry it all the way down the stairs a second time. I said good bye to Dominic and Micky, but it was not necessarily a permanent farewell since I shall be back there often, watching how the estate progresses with its New Deal plans over the next crucial years. It is still far too early to tell whether the place can be transformed in just eight years, but there are high hopes because nothing so ambitious has ever been tried before. Even if it does not all work out precisely according to the masterplan, many of its programmes are set fair to make a massive difference to the people there. Green shoots are everywhere already. There will shortly be neighbourhood wardens patrolling. Plentiful new youth schemes are about to take off. The brand-new Threshold Centre on the west side is sprouting classes of all sorts, with a crèche for mothers, computer training, keep-fit sessions for the old, activities of every kind. Before long the residents will vote on a choice of plans for redevelopment of the whole site. Sitting in on the board meetings, I am always astonished and moved by the enthusiasm and the sheer amount of time given by a hard core of determined residents and keen local managers and social entrepreneurs. Things can only get better here, the question is how much better?

I took the keys back to the housing office, signed away my lease and then set off on the ten-minute walk back to my own home. Traversing the streets between, I looked back on what it had been like to try (unsuccessfully) to live on a little above the minimum wage. I had cheated by clocking up big debts, cheated by eating some meals with family and friends, cheated by going home some weekend nights. None the less, during that time the shape of my life and the shape of the city where I have always lived altered beyond recognition. London was a sadder, duller, more impoverished place with fewer pleasures and fewer choices. I lived on the shabby side of everything that my ordinary life barely touched. Everything I did was limited by shortage of cash, from the adequate but dreary diet I ate to the lack of entertainment and alcohol. Shops simply vanished from my horizon and I realised how important they were to me, as they are to most people in modern life. Well-worn and familiar tracts of the city devoted to pleasure, art, eating, clothes and shopping disappeared off my map. Why wander down the King's Road when everything there is denied to you? Oxford Street and Regent Street vanished from my route. So did Clapham Junction and Arding and Hobbs. So did Shaftesbury Avenue, the National Theatre, the Albert Hall and the Barbican. Wherever I walked, everything I passed was out of bounds, things belonging to other people but not to me. No Starbucks sofas beckoned any more, no Borders bookshop, no restaurants, not even the most humble cafe. This is what 'exclusion' means, if you ever wondered at this modern wider definition of poverty. It is a large No Entry sign on every ordinary pleasure. No Entry to the consumer society where the rest of us live. It is a harsh apartheid. Exclusion makes the urban landscape a forbidding place where every brightly lit shop doorway designed to welcome you in to buy, buy, buy is slammed shut to one-third of the population. Shopping for the meanest food staples under rigorous cost-control is no fun, and it becomes less so every time.

True, I became keenly aware and appreciative of pleasures that are free. There are the unlimited buses once you have bought a weekly bus pass (so long as you allow the extra time, so long as they arrive). Museums and galleries are a free treat now there are no more admission charges, a reminder of the Thatcher depredations on civic life. Parks, commons and plain pavements reminded me of the pleasure of walking, as I walked far more than I was used to. But arriving home for good was nothing but sheer relief. I am glad I know more than I did about life on the other side, but gladder still, more than I can say, that I was born on the lucky side of life. I look at Clapham, my own home-territory, with other eyes now, seeing its underside everywhere, knowing more now of what lies behind a thin veneer.

Notes

Chapter 1: Starting Out

1. *Distribution of Income and Wealth. Social Trends* by Professor Anthony Atkinson, Warden of Nuffield College, Oxford, HMSO 2001
2. Office of National Statistics: www.statistics.gov.uk
3. *Changes in Intergenerational Mobility in Britain* by Jo Blanden, Alissa Goodman, Paul Gregg, Stephen Machin, Centre for Economic Performance, LSE, Number 517, January 2002
4. *Intergenerational Social Mobility and Assortative Mating in Britain* by John Ermisch and Marco Francesconi, Institute for Social and Economic Research (ISER) at the University of Essex, May 2002
5. *Social Mobility – A discussion paper,* by Stephen Aldridge, Chief Economist at the Performance and Innovation Unit, April 2002: www.cabinet-office.gov.uk/innovation/whatsnew/socialmobility,shtml
6. *Understanding Social Exclusion,* edited by John Hills, Julian Le Grand and David Piachaud, Oxford University Press 2002
7. *Report 851,* Income Data Services, February 2002
8. *Nickel and Dimed: Undercover in Low-Wage USA* by Barbara Ehrenreich, Granta 2002
9. *Employment and Poverty,* Trade Union Congress paper, October 2001

Chapter 2: A Home

1. *Rich Place, Poor Place: an analysis of geographical variations in household income within Britain* by Richard Berthoud, Working Paper for the Institute for Social and Economic Research (ISER) at the University of Essex, May 2001

Chapter 4: Spending

1. Mother Pat's Fund, donations to the Shaftesbury Resources Centre, 93, Camberwell Station Road, London SE5 9JJ

Chapter 5: Portering

1. *Employee Relations in the Public Services* by Trevor Colling, Routledge 1999
2. *Competition and Service: The Impact of the Local Government Act 1988* by Walsh, Kiernon and Davis, HMSO 1993

3. *Britain at Work: As Depicted by the 1988 Workplace Employee Relations Survey* by Cully, Woodland, O'Reilly and Dix, Routledge 1999
4. For an excellent overview of the main research into the effects of privatisation, see Sanjiv Sachdev of Kingston University Business School, *Contracting Culture: from CCT to PPPs*, Unison 2001

Chapter 14: It Doesn't Have to Be This Way

1. *Empirical evidence on the ratio of CEO compensation to employee pay* by Professor Martin J. Conyon, the Wharton School, University of Pennsylvania, Hemmington Scott Publishing 2002, commissioned by the Trades Union Congress: www.tuc.org.uk/work_life/
2. *The World We're In* by Will Hutton, Little, Brown 2002
3. *Is Rising Inequality Inevitable? A Critique of Transatlantic Consensus* by Professor Anthony Atkinson, Warden of Nuffield College, Oxford. Wider Lecture, the United Nations University, World Institute for Development Economics Research, Wider Annual Lectures 3, 1999
4. *Report 854*, Income Data Services, April 2002, p. 2
5. *Britain's World of Work – Myth and Realities* by Robert Taylor, Economic and Social Research Council (ESRC), April 2002
6. *Working Capital*, report from the Work Foundation (formerly the Industrial Society), April 2002
7. *Mapping Low Pay in East London* by Jane Wills, Dept of Geography, Queen Mary, University of London, for TELCO's Living Wage Campaign, 3, Merchant St, Bow, London, E3 4UJ
8. *Understanding Social Exclusion* edited by John Hills, Julian Le Grand and David Piachaud, Oxford University Press 2002

A NOTE ON THE TYPE

The text of this book is set in Bembo. This type was first used in 1495 by the Venetian printer Aldus Manutius for Cardinal Bembo's *De Aetna*, and was cut for Manutius by Francesco Griffo. It was one of the types used by Claude Garamond (1480–1561) as a model for his Romain de l'Université, and so it was the forerunner of what became standard European type for the following two centuries. Its modern form follows the original types and was designed for Monotype in 1929.